CITIES AS CRUCIBLES:
REFLECTIONS ON CANADA'S URBAN FUTURE

INVENIRE BOOKS

Invenire is an Ottawa-based "idea factory" specializing in collaborative governance and stewardship. Invenire and its authors offer creative and practical responses to the challenges and opportunities faced by today's complex organizations.

Invenire Books welcomes a range of contributions — from conceptual and theoretical reflections, ethnographic and case studies, and proceedings of conferences and symposia, to works of a very practical nature — that deal with problems or issues on the governance and stewardship front. Invenire Books publishs works in French and English.

This is the fifth volume published by Invenire Books.

Invenire also publishes a quarterly electronic journal www.optimumonline.ca

Editorial Committee
Robin Higham
Ruth Hubbard
Gilles Paquet (chair)

The other titles published by Invenire Books are listed at the end of this book.

CITIES AS CRUCIBLES:
REFLECTIONS ON CANADA'S URBAN FUTURE

FRANÇOIS LAPOINTE

INVENIRE BOOKS
Ottawa, Canada
2011

Les **Presses** de l'Université d'Ottawa
University of Ottawa **Press**

The University of Ottawa Press (UOP) is proud to be the oldest of the francophone university presses in Canada and the oldest bilingual university publisher in North America. Since 1936, UOP has been enriching intellectual and cultural discourse by producing peer-reviewed and award-winning books in the humanities and social sciences, in French and in English.

www.Press.uOttawa.ca

Library and Archives Canada Cataloguing in Publication
Title: Cities as crucibles : reflections on Canada's urban future / François Lapointe.
Names: Lapointe, François, 1953- author.
Description: Reprint. Originally published: Ottawa : Invenire Books, 2011. | Includes
  bibliographical references.
Identifiers: Canadiana (print) 20220285977 | Canadiana (ebook) 20220285985 | ISBN 9780776638317
  (softcover) | ISBN 9780776638324 (PDF) | ISBN 9780776638331 (EPUB)
Subjects: LCSH: City planning—Canada. | LCSH: Cities and towns—Canada—Forecasting. | LCSH: Urban
  policy—Canada.
Classification: LCC HT169.C2 L36 2022 | DDC 307.760971—dc23

This book was initially published by Invenire Books in 2012. The cover design, layout and design were produced by Sandy Lynch. Cover image: Bear66 (Dreamstime.com). The University of Ottawa Press reissued this book thanks to the support of Ontario Creates.

Invenire

Invenire Books, an Ottawa-based idea factory that operated from 2010 to 2019, specialized in collaborative governance and stewardship. Invenire and its authors provide creative practical and stimulating responses to the challenges and opportunities faced by today's organizations. The list is now carried by the University of Ottawa Press.

Profession: Public Servant
The Entrepreneurial Effect: Practical Ideas from Your Own
  Virtual Board of Advisors
La flotte blanche : histoire de la compagnie de navigation
  du Richelieu et d'Ontario
Tableau d'avancement II : essais exploratoires sur la
  gouvernance d'un certain Canada français
The Entrepreneurial Effect: Waterloo
The Unimagined Canadian Capital: Challenges for the
  Federal Capital Region
The State in Transition: Challenges for Canadian Federalism
Cities as Crucibles: Reflections on Canada's Urban Future
Gouvernance communautaire : innovations dans le Canada
  français hors Québec
Through the Detox Prism: Exploring Organizational
  Failures and Design Responses
Cities and Languages: Governance and Policy – An
  International Symposium
Villes et langues : gouvernance et politiques – symposium
  international
Moderato Cantabile: Toward Principled Governance for
  Canada's Immigration Policy
Stewardship: Collaborative Decentred Metagovernance and
  Inquiring Systems
Challenges in Public Health Governance: The Canadian
  Experience
Innovation in Canada: Why We Need More and What We
  Must Do to Get It
Challenges of Minority Governments in Canada
Gouvernance corporative : une entrée en matières
Tackling Wicked Policy Problems: Equality, Diversity and
  Sustainability

50 ans de bilinguisme officiel : défis, analyses et témoignages
Unusual Suspects: Essays on Social Learning
Probing the Bureaucratic Mind: About Canadian Federal
  Executives
Tableau d'avancement III : pour une diaspora canadienne-
  française antifragile
Autour de Chantal Mouffe : le politique en conflit
Town and Crown: An Illustrated History of Canada's Capital
The Tainted-Blood Tragedy in Canada: A Cascade of
  Governance Failures
Intelligent Governance: A Prototype for Social Coordination
Driving the Fake Out of Public Administration: Detoxing
  HR in the Canadian Federal Public Sector
Tableau d'avancement IV : un Canada français à ré-inventer
A Future for Economics: More Encompassing, More
  Institutional, More Practical
Pasquinade en F : essais à rebrousse-poil
Building Bridges: Case Studies in Collaborative Governance
  in Canada
Scheming Virtuously: The Road to Collaborative Governance
A Lantern on the Bow: A History of the Science Council
  of Canada and its Contributions to the Science and
  Innovation Policy Debate
Fifty Years of Official Bilingualism: Challenges, Analyses
  and Testimonies
Irregular Governance: A Plea for Bold Organizational
  Experimentation
Pasquinade in E: Slaughtering Some Sacred Cows

The University of Ottawa Press gratefully acknowledges the support extended to its publishing list by the Government of Canada, the Canada Council for the Arts, the Ontario Arts Council, the Social Sciences and Humanities Research Council and the Canadian Federation for the Humanities and Social Sciences through the Awards to Scholarly Publications Program, and by the University of Ottawa.

ONTARIO ARTS COUNCIL
CONSEIL DES ARTS DE L'ONTARIO
an Ontario government agency
un organisme du gouvernement de l'Ontario

Canada Council   Conseil des arts
for the Arts   du Canada

Canadä

uOttawa

[A]n attempt to make the
future a matter for public choice.

N.H. Lithwick and G. Paquet (1968)

These reflections are dedicated to:
My wife Marie, with love and admiration;
my parents, with love and appreciation;
young Canadians, with confidence and hope;
Georges Potvin, André Lessard, Pierre Blanchard,
Eugene Parent and Bill Boss, with fond memories.

A much belated, but sincere thank you to the Canada
Mortgage and Housing Corporation for its financial
support towards the completion of my Masters in Planning
in 1980 at the University of Ottawa.

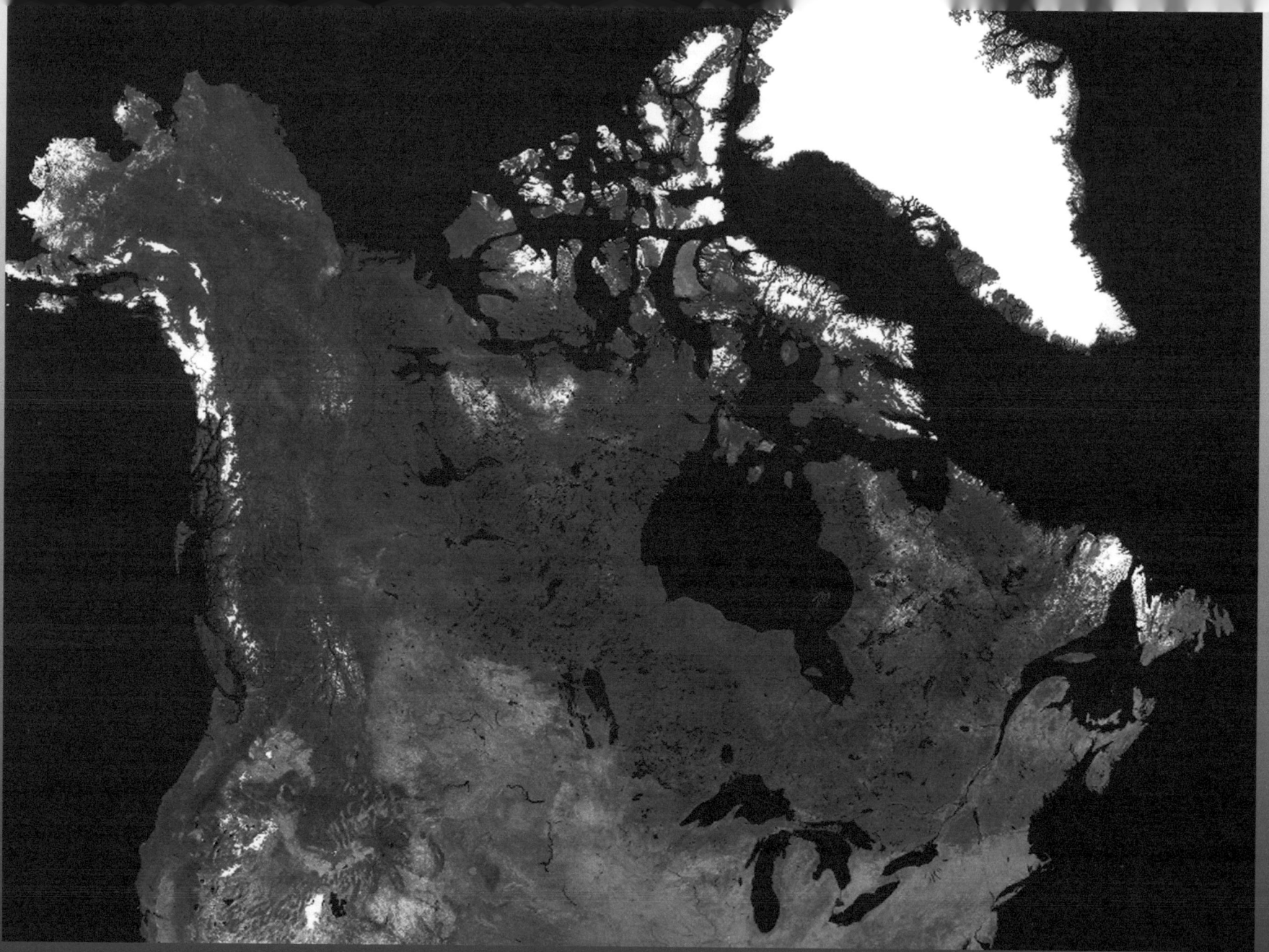

In spite of intellectual claims to the contrary, not religion, not language, not race but place is the dominant feature of civilization. It decides what people can do and how they will live.

John Ralston Saul (1997)

Cities and regions will increasingly need to invest in, and build up, their real capital — that comes from the energy and talent of their people.

Richard Florida (2008)

CONTENTS

DIAGRAMS

FIGURES

TABLES

Montreal

La ville nous impose le devoir terrible de l'espoir ... un étrange amour, l'amour secret de l'avenir et de son visage inconnu.

Jorge Luis Borges, quoted in Jodi Borja (2004)

FOREWORD

Over the course of my thirty-five year career, I have spent a lot of time thinking about cities and how they work, what makes some cities great and others just ordinary? How can we make sure that we are doing our best to shape Canada's cities so that they are wonderful places to live and work for people who are poor or rich, young or old, recently-arrived or First Nations? How can we get governments — at all levels — to work together with common purpose to address the challenges of our cities today and in the future? The answers to these questions are of course complex, burdened by history, geography, politics and human behaviour.

I was therefore quite delighted to receive François Lapointe's ground-breaking book, *Cities as Crucibles: Reflections on Canada's Urban Future*. In his unique voice, he urges us to journey with him through Canada's urban landscape, relying not only on his considerable professional expertise but also on his own personal reflections. The sweep of his vision is broad in both spatial and temporal dimensions. He does not shy away from the big questions of the day: climate change, citizenship and immigration, public debt. Like a good urban planner, François forces us to think long-term and beyond the boundaries of our individual urban realities, while at the same time, grounding us in issues that are both immediate and local.

François succeeds in weaving together the familiar hallmarks of sustainable cities — environment, economy, and society — in ways that cause us to think a little differently about the inter-connections among the three. *Cities as Crucibles: Reflections on Canada's Urban Future* is full of case studies and illustrations that make the "urban agenda" come to life. More importantly, these urban stories combine with a rich narrative to make the book accessible to a big audience — academics, urban professionals and citizens. It is an important contribution to the library of contemporary urban literature — not only for its content, but for its "gentle" pedagogical style that challenges readers to answer some questions for themselves.

Drawing from his experience in both the municipal and federal government sectors, François argues convincingly for new models of collaboration, better decision making within and between governments, and above all, for re-designing the platforms for citizen engagement. I like the way he frames the issue of participation through the broader lens of citizenship, suggesting a greater shared responsibility for our urban future among institutions and the people they serve.

I am reminded that when I first met François, he was a planner at the National Capital Commission (NCC) and I was a municipal planner at the Region of Ottawa-Carleton (now City of Ottawa). Naturally, conflicts erupted from time to time when the NCC took actions deemed to be in the federal interest but neglected to take account of local plans. François early on showed his interest in collaborative approaches, seeking opportunities to harmonize local and national plans institutionally and also informally.

François helps the reader navigate past the quagmire of political realities by setting the way forward with a proposed urban agenda. Here, we learn that he is not content to simply describe and assess; he provides us with a menu of ideas to make our cities even better places for citizens. He challenges us to conceive of a "projet de société" for Canada with the urban agenda at its core.

He reminds us — more than once — that Canada is overwhelmingly an urban nation, yet the importance of cities to our country's health and prosperity barely registers among our citizens. I, too, have pondered this conundrum and wondered if it stems from our rural beginnings when pride of place meant scenic and open landscapes.

George Eliot Clarke, in his 2006 LaFontaine Baldwin address, summed it up best:

> Our national self-image has been so indelibly constructed by the iconic Group of Seven painters and Emily Carr, not to mention by the designers of our coins, paper money, and postage stamps, we imagine ourselves as a wilderness people, not a heavily urbanized one. ... Nevertheless, we must never forget that the vast majority of us live in cities — despite what our national self-image suggests.

Anyone who lives in a city or loves cities can find something in this book to identify with and, most certainly, will learn something about how cities work. And *Cities as Crucibles: Reflections on Canada's Urban Future* will become an invaluable tool for aspiring urban planners, city managers, and others who will benefit from the experience and knowledge of a thoughtful practitioner.

Marni Cappe, MCIP, RPP

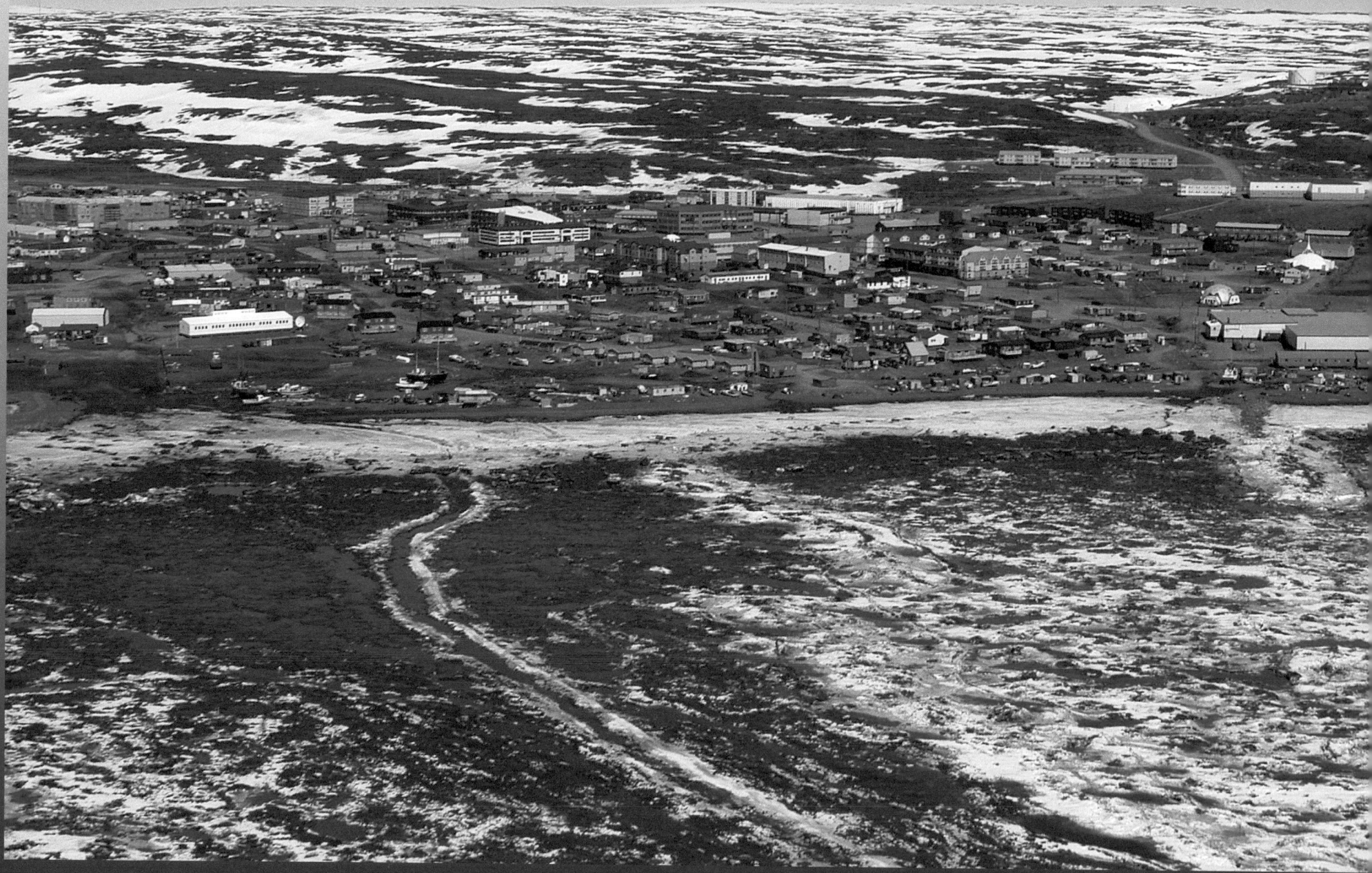

Iqaluit

Reflection means wondering, probing, analyzing, synthesizing, connecting; to ponder carefully and persistently the meaning of an experience to the self, asking not only what but why and how.

Henry Mintzberg (2004)

PREFACE

Why These Reflections?

*Canada's urban agenda —
Collaboration between levels of
government and all Canadians
to strengthen the quality of life
in cities and regions.*

Adapted from the Prime Minister's
Caucus Task Force (2002)

**Urbanism is a fairly young
discipline in Canada, having
had its beginning in the late
19th and early 20th centuries,
and taking a strong foothold
in cities after World War II.
As a professional endeavour, it
fulfills many roles and advances
many distinctive qualities
important for the evolution of
cities and the country: being
vision driven and an integrative
discipline; providing a world-
view; consisting of deliberative
and participative processes;
bridging the short- and the
long-term; and enabling the
synthesization of the social,
economic, environmental,
political, technological, local,
national and global forces
at play.**

O ften, in the course of a high-paced managerial/
professional practice, it is difficult to take the time
to step back and ponder the broader context and
meaning of day-to-day activities and actions — to combine
"praxis" with a "reflective practitioner" perspective.

What began for me as assembling and organizing my
thoughts on the practice of urbanism at the beginning
of the 21st century gradually evolved into an increasing
recognition of the need for Canadians to overcome
an heedlessness about their country and especially,
their cities.

Because of Canada's predominant urban reality, and
the emergence of a more turbulent political environment
as well as the evolution of new and different
intergovernmental relations, the requirement for an urban
agenda — that would build on the legacy of past and
more recent efforts — has been steadily gaining ground
in various quarters. However, in my view, the importance
of urban areas for the future of the country and the lives
and lifestyles of ordinary Canadians does not seem to be
registering on the radar screens of leaders and citizens
to the extent that it should.

Through the writing of these reflections, I wish to add my
voice to the collection of perspectives and opinions on the
future of Canada and its cities ... this as the 21st century
marches on.

As a practicing professional urbanist for more than
twenty-seven years in both Quebec and Ontario, I believe
that I can provide a distinctive and useful appreciation
of what underlies and could/should drive Canada's
urban agenda.

This book represents my modest contribution to this
important debate. Its goal is to:

- put forward my own reflections on the past, present
and future of Canadian cities and regions;

- address a range of topics, issues and ideas related to
the urban agenda, informed generally but not exclusively
by my professional experience and practice;

- fill a perceived void in terms of an accessible, non-
academic document on Canada's urban agenda;

- act as a true source of reflection on the part of readers, through the combination of my own thoughts with a wide range of quotes, notes and other references, coming from academic, professional and journalistic sources;

- focus on socio-economic, socio-political, socio-cultural dimensions of Canada's urban agenda, in addition to the physical and spatial considerations at the core of urbanism; and,

- emphasize the importance of combining dialogue, experience and learning in advancing and communicating the urban agenda to Canadians.

For me, this role as "reflective practitioner" has represented a long and winding journey, exhilarating but also very challenging and humbling. While I remain the eternal optimist, I have come to embrace a cautious optimism rather than runaway enthusiasm, with the fundamental

recognition that Canada and Canadians must evolve an action plan for their cities and regions. To my mind, they need to build on strengths and legacies, and address head on certain attitudes and a complacency that inhibits their recognition of necessary changes.

My overall conclusion is that if Canadians are to continue to be successful as people and as a country, they must conjure up a "projet de société" that will enable them to chart a forward-looking path in an increasingly urban world.

You are about to experience this new voice on Canada's urban scene. I sincerely hope that you will find it interesting, inspiring and thought-provoking.

François Lapointe
Fall 2010, Ottawa

Whitehorse

At its best, good city-making leads to the highest achievement of human culture.

Charles Landry (2006)

Figure 1
Urbanization of Canada and the World, 1871-2006
(%)

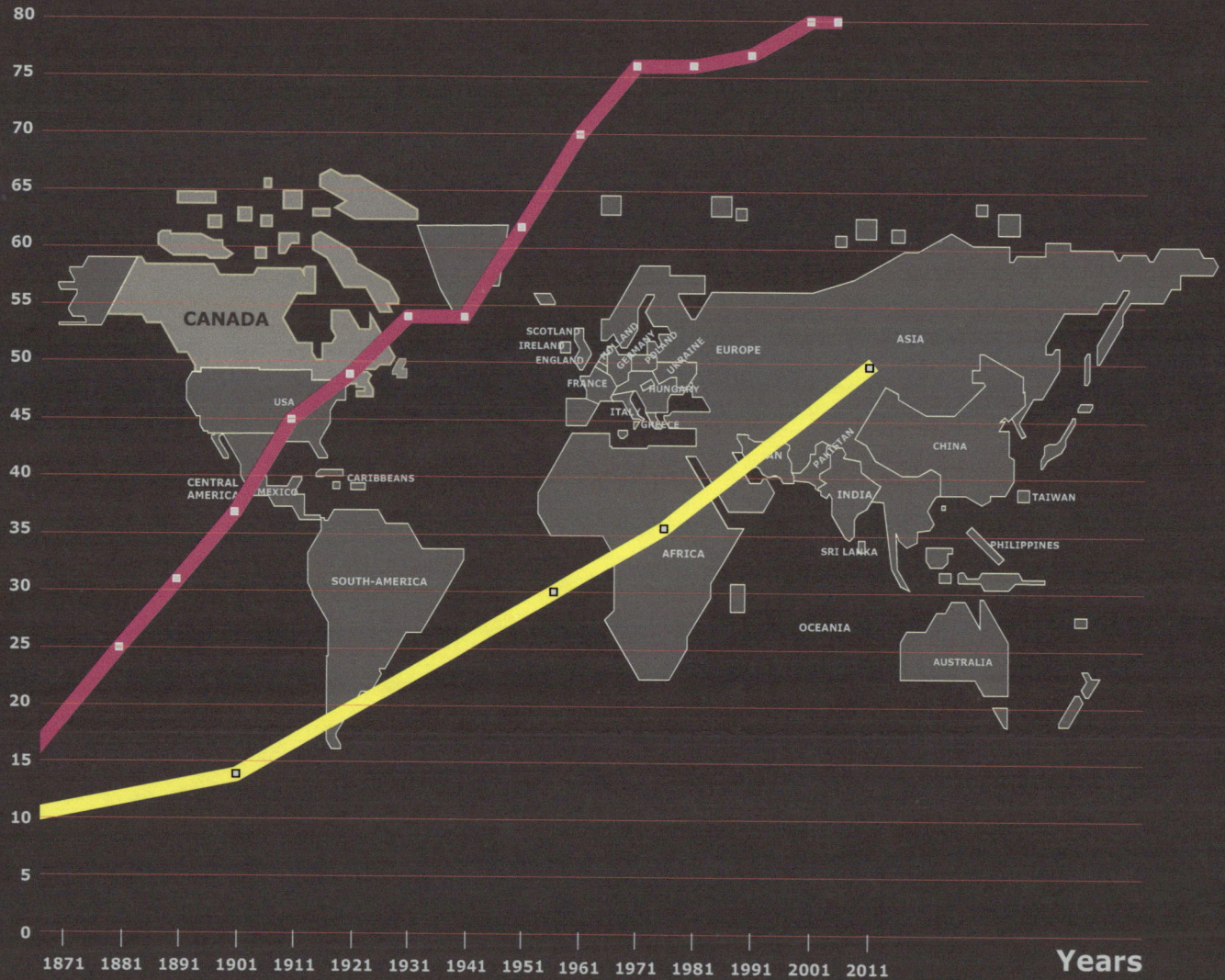

Legend
Canada
World

Sources: Adapted from *Statistics Canada, 2005* and from *United Nations Word Urbanization Prospects, 2008.*

INTRODUCTION

Why Do Cities and Urban Governance Matter for Canada?

The new century is imposing a renewed perspective on urban areas.

Cities as "crucibles" for the 21st century civilization is an apt metaphor to illustrate how the majority of people experience life in contemporary society — where almost everything begins and ends, where geography can be meaningful but also meaningless, where cultures meet and mix, where traditions compete with grand visions of the future. Canada's urbanity — in statistical terms but also in how Canadians live and perceive their lives — clearly manifests the prevalence of this "urban experience".

The fact that Canada's population is now 80 percent urban according to the recent censuses (2001, 2006) has captured the attention and the imagination of many. However, understanding the country's urban reality through geographic lenses only provides a partial and limited outlook. Canadians, wherever they live, are influenced and conditioned by this "urban reality"; expressed differently, the urban way of life permeates the daily life, expectations, needs and aspirations of all Canadians.

Figure 1 demonstrates the evolution of Canada from a predominantly rural country around the time of Confederation (80 percent rural/20 percent urban) to a predominantly urban country at the beginning of the

21st century (20 percent rural/80 percent urban). When comparing Canada's population evolution to the world's population evolution (around 7 percent in the 1870s to around 50 percent as of 2008), it is easy to grasp the extent of the "urban character" of the lives of Canadians.

Moreover, while a majority of Canadians became urban in the 1930s, by the latter part of the 20th century, the predominant human settlement form had become "suburban". The share of suburban population in Canada is estimated at between 60 percent and 70 percent,[1] and is included in the "urban" portion of the rural/urban split.

Our traditional focus when looking at cities is proving inadequate.

Not unlike what has taken placed in other developed countries and western democracies, the city development process in Canada has emphasized the physical dimension, through government policies, regulations and programs and market forces, instead of a more holistic perspective and approach. More specifically, the tension between urban and suburban living and development has been the focus of a lot of attention and debate. The seemingly irresistible movement of people, jobs and activities from central to peripheral areas has clearly dominated the inquiries regarding the challenges and possibilities associated with urbanization in Canada and other countries after World War II.

Crucible — A melting pot for metals; a test or trial.

J.B. Sykes (1980)

"Cityness" is the state most of us find ourselves in. Cityness is everywhere because even when we are nominally far away from cities, the city's maelstrom draws us in. Its tentacles, template and footprint reach out into its wide surrounds, shaping the physical look, the emotional feel, the atmosphere and economics.

Charles Landry (2006)

[1] Based on research by Dr. David L.A. Gordon, Queens University.

Sustainable Communities

Communities that provide for the needs of their current inhabitants while not compromising the ability of future generations to meet their own needs.

Healthy Communities

Communities that raise public health to a higher level of consciousness, helping people to take their health into their own hands and to support each other to achieve an improved overall quality of life.

Resilient Communities

Communities that have the inherent capacity to absorb change, ruptures and shocks; that are supple enough to adjust. They demonstrate strong adaptability. They have the right attributes of inventiveness and openness to bounce back.

City of Ottawa (2004), Gerald Hodge and David L.A. Gordon (2008) and David Witty (1994, 2002)

Through this emphasis on a simple duality in the structuring of cities, that of the central city versus the peripheral area, a whole pattern of life, experience, expectations and habitat has emerged which has conditioned the planning, development and governance of urban areas. This approach to urban planning and development has provided a specific response to the rapidly growing needs and expectations of Canadians in terms of housing, mobility, institutions and services.

However, such a narrow perspective of cities and metropolitan areas has resulted in many less appealing aspects, including the financial and fiscal costs of the sprawling suburbs, the sense of isolation and lack of identity that characterize them and, more importantly, their failings relative to increasingly recognized requirements/end-state goals of sustainable, healthy and resilient communities in the context of a rapidly changing and transforming world in the 21st century.

Understanding and approaching urban areas and urban living from a multi-dimensional perspective, that harmonizes and integrates a diversity of considerations in addition to strict geographical factors and foundations — meaning in people's life, rootedness, connectedness, healthy living, heritage preservation, environmental protection — would have reflected a more diverse urban reality and would allow different approaches to some of the 21st century's societal challenges in Canada and other countries.

The nature and quality of governance (requirements for coordination when knowledge, power and resources are widely distributed through society) is a key determinant of how effectively Canada's urban reality will find meaning in the prevailing political culture and the day-to-day life of Canadians.

The increasing denial of the unseen dimensions of the city — the culture underlying the urban fabric and urban reality, the sources of memory, identity and affection that help sustain and direct the vision and development of the future, both immediate and over the long-term — represent a fundamental deficit in our current urban civilization. It is one that requires acknowledgement on the part of leaders. A great deal of attention from all Canadians will be required if the many inter-related issues and problems affecting and threatening their valued quality of life are to be addressed and solutions proposed.

Canada's population and its complex and conflicting urban context has significant and far-reaching implications. Considering the evolving environment of people and organizations, this is especially the case when charting the country's future requirements in matters of urban governance and in providing responses to the needs and aspirations of Canadians themselves.

Contemporary Canadians want and need more say in the affairs of their cities.

Policy making in Canada has been accompanied by a degree of remoteness between people and the organizations that deliver services to them — this in terms of accessibility and capacity to influence results and outcomes.[2] Such

[2] A recent study found that only 20% of Canadians are satisfied with the level of public consultation conducted by all government levels in the elaboration of public policy. Ekos Research Associates (2006).

a gap has reduced the capacity of the Canadian public to enter into and sustain a dialogue on the future of their country and cities, leading to a chronic inability to contemplate the longer term, and resulting in a greater level of procrastination when dealing with short- and medium-term change.

Bringing policy making and the workings of institutions closer to people would force a more inclusive, cohesive and enlightened response to individual and collective needs and aspirations. It would foster, as a consequence, better understanding of what Canadians have in common and also the responsibility that they share in advancing and sustaining the development and evolution of Canada and its cities in the 21st century.

The journey towards improved planning, development and governance of cities will involve a reality check.

The future of urban planning, development and governance in Canada is and will be shaped through the responses provided to this shifting reality. In marshalling the arguments to address this changing environment of cities in Canada, I will be advancing and supporting the enactment of an "urban agenda" or a "projet de société" as a central strategic policy outcome.

FOUR THREADS

Throughout this book, four threads of thought — distinct but interrelated — will underpin the proposed diagnostic and prognostic, and the suggested courses of action:

1. Canadians generally and, their cities more particularly, are confronted with a significant and unprecedented level of change in almost all aspects and characteristics. This makes the definition and realization of a comprehensive urban agenda a national imperative.

2. Previous generations of Canadians have left an enviable legacy in terms of how national difficulties and problems are addressed, and how individual and collective will and wisdom are harnessed toward resolution.

3. The attitudes and perspectives of contemporary Canadians regarding the changes facing their society, country and cities are not always conducive to the identification and implementation of timely, workable and realistic interventions.

4. The future of Canadian cities does not rest in a monolithic set of actions, rather in a loose but integrated ensemble of building blocks, ideas and leading practices that incorporates past accomplishments, and also necessarily draws together the creativity, innovation, leadership and collaboration of all sectors and levels of Canada's society, while recognizing the importance of putting Canadians front and centre in the realization of the "projet de société".

Most of the reforms that brought prosperity [to Canada] were the results not of self-interested action but of disinterested action — citizens committing themselves beyond their personal interest in order to widen the public good.

John Ralston Saul (1994)

STRUCTURE OF THE BOOK

My reflections on Canadian cities address their past, present and future through three different sections and fourteen chapters. The conclusion wraps up these reflections through a distillation of key findings and other considerations seen as necessary for the success of Canada's urban agenda.

Part 1: What Do We See? explores the key considerations that should inform any discussion on the evolution of Canadian cities and the development of policies required to ensure that this evolution is put on a sustainable, healthy and resilient path over the longer term. Chapter 1 — Changing Cities looks at the elements of change that have influenced and that will influence the evolution of Canada's urban areas: social, economic, environmental, institutional and urban change. Chapter 2 — Some Emerging Issues and Questions for Cities identifies important issues faced by Canadian cities, requiring appropriate consideration and analysis: cities and globalization, municipal governance, delivering services to Canadians, reconciling short- and long-term decisions, range of community resources, and fiscal and financial resources of cities. Chapter 3 — The Evolving Context of Cities discusses contextual factors beyond the changes and issues previously identified that will also affect and direct Canada's urban agenda over time: climate change, aging and health, population diversity, level of debt, creativity and ingenuity, life-long learning, lifestyles and transition of generations, democratic participation, scientific discoveries and security.

Part II: What Does It Tell Us? brings into focus elements of Canada's urban reality that should underpin and help fashion the development of an urban agenda that is "made in Canada". Chapter 4 — Key Considerations of the Urban Agenda provides an overview of the situation of Canadian cities and the "road travelled" toward developing an urban agenda, and identifies seven drivers (corresponding to the dimensions of the physical/spatial reality of cities) that begin the delineation of the urban agenda: urban form, environment, housing, employment, infrastructure, community facilities and natural resources. Chapter 5 — Window on the Future of Canadian Cities examines, from a comparative vantage point, what constitutes the dominant characteristics of Canadian cities, in terms of their areas of comparative advantage (or strengths) and their areas of vulnerability (or weaknesses), and proposes a number of "pillars" for the development of an urban agenda.

Part III: What Do We Need To Do About It? gets down to the nitty-gritty of Canada's urban agenda by making the transition from the diagnostic and the prognostic to what actually needs to be done to transform the Canadian approach to its urban reality from the "déjà vu" to a "projet de société" espoused and acted upon by all. Chapter 6 — Start with a Vision initially considers the notion of vision and then articulates a vision statement for the future of Canada and its cities. Chapter 7 — Five Themes for Action moves from vision to action by suggesting fourteen possible action areas that could be acted upon by cities in the context of Canada's urban agenda, grouped according to five themes: connections, resources, generations, collaboration and institutions. Chapters 8 through 12 then deal with each of the five themes individually and their "spheres of influence" in the development of the "projet de société". Chapter 13 — Getting on Canadians' Radar Screen looks at what is required to ensure the participation and commitment of Canadians in the planning, development and governance of their cities, envisaging the urban agenda as a "place where dialogue, experience and learning" drive decisions and citizens take active responsibility for their urban environment. Chapter 14 — Pulling It All Together proposes a "call for transformation" through the implementation of an urban agenda, with a focus on perspective, roles, processes and policies.

A diagram of the various elements underpinning the development of an urban agenda is provided after each part to help readers in their journey along the proposed path to a "projet de société".

The conclusion presents a summary, identifies a number of inferences that can be drawn from the reflections and suggests essential conditions for the sustainable, healthy and resilient evolution of urban Canada. The Postface describes the "ideal Canadian city".

ADDITIONAL CONTENT

The sidebars propose a wide range of information that, it is hoped, will contribute and further the reflections proposed on Canadian cities. They consist of quotations, definitions and other materials that generally build on the content of the reflections. All the references for the information contained in the sidebars are documented at the back of the book.

Building on the metaphor of Canada's urban agenda as a "place for dialogue, experience and learning", notes, vignettes and tools are interspersed throughout the document, according to the following three categories:

Leading practices, it can be argued, are context sensitive. What is deemed a leading practice in a given situation for a project in a community may not be shared by another. Similarly, from a continuous learning perspective, the questions or issues raised by one professional as a source of enlightenment through an ensemble of leading practices may not resonate in the same way for another. The notes reflect this "relativity" of leading practices within a professional context. They have been prepared to illustrate how certain questions or issues described in the document can begin to be answered through the actions of selected individuals, communities and organizations. From my perspective, the case studies put forward in the notes are worthy of further reflection in the context of Canada's urban agenda.

Viewpoint puts forward a variety of themes that I believe are relevant and important for Canada's urban agenda. They are based on my work experience in urbanism that spans more than three decades.

Vignettes are included in shaded boxes to make some of the proposed themes or actions more meaningful and to help them come alive. They are based on the achievements and experience of distinct organizations.

Please note, the content of this book represents my personal views on Canadian cities and as such, does not reflect in any way, shape or form the views and policies of the National Capital Commission and Canada's federal government.

PART 1: WHAT DO WE SEE?

Government policies that have ignored the local knowledge of participants or underestimated their ability to solve collective action problems have done great damage.

Robert O. Keohane (1995)

Winnipeg

*Societies and civilizations in which the cities stagnate
don't flourish. They deteriorate.*

Jane Jacobs (1984)

CHAPTER 1

CHANGING CITIES

A paradigm is defined as a belief structure or ideology. It is composed of concepts, values, and perceptions shared by the members of society. Some refer to it as world-view.

W.E Stead and J.G. Stead (1992)

With more than 200 different ethnic origins reported in the 2001 Census, Canada is one of the most ethnically and linguistically diverse countries in the world. During the past century Canada welcomed 13.4 million immigrants.

Treasury Board Secretariat (2004)

In 2001, women represented 59% of college graduates aged 25 and older and exactly half of all university graduates. This represents an increase of 47% in female university graduates from a decade earlier.

Treasury Board Secretariat (2003)

Change is an inherent characteristic of urban areas, large and small. During the 20th century, and particularly in its latter half, Canadian cities witnessed many changes in the size and mix of their population, the nature of employment and economies, their physical footprint, their relationships to the broader regions, the country and the world, among others.

At the beginning of this new century, urban areas in Canada and around the world are seeing the nature of change shift and evolve in unforeseen and unprecedented ways. The convergence of local, national and global forces are both creating challenges and opportunities for cities in terms of the quality of life and the environment, prosperity, public order and the well-being of their citizens.

Because of the sheer difference in the nature of change engulfing cities in comparison to earlier eras, the scope, breadth and depth of urbanization and its links to related phenomena require better appreciation and understanding. Former perspectives, theories and approaches about cities, how they work, the needs of their citizens and how they are governed, are no longer appropriate and effective. A new paradigm, or world-view, needs to be evolved to help manage and steer cities toward new paths.

However, before considering the many dimensions of this new world-view, it is worth discussing briefly some of the key aspects of the changing Canadian cities: social, economic, environmental, institutional and urban.

SOCIAL CHANGE

The social make-up of urban areas is gradually but inexorably being transformed by such phenomena as:

- an aging population: the combined result of a reduced birth rate and higher life expectancy;

- a more diverse population: stemming from a significant increase in the number of places of origin of immigrants; and,

- evolving families and households: following an increase in the divorce rate, a reduction in the number of marriages, an increase in common law relationships, and cross-cultural and same-sex unions.

Social change is further noted at another level of Canada's urban reality — the increasing role of women in many dimensions of Canadian society, particularly in education where they have become dominant in what was formerly a male bastion. While their influence at work and in decision-making roles still does not reflect their proportion of the population, women have nevertheless made some important gains in certain professions, in politics and in business.

Certain areas of social change have resulted in some progress, such as the participation of minorities in Canadian society and the awareness of the need and the provision of universal access for handicapped Canadians.

Other areas have actually not made the progress that one might expect. The treatment of Aboriginal people, homelessness, poverty and income polarization, the precarious life of many children, and the gap in adult literacy in comparison to other developed countries, are examples where Canada must still bring about improvements.

The last twenty years or so have also seen a polarization in Canadians' view of their own life and life in their communities. On the one hand, the 1982 Charter of Rights and Freedoms has been seen as having a generally positive effect on the level of confidence in how individual citizens and minorities can go about their lives with the knowledge that their rights will be considered and respected by the majority.

On the other hand, many events, such as health scares, security threats and environmental crises, have created a sense of greater vulnerability and higher risk in the day-to-day life of many Canadians.

Implications

Although the evolving social and cultural composition of Canadian cities has been researched, documented and predicted for many years, their cumulative implications on urban policies and governance are only beginning to be understood and digested.

As an illustration, an aging and more diverse population is bringing about many transformations including: an increase in health care requirements as a result of a larger contingent of seniors; changes in the size and scope of the labour market with attendant implications for employee shortages and gaps in expertise; households growing

faster than the population following the reduction in birth rate with its implications for the housing sector and market; and deep demographic evolution as a result of the increasing reliance on immigration to sustain continued population growth.

Combined with some related phenomena — the shifting influence of different generations, different lifestyles, the emergence of life-long learning, and greater focus on cultural and leisure dimensions of life — this social change contributes to the overall enrichment of cities but also adds significantly to their complexity.

ECONOMIC CHANGE

At a broad level — recognizing that openness has always been and remains a defining characteristic of the Canadian economy, e.g., welcoming of foreign investment and adoption of ideas and innovations — the shift to a greater continental and global trading regime has had a momentous impact on the economy of cities, both favourable and less favourable.

For those cities that have participated in and contributed to this economic transformation, it has meant change to their range of productive activities and types of employment — some having grown and others having declined — as well as to their physical layout, their degree of connection to other urban centers, and their ability to attract people, tourists and investment. This greater openness of cities to the world, closely associated with the greatly expanded and influential role of information and communications technologies in economic growth and development, has provided many possibilities. But it has also meant new areas of vulnerabilities and risks,

The proportion of working age Aboriginal people with post-secondary schooling increased from 33% in 1996 to 38% in 2001. It is still well below the proportion of other Canadians, which rose from 44% to 53% over the same period. This is of particular concern because the young Aboriginal population is the fastest growing in the country.
Treasury Board Secretariat (2003)

During the 1990s, as a nation we were quick to celebrate our No. 1 ranking on the United Nations Development Program's Human Development Index ... Despite our international standing, it is evident that poverty and gross inequality persist in our own backyard ...
Louise Arbour (2005)

The rights are ... there to express the idea that individuals matter intrinsically. Democracies don't just serve majority interests, they accord individuals intrinsic respect. This respect is expressed in the form of rights that guarantee certain freedoms.
Michael Ignatieff (2004)

Tous les mois, on m'apporte des statistiques démographiques et je me dis : on a beau faire des efforts sur le plan économique, l'essentiel va nous manquer un jour, parce qu'il y aura un vieillissement accéléré de la population.

Robert Bourassa quoted in Jonathan Trudel (2005a)

especially in regard to the level of control that can be exercised locally on critical decisions related to the evolution, prosperity and welfare of these self same cities.

From a more local perspective, cities have witnessed significant changes to the nature, scope and organization of work. Key characteristics of the "new work" include the eroding difference and greater interplay between the private, public and volunteer sectors; more footloose, more knowledge-based, involving greater creativity, partnerships, and networks; and emergence, in many cities, of tourism as a key source of economic activity and employment. These have brought about new requirements and considerations in the economic development of cities (location of activities, mobility and accessibility of people, creation of wealth, quality of life, etc.) and the need for different decision-making forums and frameworks.

Implications

From a broad and a local perspective, the economic changes that have occurred in Canadian cities, while creating increased complexity and uncertainty, have also shown the importance of a close alignment between economic success and the quality of places.

Other lessons learned from economic change in Canada and its meaning for Canadian cities, include the following:[3]

- The prosperity of Canadian places is closely associated with their long-term competitiveness with, as a foundation, the continuous reinvestment in infrastructure, and a focus on quality of the environment and overall quality of life.

- Local and national decisions about cities must be closely coordinated.

- The increase in the prosperity of smaller communities, especially those associated with the extraction of natural resources, depends on raising the education level of their population and creating R & D networks and connections as close to the communities as possible to help reduce the impacts of economic cycles.

- The emergence of strong and resilient economic clusters results from the presence of a critical mass of firms, allowing the creation of economies of scale and scope, a well developed science and technology base, and a local culture conducive to innovation and entrepreneurship.

- The ability to compete for talent at the national and global levels depends on having the appropriate infrastructure for continuous learning, the capacity to overcome skills gaps in a timely manner, and overcoming the literacy gaps and the digital divide, especially in smaller communities.

- The sustainability, health and resiliency of economic development is closely associated with the creation of gateways, especially through integrated transportation infrastructure, and information and communications technology connectivity.

ENVIRONMENTAL CHANGE

Canadian cities and their citizens have undergone a sea change in terms of their relationships to the environment. Greater awareness, increased knowledge and new behaviours have driven this change.

---

[3] Adapted from External Advisory Committee on Cities and Communities (2006).

The debate surrounding the conclusion of a climate change agreement, while divisive and still inconclusive, nevertheless has encouraged new perspectives and approaches to air quality and energy use in housing, transportation, manufacturing sectors, and other areas. A renewed interest and advances in alternative energy supplies — wind, sun, hydrogen, geothermal — have also contributed to the environmental dialogue in Canada and in its cities.

The urban development process has benefited from improved environmental awareness and knowledge through a more comprehensive and integrated approach to regulations, site improvements and actual construction. Expanded application of environmental evaluations, the reclamation of contaminated sites — brownfields — for urban use and the introduction of green construction standards are additional examples of innovations in the planning and development of urban areas.

The adoption of recycling programs, the use of fiscal and market mechanisms to price resource consumption, and the protection of agricultural lands combined with the priority given to local food production, reflect the progress of environmental stewardship by many cities. Notwithstanding those advances on the environmental front, there is general acknowledgement that much remains to be done on the part of Canadian cities and regions to fully embrace the sustainable development principles espoused officially by the federal and provincial governments. The environment is still seen by too many as a constraint, something to avoid or to trade-off, and not

as a priority that must be integrated with the other spheres of activity in Canadian cities.

Implications

In order to more fully embed the environment in Canada's urban agenda, the fiscal, financial, regulatory and risk management frameworks are seen as key areas for improvement. Another area of attention and improvement is the interplay between land use, transportation and energy consumption. From a more holistic and integrated perspective, the environmental agenda warrants and requires closer connection with the education agenda and the health agenda.[4]

INSTITUTIONAL CHANGE

In recent decades, the institutional make-up and fabric of Canada's cities has undergone significant evolution, becoming, in the process, more layered, more sophisticated and also, the source of greater expectation on the part of Canadians.

While the interplay between the different levels of government has remained central to the institutional structuring and dynamic of urban areas — in terms of their governance, the provision of public goods and services, the stewardship of public resources and assets, and the oversight of private and not-for-profit sectors' activities — it has also been the subject of more scrutiny and many challenges. Specifically, the relations between governments have increasingly been faulted for day-to-day operations and decisions exhibiting too much separation, for failing to provide a shared vision of cities, for lacking clarity in the definition of roles and responsibilities, and

Proponents of green architecture argue that the approach has many benefits. In the case of a large office, for example, the combination of green design techniques and clever technology cannot only reduce energy consumption and environmental impact, but also reduce running costs, create a more pleasant working environment, improve employees' health and productivity, reduce legal liability, and boost property values and rental returns.

The Economist (2004b)

While Canadians should take credit for the gains in environmental quality since the 1970s, significant challenges remain. For example, Canadians are consuming more energy, particularly non-renewable forms of energy, and opting more for polluting vehicles such as sport utility vehicles. In addition, trends in housing development and land use are leading to more rural areas being converted in urban spaces, further fragmenting wildlife habitats.

Treasury Board Secretariat (2004)

---

[4] See "Canadian Healthy Communities Project" at the end of the chapter.

We need strong, effective government ... We can expect more rather than less government in the next decades ... [W]e will require a different form of government.

Peter Drucker (1993)

Citizens no longer see themselves as passive consumers of government policies and programs. They want their voices heard before elections. They want to participate more fully in the debate that leads to important decisions, and they want their communities to become more fully and meaningfully democratic.

Don Lenihan and Graham Fox (2005a)

for responding to the needs of citizens in an often haphazard and inequitable manner.

The demand by Canadian cities for resolution of the "infrastructure gap" — this absence of alignment between cities' needs and their capacity to provide for new infrastructure or the renewal of what exists — has forced, more particularly, the two senior levels of government to review and reassess their relationships and responsibilities to cities. The federal government through various task forces, legislative reviews and its budgetary process, has further clarified its interests and priorities. The provincial governments, for their part, have started to look at the issues confronting their cities through two sets of lenses: their own (sometimes conflicting) priorities, and federal claims for a role in the municipal agenda — this in the broader context of the dispute over the distribution of fiscal resources between the federation's partners.

The greater presence and contribution of the not-for-profit sector as a pillar of cities and their communities — facilitating a wide range of initiatives between sectors and jurisdictions, filling the gaps in public programs, promoting the interests of communities, and supporting the establishment of alliances and networks — has represented a positive area of institutional change.

Another area of institutional change that has characterized cities lately involves increasing and broadening the participation of the public in decision making. This greater involvement of citizens and, more broadly, civil society, has several important ramifications, including how the different levels of government collaborate, the balance between short-term and longer term considerations in the development of governmental policies, the nature of and

way in which priorities are established, and the delivery of public services and their quality.

Finally, the dramatic changes that have occurred in the media sector and, in particular, the explosion of the Internet, the Web and social networks throughout Canadian society, with both their centralization and decentralization dimensions and effects, have great implications and ramifications for cities. They include how people communicate, especially the younger generations; the distribution of activities in space and time; the conduct of work; how people obtain public services; and how they entertain themselves, among many others.

Implications

The combination of these considerations and others is suggestive of the need for a renewed perspective and approach to how decisions are reached and made in urban areas.

URBAN CHANGE

Urban change in Canada has followed a similar path to that of other developed countries: growth in urban areas has been higher than the average growth in the country (the inexorable push of urbanization); it has been uneven between urban centres (with the attendant socio-economic disparities); and it has fostered a concentration of people, activities, investment and wealth in a limited number of places (the rise of "city-regions" as new geo-political units). The city-regions, where population and employment growth has largely taken place, play an increasingly catalytic role in the development of Canada, acting as conduits and links between the regional and national economies and the global economy.

This pattern of evolution and development of Canadian cities is predicted to continue to prevail, with implications for smaller cities and regions located away from larger cities. Of particular significance are the opportunities (or lack thereof) to the residents of more peripheral centres to attract and retain people, economic activity, the provision and delivery of services, and overcome the different stresses imposed by far away locations. Strategic investment or re-investment in major regional centres — "hub cities" — could serve as effective and efficient conduits to help mitigate and even reduce the decline of peripheral places.[5]

Figure 2 illustrates this particular pattern of urbanization in Canada, especially this concentration of the population (as measured by its density) in a limited number of places and the existence of a limited number of city-regions in Quebec, Ontario, Alberta and British Columbia.

In the majority of Canadian cities and, especially in major and mid-size cities, the key change feature has been the expansion of their physical footprint, closely associated to the suburbanization development process.

Another change has been the broadening and greater coordination between federal, provincial and municipal governments in the establishment and application of guidelines and/or standards for the regulation and control of urban development, which has resulted in a relative improvement to the "built" environment and to the surrounding public spaces in some cities. Urbanization in Canada has also been blessed by the introduction, in selected cities and regions, of transformative actions and interventions that suggest great possibilities for emulation and adoption by others. Some of these actions and interventions include:

- residential development/re-development in downtowns and inner suburbs;

- emphasis on greater intensification and mixed land uses, allowing for better use of existing infrastructure;

- focus on the preservation of heritage assets and buildings;

- priority given to improving the quality of urban design;

- waterfront properties as key areas for investment; and,

- greening strategies, in terms of protection and enhancement of the urban forest, the use of water and the adoption of renewable energies.

Implications

In spite of these positive achievements, Canadians have failed in many respects to put in place the necessary conditions and mechanisms — regulatory, fiscal, market and community — to ensure the long-term sustainability, health and resiliency of their cities.

Some of the difficulties and problems generally associated with urban growth and change in cities in Canada include: poor integration of immigrants; homelessness; increase in criminality; shortage of affordable housing; change in economic base and lack of transition

Urbanization — Process of making urban, the removal of rural character.

J.B. Sykes (1980)

The entire urban system grew by 5.2 percent during the 1996-2001 census period while the nation's population expanded by 4 percent. Metropolitan areas (over 100,000) grew by 6.2 percent while smaller urban places grew by only 1.5 percent. The rest of the country, on balance, witnessed a declining population, for the first time in the post-war era.

Larry Bourne and James Simons (2003)

[5] See Mario Lefebvre and Natalie Brender (2006).

Figure 2
Population Density by Census Division (persons/square kilometre)

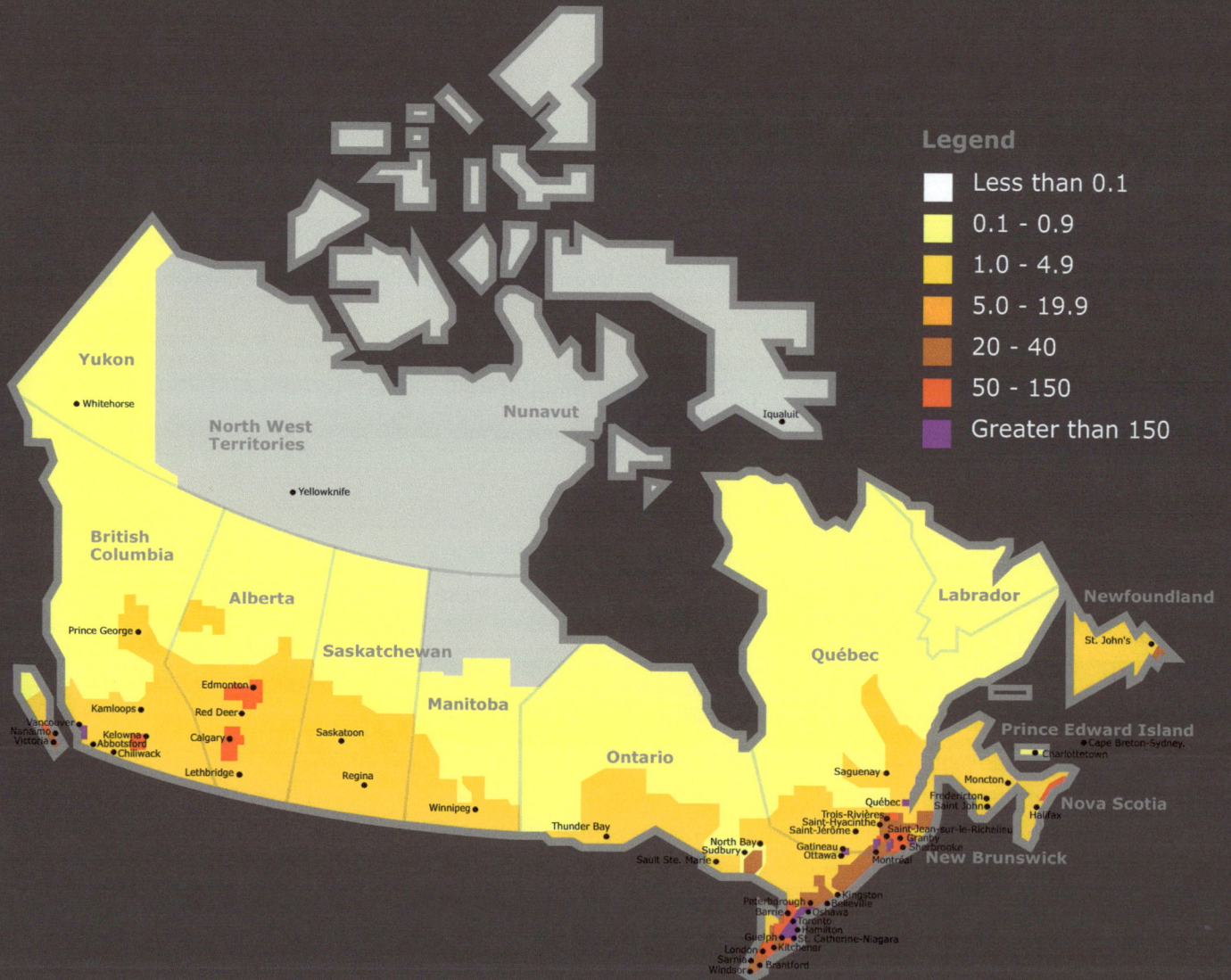

Legend

- ☐ Less than 0.1
- ☐ 0.1 - 0.9
- ☐ 1.0 - 4.9
- ☐ 5.0 - 19.9
- ☐ 20 - 40
- ☐ 50 - 150
- ☐ Greater than 150

Yukon

• Whitehorse

North West Territories

Nunavut

• Iqaluit

• Yellowknife

British Columbia

Alberta

Saskatchewan

Manitoba

Labrador

Newfoundland

Québec

• St. John's

Prince George •

Edmonton •

Red Deer •

Kamloops •

Vancouver •
Nanaimo •
Victoria •
Kelowna •
Abbotsford •
Chilliwack •

Calgary •

Saskatoon •

Lethbridge •

Regina •

Winnipeg •

Thunder Bay •

Ontario

Prince Edward Island

• Charlottetown

Cape Breton-Sydney •

Saguenay •

Moncton •

Nova Scotia

Fredericton •
Saint John •

Québec •

Trois-Rivières •
Saint-Hyacinthe •
Saint-Jérôme •

Saint-Jean-sur-le-Richelieu •
Granby •
Sherbrooke •
Montréal •

Halifax •

New Brunswick

North Bay •
Sudbury •

Gatineau •
Ottawa •

Sault Ste. Marie •

Kingston •

Peterborough •
Barrie •
Oshawa •
Toronto •
Hamilton •
Guelph •
Kitchener •
London •
Sarnia •
Brantford •
Windsor •

Belleville •

St. Catherine-Niagara •

Source: Adapted with the permission of Natural Resources Canada, courtesy of *The Canadian Atlas*, 2008.

mechanisms for the affected workers; environmental degradation; lack of investment in infrastructure; worsening traffic congestion and more air pollution through greater use of automobiles; failure to redevelop older neighbourhoods; and the continued segregation of land uses that increases the requirements for travel, among others.[6]

PLACE FOR DIALOGUE, EXPERIENCE AND LEARNING

Change in its many manifestations has been the central theme of this chapter. The following case study of the Canadian Healthy Communities Project addresses change as well, in relation to urbanism and the evolution that the project aimed to instil in its practice. Spearheaded by the Canadian Institute of Planners, it sought to reinforce and strengthen the affinities that exist between the planning, development and governance of cities and the health of their populations.

[6] Adapted from John Lorinc (2006).

Leading Practices:

Canadian Healthy Communities Project

In recent years, a positive benefit of the search for an improved and more holistic practice of urbanism has been the identification of often overlooked links and ramifications existing between cities and the broader environment in which they insert themselves and operate. One particular domain of inquiry that has garnered a good deal of attention and that has gained increasing traction in urbanists' circles is the connection between urban areas and the health of their population. Achieving healthy outcomes through the planning, development and governance of cities and regions is increasingly considered as important a goal as sustainability and resiliency.

In the late 1980s, the Canadian Institute of Planners (CIP) played a pivotal role in putting health at the forefront of the urbanists' and Canadian communities' agendas. Through a partnership with the Federation of Canadian Municipalities (FCM) and the Canadian Public Health Association (CPHA), CIP led the development and implementation of the "Canadian Healthy Communities Project" (CHCP). Although short lived — CHCP lasted only between 1988 and 1992 — it constituted an important milestone in the life of CIP, particularly in achieving a new level of maturity as a federated organization and in providing a higher profile to the profession of urbanism. It also laid the groundwork for the creation of a knowledge base, professional practices and healthy community networks that remain relevant and alive today. When looking at the challenges and opportunities of the practice of urbanism in the 21st century, it is worth remembering and drawing some lessons from the Canadian Healthy Communities Project.

Achievements

From a policy perspective, CHCP aimed to enhance the quality of life for all Canadians by involving municipalities and their citizens in ensuring that health is a primary factor in political, social, economic and environmental decision making. Other objectives included raising public health to a higher level of consciousness; to help people take their health into their own hands and to support each other to achieve an improved overall quality of life; approaching health in a more holistic manner, to move away from a strict medical definition, and recognize that healthy communities are built on a strong and viable economy, a physical environment of high quality, good public services, a respect for cultural traditions and diversity, and an active involvement of their citizens in public affairs; and, integrating health within a broader policy framework, such as the impact of the urban form and the design of the public realm in cities on physical activity and wellness.

As a process, CHCP was fundamentally a community capacity building effort. It enabled the empowerment of communities and their citizens, through the development of a shared vision, the assessment of the capacity of the community to realize the vision, and the development of strategies that can move the community's health agenda forward. It was also premised on broad-based participation of all stakeholders and of citizens, supported by partnerships and networks as well as by the use of coaching expertise to bring people forward to the new health paradigm.

Key outcomes of the CHCP comprised an implementation focus on the involvement of public schools and reaching out to different sectors of communities. Some examples of intervention areas included promoting and targeting environmental clean-up; reducing the use of pesticides; promoting the use of public transit and other alternative modes of transportation to cars; expanding recreational programs; improving air quality; fostering greater physical activity as a means to address obesity problems; and linking to crime-prevention activities. CHCP also contributed to the planning, development and governance of communities by helping to improve the relationships/collaboration between local communities and senior levels of government, enhancing the response to community need and the affirmation of a commitment to improved health, and broadening the opportunities for citizens to get involved in community decision making.

Limitations

At the time of its inception, the CHCP proved to be a truly visionary initiative, helping to connect people, communities and activities in ways not seen before. However, to this strength corresponded an important downside: CHCP literally caught politicians, administrators, professionals and the general public insufficiently prepared and equipped to assume and manage the changes and adjustments it entailed. As a result, it proved very difficult to put in place the conditions for solid constituency building necessary for its prioritization and integration in the agenda of key stakeholders.

What Was Learned

In order to ensure greater perenniality of programs such as the Canadian Healthy Communities Project, a number of conditions need to be fulfilled, including the importance of distributed leadership necessary to the emergence of credible champions; a broad-based implementation strategy that involves both a top-down and a bottom-up approach, fostering of the ongoing participation of all stakeholders and the maintenance of the necessary buy-in; the essential role and contribution of partnerships and networks; the creation of "deep ties" at all levels to successfully overcome changes in leadership and in the political arena; the need to make a difference in order to sustain interest and commitment by all stakeholders, especially the public; and, the crucial role of small projects initially, leading, in the best of all circumstances, to small wins that can be the subject of community-wide celebration. For the urbanists, the lessons learned included the need to think outside-of-the-box, to widen their professional horizons to become more responsive to opportunities beyond the traditional realm of their practice, and a willingness to extend their reach if it can make a difference in the life of communities.

Sources: Réal Lacombe *et al.* (2002), Susan Larsh *et al.* (2002), David Sherwood (2002), David Witty (1994, 2002).

Charlottetown

It takes time to make a house a home and it takes time to transform a settlement into a town and a city. There is just no substitute for time.

Hans Blumenfeld (1983)

CHAPTER 2

SOME EMERGING ISSUES AND QUESTIONS FOR CITIES

For more and more Canadians ... home is a multiple or fluid concept, a work-in-progress. They may feel attachment to a piece of territory, but they may also feel a loyalty to their partner's homeland, the country where their parents were born, the very different land where they are now stationed. Home has gone portable and invisible in the modern world and may have less to do with a house or a piece of land than with a set of beliefs or assumptions that one can share with someone in a far corner of the world or with someone one's never met. Global citizenship does not mean giving up a sense of roots so much as extending our senses of what roots involve.

Pico Iyer (2004)

In looking at the future of Canadian cities and what should guide their evolution, renewal, and in some instances, transformation, several critical issues and/or questions can be identified. Six such broad issues/questions are examined in a cursory manner below: cities and globalization, municipal governance, delivering services to Canadians, reconciling short- and long-term decisions, the range of communities' resources, and the fiscal and financial resources of cities.

CITIES AND GLOBALIZATION

Globalization is not a new phenomenon. It started in the 19th century under the impetus of significant technological innovations in transportation and communications. Its inception was also facilitated by the emergence of new political institutions, in particular, the consolidation of nation states, and a renewed economic order through the gradual development of international trade. Globalization was interrupted in the first half of the 20th century with the two world wars, the economic depression and the associated rise in trade protectionism. However, it has since regained and accelerated its momentum to become an entrenched and, most likely, irreversible element in the life of people wherever they are.

Globalization is integral to the long-term evolution of societies, economies and cultures at the national and international levels. It is a fundamental outcome of continuous and significant change in how different parts of the world interact, influence each other and transform their respective organization and institutions.

Much of the recent debate about globalization has been cast in black and white tones — some contesting its continued existence, others defending and promoting its many benefits. In light of the worldwide economic upheaval that has taken place starting in late 2008, characterized by a contraction in international trade and investment and the emergence of protectionist and nationalist reflexes in both developed and developing countries, the detractors of globalization may appear to have gained the upper hand.

But the reality remains one of many shades of grey; the future of globalization is not tied to short-term economic downturns, however serious they may be, but instead, is a function of the longer term structural evolution of world economic systems.

Local and regional development — attracting, retaining or losing enterprises, jobs and investments; sustaining improvement to the quality of life and environment over time; and creating the right conditions to integrate and nurture new people, skills and cultural diversity — constitutes generally the key area of focus and deliberation when assessing the positive and/or negative impacts of globalization on urban areas.

Opposing the evolving nature of globalization to the requirements for sustained local and regional development, a key question arises: *can this relationship between the reality of cities and globalization be approached in such a way as to bring into some kind of dynamic balance local needs and identities with the necessary trade-offs, compromises and difficult decisions resulting from the loss of cultural, economic and political oversight, and even control, to national and international organizations, institutions and networks?*

Canada and its cities have experienced some benefits out of globalization. They have also witnessed socio-economic, socio-political and environmental difficulties and problems that require societal awareness, attention and action. Looking to the future, the following challenge can be identified: *the extent or the degree to which urban and regional development can embrace globalization to further maximize and optimize local and regional returns while buffering and mitigating negative impacts.*

The interface between cities and globalization raises several additional issues/questions:

- the degree of support from senior levels of government in the provision of institutions and infrastructure in such areas as labour force skills, creativity and innovation; and the successful integration of immigrants, to sustain and lead economic competitiveness and cultural diversity;

- the role of public-private partnerships to help adjust to fiscal and financial limits and pressures;

- the level of participation in national and international forums and networks to frame and position local and regional interests;

- the role of these forums and networks in the implementation of international treaty commitments by Canada; and

- the quality of the environment and urban design considerations in planning and development decisions to reflect and protect local and regional identities.

MUNICIPAL GOVERNANCE

The governance of urban areas in Canada has witnessed some evolution and even transformation in recent times, principally in response to pressures exerted by urbanization and globalization. Two aspects more specifically of the reality of Canadian cities have proven to be fertile ground in evolving their governance:

- addressing the conflicts between central and suburban municipalities, through the rationalization of their territorial limits, the approach to urban and regional planning, and their fiscal and financial base; and

- addressing the emerging requirements of city-regions, e.g., Montreal, Ottawa-Gatineau, Toronto, Vancouver, through the introduction of more encompassing governance structures (formally or informally) as well as investments in public transportation infrastructure, among other mechanisms.

As we move deeper into the 21st century ... the name of the game has changed; instead of isolation, we are faced with the pressing reality of a single, rapidly evolving, global and multi-ethnic culture. The global culture dominates the biosphere with a logarithmically escalating effect; connections and relationships cannot be ignored, because what happens in one part of the world, whether economic, political, cultural, or environmental, affects all other parts. The built environment requires sustainable solutions that meet the needs of a network of people.

Philip N. Loheed and
Brandy H.M. Brooks (2006)

Governance is the sum of the many ways individuals and institutions, public and private, manage their common affairs. It is a continuing process through which conflicting or diverse interests may be accommodated and co-operative action taken. It includes formal institutions and regimes empowered to enforce compliance, as well as informal arrangements that people and institutions either have agreed to or perceive to be in their interest.

Commission on Global Governance (1995)

There has ... been a revival of the idea of consolidated metropolitan government after a period in which the virtues of fragmentation were preached. While the emphasis in the past tended to be on the need to expand service provision, now it is on the need for effective planning and investment to sustain economic growth and to curtail competition within metropolitan areas in order to enhance the competitiveness of the area against outsiders.

Michael Keating (2003)

In spite of a changing governance landscape, decision making at the local and regional levels is often disjointed and not well aligned with the emerging urban reality — especially from an intergovernmental perspective. Municipal governance is still very much a reflection of municipalities' 19th century origins rather than the governing institutions equipped to lead and manage in the 21st century.

The increasing interdependence that characterizes cities and their broader regions, in socio-economic, socio-political and environmental terms, does point to a key governance issue: *the extent of the collaboration between cities and other levels of government in finding the appropriate governance framework, responsive to cities' individual requirements, e.g., right size, appropriate decision making, context-sensitive policies, relevant programs, efficient services delivery, appropriate communication channels, etc.*

Other municipal governance related issues/questions include:

• the involvement of the public in the management of change;

• the use of consensus building and conflict resolution to bridge differences and gaps between groups and their interests;

• how to foster power sharing between levels of government towards the establishment of an optimal governance of urban areas;

• new perspectives, solutions and frameworks that can nurture and further advance a culture of collaboration; and

• whether the roles and responsibilities of the different participants in urban governance can be better defined and agreed upon.

DELIVERING SERVICES TO CANADIANS

The provision of public goods and services in Canada, in comparison with the delivery of public goods and services in other developed countries, is generally rated highly and is well appreciated by Canadians. Upon closer scrutiny, however, the performance of the current system is not always optimal in terms of the quality and quantity of goods and services delivered.

As has been documented over the last few years, the focus for the delivery of these goods and services has been on the needs and requirements of the providers: the different levels of government and other institutions, and to a lesser degree on the needs and aspirations of the users: the people of Canada.

Learning from and building on successful examples of integrated service delivery, such as Service Canada, Ottawa's government service centres, and BizPal, as well as the early adoption and use of Web 2.0 tools, would constitute a good starting point to reduce this service delivery gap.

More importantly and fundamentally, a service delivery transformation spanning all levels of government and other institutions, would eliminate duplication as much as possible, enhance the effectiveness and efficiency of supply mechanisms, improve responsiveness to citizens' rapidly changing needs and, finally, make the provision of public services more equitable, especially between larger and smaller cities.

Therefore, the reorientation of service delivery from a provider-centred to a user-centred paradigm raises the following issue: *the level of integration and coordination achieved by the different levels of government and other institutions in the delivery of public services to Canadians.*

Additional issues/questions related to the delivery of public services to Canadians include:

- to what extent can the involvement of users in the design and decisions on delivery of public goods and services be improved and expanded;

- how can the good standing of Canada in the provision of online services be enhanced;

- can renewed approaches to public goods and services delivery help address and alleviate fiscal and financial pressures; and

- could improved and decentralized people services contribute to keeping more residents in peripheral regions?

RECONCILING SHORT- AND LONG-TERM DECISIONS

Provincial planning acts and other legislation mandate municipalities to undertake short- and long-term planning and development. While obviously very diverse in application and scope, this planning and development authority has enabled many municipalities to successfully establish inspiring future visions based on community values, and determine key policies to help future decision making, while supporting their day-to-day activities and operations.

Balancing short-term development decisions with the long view consistent with a future vision is a key requirement if cities, for example, are to attain goals such as sustainable, healthy and resilient development *and* maintain their infrastructure. This demands enlightened leadership, political will, and a culture of planning and development that provides for flexibility and a capacity for evolution in the face of changing conditions.

Because of electoral politics — with its short-term focus at federal, provincial and municipal levels and concomitantly, the often intractable difficulty of balancing local issues with broader community goals — the overall record of Canadian cities and regions in balancing the short- and long-term aspects of their planning and development has not been all that successful and needs improvement.

Some of the current problems facing both small and large cities — conflicting land uses, congested roads, aging infrastructure, environmental risks, unsatisfactory provision of services, difficulties in controlling costs — can be directly associated with the failure to master this balancing act.

Two specific examples will illustrate this problem:

1. The failure to adequately supply affordable housing is linked to insufficient attention to such long view

A good e-government scheme starts off from the citizen's eye view, not the bureaucrat's one.
The Economist (2008)

What people perceive and how they perceive it determines how they react to it … [I]f a person perceives time in terms of a human life span, then 100 years seems to be long time. Using such a time horizon means that 5- or 10-year periods are considered long-term planning. What if time is perceived in terms of the age of the Earth though? In that case, a 100-year life span amounts to only 1/45,000 of the total 4.5 billion years survived by the Earth thus far. Such a perception makes 5- or 10-year periods anything but long-term. Obviously these widely varying perceptions of the same 100 years can lead individuals to make vastly different decisions about how they use the Earth's resources.
W.E. Stead and J.G. Stead (1992)

The time horizon implicated in a decision materially affects the kind of decision we make. If we want to leave something behind, or build a better future for our children, then we do quite different things than would be the case were we simply concerned with our own pleasures in the here and now.
David Harvey (1993)

... [A] fundamental problem in democracies [is that] [t]hey have great difficulty solving the long-term problems created by policies that provide short-run benefits. Once people receive the benefits, they do not want to give them up. But they cannot agree how to distribute the long-run costs necessary to sustain the benefits. Each group of beneficiaries tries to shift as many of the costs as possible onto other groups. In some cases the costs are not paid at all. Ultimately, such a failure undermines or offsets the short-run benefits. Increased traffic congestion and air pollution offset some of the benefits people sought when they moved to low-density suburbs. Yet these problems are partly caused by the very low density these people insisted upon.
Anthony Downs (1994)

considerations as the provision of social housing programs, the protection of tenant rights, the control of conversion from apartment to condominium tenure, and the existence of land use and fiscal policies to foster a mix of housing.

2. The sprawling metropolitan areas, while reflecting the interplay and results of market forces, nevertheless have failed to integrate the financial and fiscal costs inherent in this model of development and, more importantly, their systemic implications for human health, access to services by the less wealthy and other related dimensions of urban living.

On the basis of the above considerations, how shorter term and longer term decisions are reconciled in the governance of cities and regions can be seen to depend on addressing properly the following challenge: *the creation of the conditions to support a culture of and commitment to a long view, one that guides and informs short-term decisions.*[7]

Other issues/questions related to the necessary link between short-term and long-term decisions include:

• how to create the constituency and discipline required to implement the future vision over many generations;

• what changes to the tax systems would help harmonize longer term policy directions with ongoing city development;

• can the use of high-level planning at a broad community level and more detailed planning at the area and site levels achieve the benefits of balancing the short- and long-term planning perspectives; and

• what types of leadership and new institutional arrangements can be nurtured to support the integration of the long view in short-term development decisions?

RANGE OF COMMUNITY RESOURCES

Some of the key aims and aspirations for cities and their citizens are well-being, prosperity, order and sustainability — in other words, quality of life.

Traditionally, the creation of economic wealth through physical improvements such as manufacturing plants, office buildings, infrastructure, and transportation facilities, along with a positive regional and national trading balance, were seen as most important to support these aspirations. The quality of the relationship between the private and public sectors was also considered critical to the economic success of urban areas.

Achieving a quality of life for the country as a whole, its regions and its cities has, in reality, always been a much more complex undertaking. The economy, while a critical measure of success, must be approached from a larger and more diverse perspective, in which economic resources are combined with social, cultural, intellectual, political and environmental resources, acting in synergy or as catalysts for each other. Only by considering these many "layers" can the conditions for the creation of resources for the community be appropriately understood.

[7] See "Promoting the Long View" at the end of the chapter.

As well, the rich and diverse make-up and concomitant dynamism of urban areas must be seen through different "lenses". The limited perspective of the immediate, "on the ground" experience of Canadian cities and regions can be substituted for a more balanced view, one that combines the hard and also the soft sides, the latter finding specific expression in formal as well as informal relationships, and their tangible and intangible achievements.

Emerging from this broader definition of community resources is the following key governance challenge: *the creation and sustenance of a culture of conviviality that can successfully harness these different kinds of resources.*

Other issues/questions related to the management of the diversity of community resources include:

- how can cities better nurture the different networks that can underpin this culture of conviviality;

- where to begin in order to reverse the factors that inhibit community cohesion and integration; and

- what can be done to help bridge the different perspectives that society and people hold of "resources" and what underpins their creation?

FISCAL AND FINANCIAL RESOURCES OF CITIES

The fiscal and financial situation of cities has been an important topic of discussion and debate in Canada for a long time, constituting a key claim for change on the part of municipalities to senior levels of government and, more recently, as a core item of the intergovernmental agenda.

In the wake of a renewed interest in urban areas by the federal government — one not seen since the 1970s and early 1980s — the issue of municipal resources and funding has gained even more visibility and, at times, controversy. This is especially so for two distinct but related reasons.

First, because cities are the "creation" of the provinces in our existing constitutional framework, unilateral relationships between cities and the federal government are not permitted, at least in theory.

Second, the debate about the "fiscal imbalance" between federal and provincial governments — the outcome of reductions in federal transfers to the provinces since the mid 1990s — casts a shadow over new funding solutions for cities. It also limits the possibility of identifying any longer term change in intergovernmental funding arrangements in the near term.

Bringing about improvements to the fiscal and financial balance sheets of cities must be further considered in light of two competing realities. While everyone acknowledges and recognizes the crucial role of urban areas in the development of the country, they compete for scarce fiscal and financial resources with many other problems, issues and opportunities. The fiscal and financial plight of many cities is a direct outcome of this competition for resources, which has triggered successive rounds of downloading of funding responsibilities, initially, from the federal government to the provinces, and subsequently, from the provinces to the municipalities.

[T]he close physical proximity of intensely varied human experiences and conflicting aspirations ... is the engine that imbues urban life with its particular vitality: the city of opportunities, the city of ideas.

Jane Jacobs quoted in John Lorinc (2006)

[L]ocal government should be responsible for public services that benefit the local community ... [M]unicipalities should have access to local revenue sources so that they can fund those expenditures and taxpayers should pay for them according to the benefits they receive ... Provincial and federal governments should be responsible only for services that are primarily redistributional or for which there is a distinct provincial or national interest.

Harry M. Kitchen (2002)

In the United Kingdom, Europe, Japan and the United States, local governments have gained access to more stable and broad-based source of revenues than is available to most Canadian cities.

John Lorinc (2006)

Achieving consensus on municipal funding is absolutely essential to maintaining and enhancing the global competitiveness and prosperity of Canada — through renewed infrastructure and institutions, and by nurturing and retaining the talented and ingenious people, key to the emerging knowledge society.

A solution must be found in the affirmation and application of a number of principles related to the fiscal and financial resources of cities: budgetary and monetary stability; revenue sharing between levels of government; revenues linked to growth that can be the basis on which to develop cities; and a diversity of sources of revenues.

With these principles as guiding posts, the key challenge for the future resourcing of Canadian cities can be stated as follows: *there is a requirement for municipalities to have sustainable funding, corresponding to their expanded role in the 21st century, and to ensure that they can meet the many challenges of an urban-centric world.*

Other issues/questions related to the fiscal and financial resources of cities include:

• the strategic imperative to align the increasing number of responsibilities of cities with the appropriate fiscal and financial tools;

• how can cities better balance the use of regulatory and market mechanisms to address and meet their financial requirements;

• how should the fiscal paradigm of cities be reframed to create the necessary alignment with planning, development and governance policies;

• what new intergovernmental funding arrangements should cities be able to use in order to deliver programs and services;

• what new intergovernmental collaboration frameworks can be created to better confront the emerging fiscal and financial aspects of the urban agenda in Canada; and

• what types of public-private partnerships could be evolved to support the provision of additional resources to municipalities and how can such partnerships be structured so that risks and benefits are equally shared between the public and private sectors?

PLACE FOR DIALOGUE, EXPERIENCE AND LEARNING

Bridging the short- and the long-term in the planning, development and governance of cities was one of the issues addressed in this chapter. The following note demonstrates the challenges and the opportunities associated with this time dimension in the practice of urbanism.

Viewpoint:

Promoting the Long View

I have always found addressing and incorporating "time considerations" in urbanism both intellectually stimulating and central to any successful professional practice. If the expression "time is of the essence" has any true meaning, it is certainly to be found in the discipline of urbanism. My exploration and application of the time dimensions — short- and long-term — has taken place in many guises, in formal and informal work endeavours.

In the early 1980s, my work in the context of the federal-provincial Neighbourhood Improvement Program (NIP) led me to co-author a white paper that looked at the future of housing rehabilitation in Quebec to the year 2000. This reflection brought home the need to carefully and proactively consider the situation of the housing stock over time, especially the aging factor, and the key requirements to ensure its preservation over the long-term, among others, incentives to owners, private and public investments, skill sets of technical trades, design aspects and types of materials.

The development and use of project management and portfolio management in urbanism and real asset management provided another important window into my conceptualization and grounding of time and, in particular, in how to bring into focus and link short- and long-term considerations. Project management as a methodology based on discrete actions integrated in time through the use of schedules helps to discern and handle key factors in planning and managing project lifecycles. For its part, portfolio management, also with a strong lifecycle dimension, contributes to furthering the learning process in balancing short- and long-term factors in the stewardship of real assets, including financial, technical, environmental and material factors.

Finally, realizing the mandate of the National Capital Commission (NCC) clearly calls for the establishment of a comprehensive planning framework that permits bridging and coalescing past, current and future visions of Canada's Capital Region (CCR) by successive generations of Canadians and their leaders. In my capacity as the NCC Planning Director, I have found understanding and scrutinizing the previous work of capital planners very useful and insightful in helping to consider and chart possible future paths for the long-term development of the CCR. The past, as a key source of knowledge and learning of and for the future, constitutes for me much more than evidence; it is a golden rule worthy of closer attention and consideration by urbanists.

The focus on the short and narrow view that characterizes our current society is incompatible with the achievement of the goals of sustainable, healthy and resilient societies and cities. A different perspective of time — not animated by particular positions and interests but one espousing a generous world-view that transcends social, economic, political, environmental and geographical horizons — is clearly called for. The action of linking different experience and learning processes that involve debating and sharing a wide range of visions and ideas can offer insights that help bring into better balance and focus short- and long-term views of societies and cities.

Toronto

At the dawn of the twenty-first century, it is only a small exaggeration to say that cities are us, and we are cities.

Mark Kingwell (2008)

CHAPTER 3

THE EVOLVING CONTEXT FOR CITIES

Climate is, and always has been, a powerful catalyst in human history, a pebble cast in a pond whose ripples triggered all manner of economic, political, and social changes ... [H]uman relationships to the natural environment and short-term climatic change have always been in flux. To ignore climate is to neglect one of the dynamic backdrops of the human experience. The past 15,000 years provide many instances of climate change as a major historical player ... [H]umanity has become more and more vulnerable to long- and short-term climate change, as it has become ever more difficult and expensive for us to respond to it ...

Brian Fagan (2004)

Emerging from the previous chapters is a clear recognition and understanding that what can influence the evolution of cities and regions, their development, progress and growth has become inherently much more complex and also much more difficult to decipher for the formulation of future policies.

Indeed, beyond the types of change and the issues outlined before, there exist factors of evolution and trends that must be taken into account in order to gradually refine and complete the identification of the dimensions of Canada's urban agenda.

Some of these factors and trends are already manifest and significant in terms of their effects on urban areas. Others are not yet fully in play at this time but have been recognized as important future contributors to urban change in Canada and other countries.

Ten key factors or trends that provide the context for cities will be described in this chapter, not in any order of significance. They are: climate change, aging and health, population diversity, level of debt, creativity and ingenuity, life-long learning, lifestyles and transition of generations, democratic participation, scientific evolution, and security.

CLIMATE CHANGE

Of the many dilemmas and risks confronting societies and the world in the early years of the 21st century, perhaps none is being as contested and debated as climate change. The discussions around the implementation of the Kyoto Accord (1997) exemplify very well the contradictory stands that climate change elicits in individuals, groups, governments and societies.

Although the effects of human activities on the past, the current, and especially the future climate of the planet are generally recognized, no consensus exists on the exact scope of these effects, and the approaches that should be adopted in order to address and resolve them.

Agreement on a clear and well-articulated global action plan for climate change is unlikely to happen in the short- to medium-term. This is mainly because of the distance that separates the developed and developing countries in terms both of their relative contribution to the problem and more significantly, in their ability to make the necessary trade-offs — environment versus economy — required to affect changes that could help stabilize the climate.

As a result, and acknowledging their inherent limitations, continental and national plans and strategies will initially play a critical role in contributing to the reversal of some of the threats associated with climate change, and the reorientation of some of the activities that are at the source of climate problems.

Cities will obviously make an important, even significant, contribution to the success of any national or continental plans because of their concentration of population and activities, particularly the larger metropolitan areas. Some of the proposals and strategies to address both the threats and the reorientation of activities could very well be aligned with the emerging urban agenda. Others could have the opposite effect of diverting valuable resources away from the priorities of the urban agenda. Examples of the former include greening interventions, denser urban form and improved interface between land use and transportation planning. Any project specifically geared to mitigate the consequences of climate change — that otherwise would not have been necessary or initiated, such as to deal with shoreline erosion or to partially or completely relocate human settlements — represents an example of the latter eventuality.

At a more specific level, the environmental effects of climate change and the actions taken to mitigate them or to adapt to them, will affect cities' revenues and expenditures, their operations, and how they organize and deliver services in such areas as transportation, infrastructure, housing and economic activities and development, among others.[8] A commitment to sound and coordinated urbanism practices will help ensure that cities are adequately equipped and provided with the necessary capacity to mitigate or adapt to climate change.

AGING AND HEALTH

The gradual aging of the population as a fundamental demographic trend in most societies will be the most significant demographic change to take place over the coming decades — in developed countries in the short term, but also in developing countries within the next two decades. While some countries in the aftermath of wars have experienced deep demographic transformations, such a shift in the structure of the population will nevertheless be unprecedented in the history of the world.

Often associated with the aging phenomenon — for the right but also for the wrong reasons — is the emergence of health care as the number one preoccupation of people in developed countries, including Canadians, at the beginning of the 21st century. Over the last two decades, the share of health expenditures in Canada, as measured against its gross domestic product, has risen consistently, with the result that it is now one of the highest in the world.

Historically, a direct linkage has been established between older populations and the increased level of required health services. In the debate about health in Canada, the hypothesis is that this correlation will be maintained in the future and that health care budgets will indeed need to continue to rise — taking into account the other cost factors of health services, especially research and development, technology and human resources.

The "baby-boomers" are often recognized as having a better overall health profile than the generation that preceded them. Also, the younger generations — X and Y — espouse certain lifestyles — such as the importance

The rising atmospheric concentration of GHG's is causing the atmosphere to warm and climate to change. In Canada, the effects that can be related to change in the climate can already be noticed; these include an increasing number and intensity of heat waves, declining water levels in the Great Lakes, melting of Arctic sea ice, changes in fish stocks and migration patterns, increasing frequency and severity of fires and insect infestations in forests, increased heat-related weather problems, and more extreme weather events.

Treasury Board Secretariat (2003)

[I]f we are to look to demography as a tool to help us anticipate the future and plan accordingly, it is time we stopped simply counting noses and began to carefully consider how the presence and behaviour of great numbers of a new type of old person will fundamentally alter society ... [W]e're ... finding that the predictive power of age is diminishing because North Americans aren't behaving as past generations did at the same stages of life ...

Allan R. Gregg (2004a)

[8] See "Bio-climatic Urbanism — Profiling the work of Norman Pressman" at the end of the chapter.

[U]ne bonne partie de la population n'a pas encore pris acte de la décroissance démographique. Les politiciens doivent aussi tenir compte des personnes âgées, qui ont un poids politique important dans la plupart des démocraties. Comme elles sont directement touchées par les changements qui seraient nécessaires pour faire face au vieillissement de la population, il devient plus délicat d'agir politiquement.

Jonathan Trudel (2005b)

In February 2005, the Heart and Stroke Foundation released its latest Report Card on the Health of Canadians, which looked at the relationship between community, transportation and health ... The study found that Canadians living in major centres were twice as likely to walk, bike or use the public transit to commute to work than those living in suburbs or in the country. Over three-quarters (77%) of urbanites also reported they walked or biked to do daily chores, compared to 60% of other Canadians...

Corrine Hodgson (2005)

of balance in their life — that could yield a more preventive approach to health care than was the case before. However, while a more intense demand for health care may be delayed perhaps for a decade, it will come as the need for "assisted living" (including housing) increases with the baby-boomers living longer.

Although the link between aging populations, health services, and the role of cities is not necessarily direct and of the first order, it will assume much more prominence, as the requirement for a more effective and integrated approach to governance becomes key to the success of the urban agenda.

Addressing the implications of aging through activities and relationships between generations and enhanced accessibility and mobility for older people can contribute in a significant way to the achievement of sustainable, healthy and resilient communities. Redirecting to a certain degree the approach to health care, by way of a more holistic perspective that clearly associates healthy people with healthier lifestyles, healthier work environments, and healthier living conditions, can also help achieve similar outcomes. The importance of good planning — that can provide for seniors to age in place, to be mobile and to remain active — needs to be underscored. Any impediment or threat to the fulfillment of any of these dimensions of the lives of our seniors will contribute to the overall reduction of their quality of life.

Obviously, to successfully navigate such an evolution in urban areas will also demand difficult trade-offs between different priorities, including economic development and employment, infrastructure investment, how transition between generations is handled, and resource allocation.

DIVERSITY OF THE POPULATION

The development of Canada as a modern country has been founded, to a large extent, on the welcoming of immigrants from all over the world, and their successful integration into the fabric of our society, with all the benefits but also with the many challenges this entails. Noteworthy is the shift, throughout the 20th century, from the predominantly European origin of immigrants to a more decentralized/distributed origin, mainly from Asia but also from South America and Africa.

As a result, Canada finds a great deal of its identity based on the diversity of its people. From a global perspective, this openness to the world and the close relations it enables and facilitates with numerous countries located on the five continents, represents a definite strength at the beginning of the 21st century.

When considering the changing makeup of Canadian society, immigration has for a long time been, and will continue to be, a substitute for the natural increase in population, since Canada has experienced a continuous decline in the birth rate of the population over the last decades of the 20th century.

Although immigration is a shared responsibility between the federal and provincial levels of government, cities, as gateways to immigrants, have been and will remain key players in their successful integration into Canadian society.

Lately, following the sheer increase in the number of immigrants — between 200,000 and 250,000 on an annual basis so that 20 percent of Canadians are now foreign born — the integration process has experienced some shortfalls, particularly in the provision of adequate housing and access to relevant employment.

While greater coordination between stakeholders is helping to remove some of the barriers to immigrant settlement, over the medium-term Canadians will have to discuss and decide what is a viable absorption rate for new immigrants in order to fully benefit from the social energy and the creativity they bring and, at the same time, to ensure that their integration is achieved, respecting Canada's cohesion and values.

Ultimately, the continued successful integration of immigrants hinges on Canada's ability to coordinate the basic requirements for integration (being a "welcoming community") — housing and employment, and also education and people services, among others. These integration requirements will need to be set within the broader environment of the country, such as the course of evolution of the urbanization process, the possible fluctuations in global trading, and the increasing attention devoted to national and continental security.

LEVEL OF DEBT

The use of debt as an instrument by federal and provincial levels of government to fund programs has been a key but also a problematic factor in the governance of the country. When considering public sector debt in combination with corporate and individual debt, the financial outlook of the country becomes even more challenging for future generations.

While deficit-free budgets constituted a key policy of the federal and provincial governments over the last decade and have helped to significantly reduce Canada's debt/GDP ratio, the recent economic/financial crisis and its implication for debt management, represents a significant set-back for the country's ability and capacity to put its fiscal house on a normalized path.

As a result, the burden of debt will remain a significant preoccupation for the medium- to the long-term when considering the liabilities that are likely to arise from future demands for spending in such areas as pensions, health care, climate change, infrastructure and security.

From the perspective of the emerging urban agenda, the present and future levels of debt constitute a major area of risk for the country. As such, improved planning and coordination will become increasingly critical if any aspect of the urban agenda is to be realized within the financial and fiscal pressure that high levels of indebtedness bring.

CREATIVITY AND INGENUITY

In many fields of endeavour — science, medicine, energy, aeronautics, aerospace, culture, social and political institutions — Canada has an admirable record in terms of innovation, invention and creativity. The country has evolved, in particular, a superb ensemble of colleges and universities that make a significant contribution to the knowledge and innovation infrastructure of all major Canadian cities. These post-secondary educational institutions have also developed close links with the private and not-for-profit sectors in building their research capacity.

[T]he very notion of a mosaic society, as opposed to a melting pot, tells new Canadians that they can think of citizenship in a less exclusionary way than they did before.

Pico Iyer (2004)

In a landmark 2001 study, the Conference Board of Canada estimated the country loses $4.1 billion to $5.9 billion in income annually because it does not recognize the professional qualifications of 540,000 people. That includes almost 350,000 immigrants, most of them from China and India ... The reasons for this dilemma are complex. The educational system somehow works for dewy-eyed high-school graduates; but it is ill-equiped to assess adults with degrees from foreign lands. Then there are the regulatory bodies themselves: understandably cautious about maintaining quality, some have taken refuge in rigid formulas that protect existing members. Finally, there is the Canadian curse of multiple jurisdictions: there are more than 50 regulated occupations, each with its own provincial and territorial organization ...

Mary Janigan (2003)

La norme internationalement reconnue pour évaluer l'endettement d'un pays demeure le ratio de sa dette sur son PIB. À ce chapitre, le Canada se compare très avantageusement au reste du monde : de presque 70% en 1994, son ratio est passé à 42% (en 2004) … [L]e renversement des 10 dernières années est spectaculaire.

Emmanuelle Garnaud (2004)

Being creative means being able to relax into uncertainty and confusion. In most organizations this is becoming increasingly difficult because things move far too fast. People feel that they have hardly any time for quiet reflection, and since reflective consciousness is one of the defining characteristics of human nature, the results are profoundly dehumanizing.

Fritjof Capra (2002)

[L]'apprentissage tout au long de la vie [est] la condition essentielle pour qu'une société entre vraiment dans l'ère du savoir.

Déclaration de Hambourg quoted in Valérie Borde (2004b)

However, when compared with other developed countries, especially the United States, and using a common benchmark — number of patents per capita per year — our performance is less enviable. Historically, Canadians have not stressed investment in research and development activities. This situation results, to a large extent, from the greater preponderance of the public sector in the working of the economy, the absence of fiscal and financial incentives to foster and sustain research and development, and the related implications for the development of an entrepreneurial ethos. It should be mentioned, though, that in recent years, governments, with leadership from the federal government, have made significant strides to turn around this underinvestment in R & D funding.

The solution to many of the issues facing the country and its cities will require constant and renewed funding of original solutions — involving more creativity, ingenuity and innovation. In consideration of the interrelated nature of most of the key challenges posed by the emerging urban agenda, it is becoming increasingly clear that traditional approaches will not work.

The public, private and volunteer sectors must encourage and support creativity, ingenuity and innovation in all aspects of their activities. This is especially important when the financial and fiscal pressures identified above are considered as part of the development and realization of urban plans and strategies.

LIFE-LONG LEARNING

The transition from an industrial to an information age — with a change in focus from physical to intellectual products — has long been heralded and promoted. More recently, the "knowledge society" has become the key moniker of the transformation of life in the late 20th and early 21st centuries.

In global and national societies, founded on constantly evolving and increasing knowledge, the act of learning has had to take new forms. While in the not too distant past, learning was mainly associated with the early stages of life, in a knowledge-based society the requirement becomes one of continuous, life-long learning.

The competitiveness of cities depends to a large extent on the successful adaptation and transition of all educational institutions, especially colleges and universities, to this new world-view.

In Canada, formal education is not a municipal responsibility. It falls under the jurisdiction of the provincial government and the mandate of local school boards. The movement to a knowledge society and economy requires transforming learning in cities from a context dominated by educational institutions to an environment enabling all individuals to access life-long learning.

A good example of this transformation is the important contribution made by public libraries for the first learning experiences of newcomers, including their apprenticeship and mastery of English and French. Similarly, a more optimal use of existing public facilities — making schools accessible for community activities on a 12-month, day and night, and weekend basis — would support more transformation of learning in Canadian cities.

Although this new approach to learning is gradually being acknowledged and accepted by individuals, businesses and institutions, its ramifications and implications for the emerging urban agenda are not well understood nor well grasped.

Setting the stage for life-long learning represents many changes for cities — in terms of their overall culture, what it means for the life of their citizens, but also their physical structure, their infrastructure networks, their urban form, their organizations and their governance.

LIFESTYLES AND TRANSITION OF GENERATIONS

It has been observed that a key influence in the evolution of Canadian cities after World War II involved rapidly changing lifestyles — especially the aspiration of families to own a single family home. These new lifestyles were nurtured through the interplay of a growth in wealth, regulatory instruments and financial conditions encouraging home ownership, the increasingly dominant role of the automobile, the decentralization of employment and retail, and the rise of mass communication and consumption, among others.

Lifestyles are still an important but also a changing contributor to the shape and structure of urban areas at the beginning of the 21st century. In particular, the increased awareness of the environmental implications of "sprawl", generally associated with the suburban model of development, for both housing and employment, has resulted in a stronger appreciation for older community areas, including central areas and downtowns, as good alternative places for "working, living and playing".

The consolidation and intensification of urban areas, albeit only in its early stage, is an important trend. Accounting for this are the financial and fiscal costs of sprawl and the greater linkage made between land use and transportation (the latter is increasingly seen as a means rather than an end in providing accessibility and mobility in cities). The transition from a dominance of single uses to mixed uses is also considered increasingly as an ideal model for communities. Furthermore, the transformation of the real estate industry in terms of the diversity of legal and financial development instruments, has contributed to the intensification of cities through the construction of infill projects and the rehabilitation of brownfield sites.

In parallel with these changes is an interesting phenomenon of "convergence" between the "baby-boom" generation and the younger generations. While differing significantly from financial and socio-cultural points of view, these generations have similar aspirations with regards to their preferred type of urban environment. This phenomenon, in combination with the wealth transfer between generations

In a knowledge-based economy, we need people who know how to learn and who keep learning throughout their working lives. The universities and colleges will be an integral part of this new economic system because many people are going to need retraining and re-educating during their working lives. Our post secondary institutions will have to become more responsive and flexible to meet the changing needs of their clientele ... If the demand for continuing education is coming from the workplace, then it makes good sense to take courses to the source of the demand and present them in the workplace or close to it.

David Foot and Daniel Stoffman (1996)

Les organisations qui excelleront vraiment dans l'avenir seront celles qui auront découvert l'art de faire appel à la motivation et d'exploiter la capacité d'apprentissage des gens à tous les niveaux organisationnels.

Peter Senge quoted in Government of Canada (1993)

[T]he boomers' ballyhooed inheritance windfall is not panning out as planned. In 1990, many leading economists predicted that, over a 20-year period, the amassed assets of the frugal and debt-shy Depression and wartime generations would enrich their free-spending offspring ... But far less — perhaps as little as half — is actually being passed on ... [F]orecasters had failed to take into account the impact of parents living longer, or the possibility of a prolonged period of historically low interest rates that would hurt retirees' income.

James Deacon (2004)

When electors cease to go to the polls, it weakens the foundations of democracy because they are tacitly saying: the individual has little impact or say in our national affairs; the welfare of the collective has little bearing on individual well-being, and individual well-being can flourish or flounder independent of decisions initiated through legislative democracy ...

Allan R. Gregg (2004b)

that could take place over the coming decades, are indeed very promising and encouraging trends in what is generally presented as potential sources of problems and conflicts.

These positive dimensions of relations between generations will hopefully influence future intergenerational dialogue on such topics as education, employment, technology and the place of Canada in the world. They can also ensure that issues affecting future generations, such as the payment of the public debt and the level of contribution to public pensions, will be dealt with in a more open and positive frame of mind.

DEMOCRATIC PARTICIPATION

At the municipal, provincial and federal levels of government, participation in the electoral process has fluctuated in recent years, with a definite downward trend being observed. Overall democratic participation appears also to be diminishing, eliciting pointed warning signals from academic and non-academic observers. A key consideration raised in that context is the ability of the different mechanisms for democratic participation to reflect not exclusively special interests but a broader view of community interests.

It has been demonstrated again and again that broader participation makes for much better decisions. A dialogue involving all concerned parties in an issue enables the consideration of many more dimensions as well as allowing for a greater variety of points of view and possible solutions to a problem.

Broader participation not only helps create the right conditions for many different decisions but also a constituency that will help sustain the dialogue over time, the balancing of different interests, and the achievement of the longer term community agenda and vision.

Leadership — shared and distributed — is a key ingredient for healthy democratic participation, in terms of commitment to the institutions but also in ensuring the creation of networks, enabling wide involvement of people, and demonstrating that their opinion counts, not only the opinion of a selected few.

The problems encountered in establishing strong democratic participation as a part of the communities' culture have many sources and causes, including the preference for a hierarchical, top-down approach. It is an approach to participation that expects people to come to the institutions all the time instead of having institutions come to the people some of the time.

Many consequences result from this reduction or absence of broad participation: the bonds of community spirit become more fragile; cynicism and skepticism towards community institutions is the norm rather than the exception. In addition, community memory risks disappearing at a time when it should be maintained and strengthened, in order to help create a new future and also face difficult situations.

Considering the many challenges that lie ahead for Canadian cities, the nurturing and rekindling of democratic participation will be very important — a key priority for municipalities and senior levels of government to address, along with other participants. This will require vision, leadership, flexibility and creativity to invent new institutions, a longer rather than a shorter view, an ability to consider different interests but at the same time move away from self-interest, espouse consensus building, and an inclusive approach to decision making.

SCIENTIFIC EVOLUTION

Cities in Canada and elsewhere, are constantly confronted with challenges, unforeseen events and crises, in physical, socio-cultural, economic and political terms. In the past, many challenges faced by cities, such as public health in the late 19th and early 20th centuries, have been the source of many protracted efforts to arrive at solutions. The supply of renewable energies and the replacement of aging and inefficient infrastructure illustrate some of the dilemmas of the 21st century.

The uncertainty generated when efforts to resolve urban problems result in failure, can be a source of pessimism, anxiety and despair. When looking at the history of cities from a broader perspective, a brighter side can be painted on this darker picture — scientific evolution, discovery and technological innovation have helped improve a sustained quality of life and environment in cities.

The contribution of scientific discovery and technological innovation to the development of cities has been both a response to this search for solutions to specific problems, and also as a facilitator of totally new directions — improvements to water and waste-water infrastructure are examples of the former, while computer technology and the Internet can be cited as examples of the latter.

Based on the issues confronting Canadian cities at the beginning of the 21st century, it can be safely asserted that solutions will benefit from upcoming scientific discoveries and technological development in fields as varied as genetics, new materials, ecology, biology, medicine, energy, pharmacology, physics, psychology and information/communication technologies, among others.

The approach of future public, private and volunteer sector leaders to the solution of urban problems can take many forms. This includes acceptance of problems and correction or mitigation within a more integrated approach. The combination of imaginative actions that benefit from scientific discoveries and technological development will constitute a key area of priority. It should contribute many solutions for cities, in accord with the many choices and trade-offs that the urban agenda will require.

SECURITY

Following the disturbing and painful events of September 11, 2001, the security of people, property and country was raised to the top of governmental concern in North America and elsewhere. Because of the

[T]he internet seems to have had remarkably little impact on mainstream politics. That will not remain true for much longer. Communication is the lifeblood of politics, and every big change in communication technology, from the printing press to television, has eventually produced big, and often unexpected, changes in politics. As the internet becomes mobile and ubiquitous, it will bring about changes of its own. Precisely what these will be is not yet clear, but the ... claims ... that the internet will produce a shift of power away from political elites to ordinary citizens may well become reality.

The Economist (2003)

Canadian scientists have contributed immensely to the beauty and marvel that are science's legacies to humanity ... There are myriad Canadian scientists whose work justifies the idea that discovering the intimate, detailed nature of the universe is essential to ... humanity ...[M]uch of the work of Canadian scientists had practical effects ...

Larkin Kerwin (2004)

*Without security, democracy
is impossible.*

Fareed Zakaria (2004)

*Closing streets and sidewalks
destroys the vitality of our cities and
should be used only as a last resort.
Finding effective long-range security
solutions for our cities must become
a top government priority. If we
allow our public realm and national
civic spaces to look terrible, then
the terrorists will have succeeded.*

Mike Sheridan quoting
Richard L. Friedman (2004)

important role that safety and security play in the working of democracy, and also the diffuse, intractable nature of terrorism and acts of organized crime — that can strike anywhere, anytime — such a focus on security was, and is, totally understandable.

Furthermore, the security risks posed by large cities — because of the possibility for terrorists to hurt many people — is of special concern and cannot be underestimated nor minimized.

The need to integrate both corrective and preventative actions in the area of security is key to the aim of government to foster and provide quality of life and environment for its citizens. When safety and security dominate all other aspects of society, these goals become less and less achievable and sustainable. The pervasive presence of surveillance cameras in the United Kingdom is illustrative of this dilemma.

Because of the values espoused by Canadians, and our history of collaboration and peaceful approaches to the resolution of differences and conflicts, combining corrective and preventive approaches to the response to security and safety issues and concerns is easier to envision and realize. When superimposing the security agenda on the life of cities and the operations of municipal governments, the balance between the protection of people and property and freedom — symbolized by openness, quality of development, and good design — takes on a special meaning and importance.

By their nature, cities that work well offer an excellent model for preventative security measures. Through the combination of design, density, spread and mixing of activities and land uses, any security threat can be minimized and mitigated through the constant provision of "eyes on the street". If security dominates the design of cities, it reduces the mixing of people and their activities through the creation of separate spaces and "no man's land" — which can have the opposite effect of heightening insecurity in people and creating opportunities for unwanted acts.

Also, cities that have benefitted from enlightened leadership have participated in various national and international networks of cities. Through these networks they can contribute to better understanding between cultures, and promote international collaboration and awareness — important elements to prevent the insularity and separation that are often at the root of conflicts and security risks.

Diagram 1 provides a visual tool to view the many complex elements that constitute our cities, and to build our appreciation of what changes need to be undertaken to place cities on the path to a "projet de société" (the urban agenda) as the 21st century further advances. The overarching metaphor for the city is the large circle, with the notion of a "world-view", as introduced in the beginning of Part 1 of this book. The vertical line represents our path towards the urban agenda and the horizontal line, the time continuum. Their waviness reflects the shifting nature of the journey of Canada's urban reality.

Diagram 1
Schematic View of the Development of the Urban Agenda, Part I

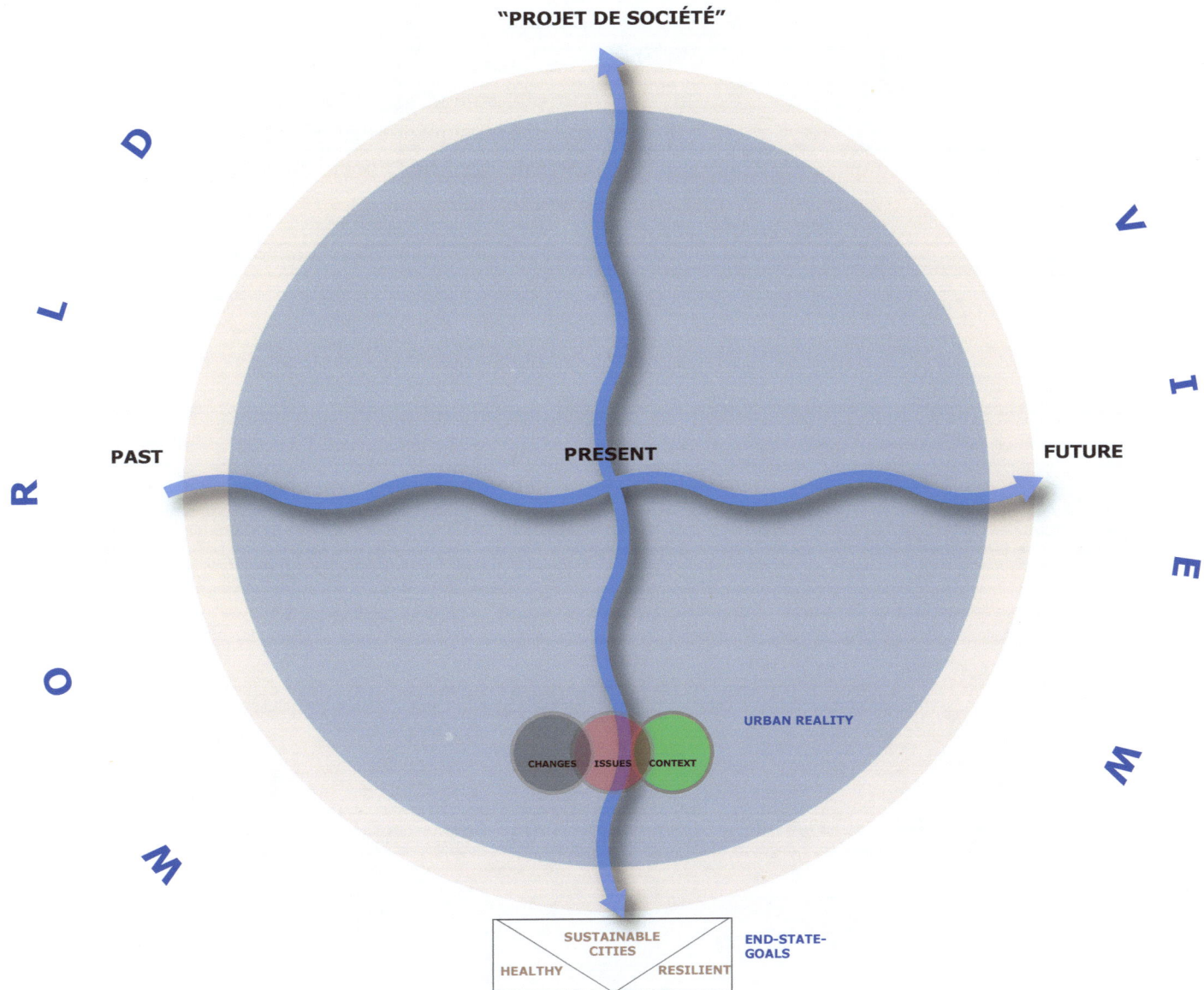

The ultimate "end-state" goals, those of sustainable, healthy and resilient cities, are represented at one end of the vertical line, and were proposed in the Introduction. The circles just above the goals — the changes, issues and context — are discussed in detail in chapters 1, 2 and 3. They represent one aspect of the urban reality which will be further elaborated in Part II.

PLACE FOR DIALOGUE, EXPERIENCE AND LEARNING

Climate change was shown as one of the most significant factors of evolution for cities over the coming decades. The following case study documents the important work of a Canadian scholar, Norman Pressman, in bettering our understanding of the relationships between climate and the design of cities and in helping Canadian cities prepare for the transformation that climate change will represent.

Leading Practices:

Bio-climatic Urbanism: Profiling the Work of Norman Pressman

One of the most important dimensions of the Canadian *oekoumène* (human habitat) is its Nordic environment and character. While human settlements in Canada have evolved with climatic conditions as an incontrovertible consideration in the planning and development processes, as a general rule, climate has been envisaged in a narrow perspective — as a limiting factor that must be overcome, rather than in a more holistic context, presenting both opportunities that need to be optimized and constraints that can be mitigated with appropriate design and technologies. When looking to the future, with climate change looming as a defining factor for the planning and development of Canadian cities — through mitigation and adaptation measures — the place of climatic considerations will, by necessity, have to be amplified and given much greater priority.

Norman Pressman, Professor Emeritus of the School of Planning at the University of Waterloo, has dedicated much of his career as a researcher and teacher to the improved understanding of the role and influence of Nordic climate conditions on the planning and development of human settlements. Through his leadership role in the Liveable Winter Cities Association and his work as a consultant in Canada and abroad, he also contributed in a major way to the identification and elaboration of policies, strategies and measures for the optimal integration of climatic factors in the design of habitable, sustainable, healthy and resilient environments. The main contribution of Norman Pressman's body of work has been to articulate and define

the following three tenets of the theory and practice of bio-climatic urbanism: good bio-climatic urbanism is good urbanism; climate-sensitive design is integrative by definition; and climate-sensitive design is based on a number of key characteristics.

Achievements

Good bio-climatic urbanism is good urbanism, with appropriate coordination of human, natural and built design elements. Climate considerations need to be integral to the design process, addressing inherent constraints but at the same time proactively incorporating responses to possibilities offered. The development of place-specific, climate-sensitive design must combine traditional, vernacular knowledge and experience with appropriate scientific and technological aspects and inputs. It must also reflect and balance the requirements placed by seasonal variations and fluctuations. Through culturally based vocabularies, climate-sensitive design contributes in important ways to communities' sense of place and helps convey meaning and identity.

Climate-sensitive design is a four-pronged integration effort: level of the region, of the community, of the neighbourhood and of the site. It is by definition locally driven instead of relying on the importation of international standards and guidelines. Involving citizens in climate-sensitive design processes helps not only in nurturing awareness but also shaping climate-responsive perceptions and behaviours. It can also help make urban living more dynamic by energizing the use of public places throughout the year, in all four seasons. The influence and imprint of the climate on the activities and the design of communities should be the subject of celebrations — through festivals as an example — rather than the focus of criticism.

Key characteristics of a climate-sensitive design approach include using compact rather than dispersed spatial configuration; using vegetation as wind screen; siting buildings on the basis of sun and wind orientation; allowing sunlight to penetrate between buildings; shielding sites and buildings from winter winds; locating and sizing building openings to optimize natural lighting conditions and contribute to energy efficiency; and, using various protective devices to make the use of public spaces more climate-responsive, such as public transit shelters, archways and colonnades.

Limitations

Because Norman Pressman has always advocated a holistic perspective and approach to climate, the integration of climate change considerations to his body of work on the theory and practice of bio-climatic urbanism can be envisaged more as extensions of it rather than limitations. However, a more focused attention on climate change principles, strategies and guidelines will necessitate closer consideration of "resiliency" as an end-state for the planning, development and governance of cities and regions — in addition to the goal of comfortable, habitable, sustainable and healthy cities and regions. In the development of mitigation and adaptation measures to climate change events, risk management and emergency management will broaden the tool kit for climate-sensitive design.

What Was Learned

The current perspective and approach to the planning, development and governance of cities and regions is often characterized by an absence of a comprehensive framework for the management of climate issues and challenges. Climate is an important mediating aspect between living conditions and design considerations.

Appropriate attention to climate conditions through a climate-sensitive design approach can make living, working and playing in Nordic environments more comfortable and interesting during the four seasons, extending the comfort-zone of people in their day-to-day lives. The failure in the past to properly integrate climate in the planning, development and governance of cities and regions may account to a certain degree for the time it has taken Canadians to appreciate the reality of climate change and the extent to which its effects will impact and transform their lives.

Sources: Norman Pressman (1995, 1996, 2004, 2005).

PART II: WHAT DOES IT TELL US?

[W]e must look beyond the bricks and mortar to the issues underlying the physical organization of urban society if we want to know what instils a sense of pride and belonging in citizens.

Eleni Bakapanos (2005)

Quebec City

The process of seeking equilibrium is the essence of civilization.

John Ralston Saul (2001)

CHAPTER 4

KEY CONSIDERATIONS FOR AN URBAN AGENDA

In this chapter I begin to make the transition from the broader context of Canadian cities to a review and discussion of the scope and scale of the urban agenda and some of its "key drivers". It includes a cursory examination of some of the factors that underpin the "shifting reality" of urban Canada and selected guide posts on the "road traveled" toward charting an urban agenda.

On the strength of these considerations, a number of urban outcomes and results (or "key drivers") are identified that can help Canadians grasp the essence of Canada's urban agenda.

URBAN CANADA: A SHIFTING REALITY

The following observations distill some of the important characteristics of Canada's urban reality:

• Canadian cities have changed significantly and will continue to change.

• Canadians have successfully navigated some aspects of this urban change but have also experienced difficulties and registered setbacks in dealing with some other changes.

• Increasingly, and this has been the situation for a while, some of the factors influencing the evolution of cities are less and less, if not at all, under the control of local decision makers, i.e., stemming from increased urbanization and globalization.

• The differences between cities — their unique factors of change, their issues, and the other influences that manifest themselves in some and not in others — make a "one size fits all" approach to their planning, development and governance even less desirable and acceptable.

• The interplay between the different contextual elements of urban areas is creating greater complexity and blurring traditional roles and responsibilities of the different levels of government.

• The pace of change has increased and continues to increase, and there are many who wish to participate and have a say in decisions concerning cities. As a result, cities face much more complex governance, with a great deal more uncertainty and risk for decision makers.

• As some large cities have evolved into city-regions, their size and complexity have made it particularly difficult to find the appropriate and most viable governance structure.

• The fragmented delivery of public goods and services in urban areas is increasingly challenged by users, who are demanding simpler, more integrated and cooperative approaches from their governments and institutions.

- A key aspect of the evolution of urban areas is the need for new ways to address future challenges, with a clearer sense of priorities for the short- but also the long-term.

- Transitional approaches, experimentation and consideration of "leading practices" will play a key role in steering urban areas.

- Leadership will be an essential ingredient in the successful evolution of urban areas — to ensure that all necessary communications take place from the top as well as from the citizenry. Also, leaders will play a key role in facilitating a shift in the perspective of Canadians towards an increased awareness of the reality of cities.

- More specifically, there is a requirement to break away from the past in order for Canada to succeed in an urban world, and foster in Canadians a full understanding, commitment and role that can ensure this success.

- A new approach to the planning, development and governance of cities — more collaborative and integrative — must be substituted for the traditional perspective and approach, which was focused and arranged around distinct areas of municipal organization and separate operational units, e.g., making the transition from bureaucratic silos to networks fostering and promoting lateral/horizontal coordination and cooperation.

- Three key "end-state" goals — sustainable communities, healthy communities and resilient communities — are increasingly recognized for the purpose of guiding the planning, development and governance of Canadian cities in the 21st century.

CHARTING AN URBAN AGENDA: THE ROAD TRAVELED SO FAR[9]

The evolution towards the enactment of an urban agenda in Canada has been a long, winding journey, confronted by many challenges and barriers. "The road traveled so far" can be broken down into five parts: initial attempts, environmental agenda, macroeconomic considerations, recent intergovernmental dynamics and looking ahead.

Initial Attempts

1950s-1960s

The postwar economic expansion in Canada was, in important ways, an urban phenomenon. The concentration of people and activities in cities led to the emergence of new needs and aspirations that the different levels of government had to acknowledge and address, in conjunction with the private and, increasingly, the not-for-profit sectors.

Accommodating the growth and physical expansion of urban areas found responses through a variety of governmental actions and interventions. Because of the absence of a strong planning tradition — a consequence of the economic depression and the focus on the war effort, combined with the very limited collaboration/coordination between the different levels of government — new policies and programs were rapidly put in place by the federal government, in particular, in housing and infrastructure.

If we are not clear about what we think is wrong with our democracy we will be in no position to decide whether changes we are considering will make it better ... [T]here are elements of the system that are working well ... At the same time, the current system was designed for the 19th century. It needs to be updated for the 21st. The real challenge will be sorting out ... what works from what doesn't. We ... cannot do that if we are not clear on the problems we are trying to solve ... Our democracy needs to be reinvigorated and modernized — that is clear. But we must take the time to be sure that we get it right.

Donald G. Lenihan and Graham Fox (2006c)

---

[9] Key source for this section is Gerald Hodge and David L.A. Gordon (2008).

Urban renewal emerged in recognition of the fact that a large portion of the buildings in Canadian communities were half a century or more old ... The central parts of many cities, which were also the oldest sections, suffered most from physical deterioration. Urban renewal was an effort to restore the commercial attractiveness of downtown areas and avoid the loss of investment they represented.

Gerald Hodge and David L.A. Gordon (2008)

With an expanding real estate market, older areas in cities — where most urban planning, development and governance problems were to be found — became the subject of particular attention by the Central Mortgage and Housing Corporation.

The "urban renewal" program was launched in the late 1950s with the aim of restoring the physical fabric and the socio-economic vitality of older areas in Canadian cities. Through the use of a "shared cost" approach, the urban renewal activities pioneered a closer collaboration between the different levels of government for the purposes of program delivery and implementation.

Because urban renewal interventions had a significant negative impact on communities — uprooting families, destruction of heritage buildings, insufficient attention accorded to quality of design, deleterious effects on local identities — it rapidly drew a great deal of criticisms. By the late 1960s, "urban renewal" was abandoned as it no longer corresponded to prevailing societal values. From this urban renewal pushback would emerge the first social movements and interest groups, and this would also trigger an increasing demand for the participation of citizens in the affairs of their communities.

On the other hand, the "shared cost" approach would prove the precursor to future, more successful intergovernmental programs, e.g., Neighborhood Improvement Program (NIP), Residential Rehabilitation Assistance Program (RRAP), and urban development agreements.

1970s-1980s

In the early 1970s, a more activist federal government established the Ministry of State for Urban Affairs (MSUA). With the intent of determining the interest of the federal government in urban areas, MSUA, over the following decade, would become known for leading-edge research on cities and the source of extensive policy analysis, with the aim of re-imagining the planning, development and governance of urban areas within national and international contexts.

However, the provincial governments never warmed to the mandate and role of MSUA, claiming an infringement of their jurisdiction over municipal affairs. This resulted in a standstill over how the senior levels of government approached cities and their evolving governance requirements. This failure in credibility and in achieving results brought about the dismantling of MSUA in the early 1980s.

Despite the absence of clear success through these initial attempts at fostering an urban agenda for Canada, not everything was for naught from an intergovernmental perspective. In response to the criticisms to and collapse of the urban renewal program, federal policy reviews in the early 1970s resulted in the installment of new intergovernmental housing and urban redevelopment programs. The NIP, providing grants to cities to upgrade civic amenities and infrastructure, and the RRAP, providing grants geared to the renewal of existing housing stock, enabled significant improvement in the fabric of the older parts of Canadian cities up until the late 1980s/early 1990s.

Environmental Agenda: 1970s-1980s

An emerging environmental consciousness in the early 1970s, which fostered a new policy environment in Canada in the decades that followed, has had far reaching implications for cities and the eventual transition toward an urban agenda.

At the international level, the energy crisis combined with the publication of several influential books and reports, and the organization of United Nations' sponsored conferences related to the environment and urban areas, provided, initially, important policy stimulus and direction to the different levels of government in Canada.

This highly charged environmental agenda created an impetus for innovative legislative actions, e.g., the adoption of federal and provincial environmental evaluation acts, active Canadian involvement in the international dialogue on cities, e.g., Vancouver Habitat Conference, and the adoption of "sustainable development" as a guiding policy principle and framework at the federal, provincial and municipal levels of government.

While the influence of the environment has only been indirect in advancing an urban agenda for Canada, it will continue to play a catalytic role in bringing the different levels of government to assess and ascertain their respective responsibilities for the long-term quality, order and sustainability of urban areas.

Macroeconomic Considerations: 1980s-1990s

A number of macroeconomic factors have had a significant influence over Canadian urban areas and the evolution toward an urban agenda. Similarly to the environmental agenda, this influence has proven also more indirect but of consequence in how the prosperity of Canada and its cities is approached from a policy perspective.

Canada entered the 1980s in the throes of a deep recession, with inflationary pressure rarely seen in the economic evolution of the country. The prospects of the Canadian economy — productivity, trade balance, ability and capacity to change from a resources-base to a more diversified economic base — were the source of a great deal of concern and anxiety at the time.

The election in the mid 1980s of a federal government espousing a more market-driven ideology — in contrast to the earlier interventionist ideology — lead to the consideration and adoption of new macroeconomic strategies for Canada.

The strengthening of the trade relationship with our continental neighbours, the United States and Mexico, proved to be the most important and transformative economic policy platform during the late 1980s and early 1990s. The trilateral North American Free Trade Agreement (NAFTA), that ultimately came into effect in the mid 1990s, has had a momentous effect on Canada's trade volume and trade balance. Because of the dominant role of urban areas in the Canadian economy, this new trading framework has exerted significant pressure on municipal

The 1987 Report of the World Commission on Environment and Development [...the Bruntland Report] defined sustainable development as: "ensur[ing] that [development] meets the needs of the present without compromising the ability of future generations to meet their own need". This broad concept became a primary goal in many Canadian community plans at the end of the 20th century, pushed along by public concerns about global warming, climate change, and other future legacies.

Gerald Hodge and David L.A. Gordon (2008)

[The British North America (BNA) Act of 1867] did not provide communities with the right to a local government, but only specified that the responsibility for establishing municipal institutions lay with the provincial governments. Section 92 of the BNA Act defines this prerogative. [The 1982 Constitution carries forward the same section].

Gerald Hodge and David L.A. Gordon (2008)

governments to adjust their resources, infrastructure, fiscal and amenities foundations. It has also forced senior levels of government to consider the needs of cities in a new light, if the economic benefits of more open trade are to be sustained in the future.

But at the same time as free trade was dominating the economic and political agenda, another macroeconomic factor was rearing its ugly head: the structural dependency on deficit financing and the alarming increase in the size of the Canadian debt (especially at the federal level) in relation to the gross domestic product.

Some initial efforts were made in the late 1980s to begin to address this problem — mainly by the downsizing of the federal government — but the actual reality check and frontal assault on deficit and debt occurred in the mid to late 1990s, fueled by both national and international pressure points.

While addressing this structural imbalance was clearly urgent and important, the solution not only affected the organization and operation of the federal government but also, and more importantly, the whole fiscal and financial redistribution system that underpins Canada's federalism and its intergovernmental relations regime.

In the same way that the renewed trading framework would have significant implications for the prosperity of urban Canada, this new fiscal and financial reality between senior levels of government would also trickle down to the municipal level, through downsizing, downloading or reduction of services, and the elimination of housing and urban redevelopment programs.

Notwithstanding the reversal of some of these policy and program decisions over the ensuing years, Canadian municipalities are still coming to grips with the consequences and ramifications of these transformative changes. From an urban agenda perspective, the role of cities in Canada's governance structures, in relation to how important macroeconomic and socio-economic decisions are made, remains an open ended question.

Recent Intergovernmental Dynamics: 1990s-2000s

Over the last two decades, three events marked the intergovernmental milieu and calendar in Canada in a significant way, and contributed in distinct but related ways to the progress — or lack thereof — towards charting an urban agenda: constitutional discussions, fiscal transfers to municipalities, and the climate change debate.

In the aftermath of the 1982 constitutional amendments — which failed to achieve unanimity and contributed, instead, to the creation of a divide between senior levels of government — national unity and jurisdictional issues rapidly came to dominate the intergovernmental relations.

As a consequence, the resumption of constitutional discussions in the late 1980s and early 1990s was dominated by the search for a new balance of power and dynamic between federal and provincial governments. The Meech Lake and Charlottetown accords reflected this narrower constitutional agenda and left other important dimensions of Canada's governance unattended. Particularly absent from these discussions was the role of cities in a changing country and what place they should occupy at the intergovernmental table.

On the fiscal side of the intergovernmental ledger, the claim by Canadian municipalities for more diversified sources of revenue — revenue options that would allow them to address and better manage the cyclical nature of urban economies and move away from a strict structural perspective represented by property taxation — has been a constant source of tension between senior levels of government and municipal leaders.

The permanent transfer of a share of the gasoline tax by the federal government to municipalities, with the cooperation of the provinces, in the mid 2000s, was obviously a source of relief for municipalities, providing them with a little more fiscal room to address many of the issues confronting urban areas, including the infrastructure gap. In as much as these new funds contributed to the revenue diversification objective, much more dialogue and negotiation between levels of government needs to take place if urban areas are to see improvements to their governance, and if they are to be called upon to contribute their share to the ongoing prosperity and sustainability of the country.

Climate change has represented another challenge in recent intergovernmental relations, more particularly in how contemporary environmental considerations are to be factored into the future evolution of Canada's governance. The debate surrounding the implementation of the 1997 Kyoto Accord, through the requirement for national, provincial and municipal action plans, has proven to be divisive, culminating in the conflict within the Canadian delegation at the 2010 Copenhagen climate conference. Similar to the constitutional and fiscal conundrums characterizing the intergovernmental dynamic in Canada in the early years of the 21st century, the way the country and Canadians will respond to the environmental/climate challenges will dictate, to a great extent, the scale, scope and shape of the evolving urban agenda.

Looking Ahead

The lack of recognition of cities as a force to be reckoned with in the Canadian intergovernmental, environmental, macroeconomic and socio-economic contexts is a good illustration of missed opportunities in the recent evolution of Canada's governance.

The limited autonomy of municipalities and the push by the provinces to exercise increasing control over them during the 19th century and the first decades of the 20th can be understood due to the predominantly rural character of Canada at the time. But the changes that have taken place since — essentially, Canada having become mostly an urban country — and the important role that cities play and will increasingly play in Canada's future, especially the larger ones, explains the claim by municipal authorities for a fresh approach to governance in Canada. They no longer want to be a sideline observer. They feel entitled to a full and legitimate place at the intergovernmental table, in charting a future course for the country and the role of cities within it.

Despite the strongly held differences of opinion on how Canada should be governed, the urban agenda represents many opportunities and positive energies that can help bring Canadians together. These energies

By the end of the 19th century, provincial governments were beginning to limit the discretion of municipalities. This process, which would continue throughout the 20th century, came about through a complex interrelationship among changing technology and material conditions, the growing interventionism of provincial governments, the increasing strength and organization of professionals, perceptions of municipal inefficiency and corruption, and changes in ideology and definitions of citizenship.

Caroline Andrew (1995)

By the end of the twentieth century, interdependence in federations was increasingly coming to be seen as applying ... not just to the two orders of government within federations, but to their international relationships and the operation of local governments ...

Ronald L. Watts (2003)

Forward-looking urban leaders ... recognize that constructive, locally driven partnerships between governments, academic institutions, not-for-profit organizations, ethno-cultural groups, businesses, and neighbourhoods are much more in tune with the orchestral rhythms of city life than those cacophonous partisan political feuds over archaic jurisdictional boundaries.

John Lorinc (2006)

Smart cities are re-inventing themselves for people — and where, and how, people live. Smart cities are becoming "cities by design".

Larry Beasley (2004a)

should be harnessed outside the realm of constitutional modifications. Coming to grips with the urban agenda could help transform intergovernmental relations into a more collaborative climate that could pave the way to a fruitful reopening of constitutional discussions down the road.

Moreover, in undertaking this exploration of solutions to some of the urban problems confronting Canada at a very basic level, we must consider carefully the recent experiences and decisions of countries around the world with respect to the transfer of responsibilities to municipalities as a lever for addressing and dealing with the consequences of globalization through more effective governance at the local level. Over time, inherent to the urban legacy that we wish to bequeath to future generations of Canadians, there should be governance arrangements that provide municipalities with the necessary autonomy, flexibility and range of resources to make the best local decisions and provide the best services to their citizens.

What is required in the short- and medium-terms is not a wholesale transformation of how different levels of government work together, but a pragmatic approach to the identification of the actions that will ensure the sustainability, health and resiliency of cities and allow them to play their critical role in the development and prosperity of Canada. A clear sense of direction and a capacity on the part of political leaders to re-imagine and reposition the place of municipalities in Canada's governance, will be key ingredients for such change in intergovernmental relations and thinking.[10]

A new vision for Canada and its urban areas, based on collective and individual will and effort, and the benefits of a renewed cooperation between the different levels of government, is clearly discernible, if we really care to look and consider it. Compromise and tripartite approaches to problem solving should be the hallmark of this new beginning — nothing revolutionary there. The revolution will lie in the reconsideration of who should be at the centre of attention, in the search for solutions and new ways to deliver the urban agenda.

When this question has been properly and serenely answered by Canadians and their governments, we will likely be closer to a governance breakthrough.

KEY DRIVERS OF THE URBAN AGENDA

To begin to capture and discern the essence of Canada's urban agenda, it is useful to examine some key outcome and result areas that are increasingly recognized as fundamental drivers for coherent and sustainable urban policies and action plans. Currently, there appears to be a prevailing hesitancy on the part of Canadians to fully embrace them. Nevertheless, taken as a whole, they can help set the stage for a more detailed discussion later on future urban goals and objectives for Canadian cities.

Seven drivers that focus on the physical dimensions of the urban agenda are described in this chapter: urban form, environment, housing, employment areas, physical infrastructure, community facilities, and natural resource areas.

---

[10] See "Repositioning Strategies in Urbanism" at the end of the chapter.

Urban Form

Urban form is a major structuring element of cities that reflects incremental community decisions and actions. The overall outcome sought in evolving the ideal urban form in cities: *is the achievement of sustainable and healthy urban areas, including quality urban design, that makes an important contribution to people's quality of life, through the balancing of continued progress and growth of cities with the creation of new "smart" communities and the revitalization of older ones, via adherence to contemporary principles, guidelines and standards of "good urbanism".*

Some of these principles, guidelines and standards, representing urban form key results, include the following:

- the physical footprint of cities has been reduced through increased intensification of land uses;

- mixed uses are thoughtfully used and account for an increased share of new development;

- densities reflect sensitivity not only to the economic value of lands but also to human scale and their local impacts;

- quality of design — derived from the application of design reviews and professional peer reviews — is not only inspired but also inspires a sense of identity, helps contrast the public from the private realms, and contributes to a positive civic image;

- land uses are integrated with accessible, affordable and energy efficient transportation;

- public transit is accessible in less than 10 minutes on average from all residential, employment and other public use areas;

- modal share of public transit has increased over recent years relative to private vehicles;

- universal accessibility is a standard feature of all development projects; and,

- cultural, heritage and/or archaeological resources are preserved and/or rehabilitated.[11]

Environment

The environment constitutes the foundation layer of cities. The overall outcome sought in incorporating environmental values and considerations in the city-making process: *is to create a sustainable, healthy and resilient environment, one that reflects a layered, multi-dimensional and meaningful character and identity, through the balancing of the protection, preservation and good stewardship of air, water and soil community resources with an excellent city design and building framework, via adherence to contemporary environmental principles, guidelines and standards.*

Some of these principles, guidelines and standards, representing key environmental results as well as environmental management and stewardship mechanisms, include the following:

- the urban environment:
  - ▶ is respectful;
  - ▶ minimizes the production of CO_2 and other greenhouse gases while fostering the maintenance of air of quality;

If we want to maintain a high quality of life in our cities, we have got to be more effective in building a different kind of place that is less dependent on cars, more walkable, more dense and more appealing to the needs of people throughout their life cycle. Our vision must embrace authenticity of place ...

Paul Bedford (2005)

[F]ertile ground can be found in ... improvement of the existing "built environment", with the highest profiles being in "heritage" properties and districts ... Although legally designated "heritage" properties represent only a tiny fraction of [Pre-Wold War II buildings] ... their catalytic effect on development patterns is dramatically disproportionate to their numbers ... [T]he fundamental planning question is how they will be used and maintained? ... [H]eritage is not an alternative to development; it is an alternative form of development. Instead of the 1960's pattern of flattening buildings to start over ... heritage-type work makes exteriors look as they were intended while upgrading interior systems and livability to today's standards ...

Mark Denhez (2003)

---

[11] See "Heritage Rehabilitation — The Lachine Canal in Montreal" at the end of the chapter.

[B]rown-fields represent a significant lost economic opportunity. Left untouched, they can damage local economies and in some cases, pose threats to human health and environmental quality. Cleared up, and returned to productive use as sites for new housing, offices, parks or recreational facilities, redeveloped brown-fields consistently generate economic, social and environmental benefits ... [R]e-development of brown-fields across the country could deliver the equivalent of $7 billion in public benefits, not including direct commercial gains realized by those responsible for development. Redeveloping one hectare of brown-field can avoid the development of approximately 4.5 hectares of green fields. The resulting public "windfall" results from more compact, efficient urban growth, and ultimately, more competitive cities.

National Round Table on the Environment and the Economy quoted in Sara Melamed (2003)

▸ emphasizes renewable energy sources and minimizes the production of ambient light through the protection of the dark sky;

▸ fosters a water consumption regime maximizing recycling and reuse measures;

▸ uses context sensitive storm water management methods; and,

▸ enables the recycling and reuse of urbanized lands, including soil decontamination through brownfield site redevelopment.

• environmental assessment instruments and processes are appropriately and consistently used;

• fiscal, financial and regulatory aspects of environmental planning, management and stewardship are fine-tuned and the source of incentives;

• funding and financial incentives are available for the redevelopment of brownfields;[12]

• environmental decision making supports international environmental commitments made by Canada; and,

• public incentives combined with market mechanisms support the integration of environmental preservation with urban development.

Housing

Housing is an important component of the urban form and provides a response to a basic social need of urban residents — the requirement for shelter accommodation. The overall outcome sought in reconciling the supply and demand of housing in cities: *is to deliver a sustainable and healthy housing stock, through the balancing of the response to individual circumstances and lifestyle choices as well as an appropriate variety of dwelling types and tenures with accessibility, affordability and quality considerations and conditions.*

Some of the key results targeted through the housing sector of cities include the following:

• supply of land provides for short- and long-term housing needs on a market absorption basis rather than a jurisdictional basis which often creates an oversupply situation;

• the range of housing types and tenures affordable to people at different income levels, including "special needs" programs that are created to support residents with temporary or more permanent accessibility and affordability problems;

• efforts that are coordinated among all concerned stakeholders to address and reduce homelessness;

---

[12] The importance and role of incentive/disincentive systems for the future planning, development and governance of Canadian cities will be a recurring theme throughout the book. In this regard, I would reference the leadership taken by the National Roundtable on the Environment and the Economy (NRTEE) in reflecting on and proposing a range of incentive/disincentive approaches, with a particular focus on the environment/ urban development interface.

- development of housing reflects proximity between employment and residential areas, and supports public transportation and other alternative modes to the automobile; and,

- development of housing integrates other goals such as mixed land use, "green construction" and a life-cycle perspective and approach.

Employment Areas

Employment areas represent a component of the urban form and provide a response to a key socio-economic need of urban residents — meaningful and remunerative work. The overall outcome sought in determining future locations for employment areas in cities: *is to supply a sustainable, healthy and resilient range of employment opportunities, through the balancing of a diversified economic base with the requirement to integrate employment activities across the broader community.*

Some of the key results targeted through the employment sector of cities include the following:

- diversity of employment locations are supported by an adequate supply of land for a range and mix of office, retail and industrial uses;

- vitality of central areas and main streets is maintained and enhanced;

- locations for employment growth are identified and prioritized;

- transport demand management measures constitute a key stewardship strategy at the majority of major employment centres; and,

- employment areas are conceived and integrated in the context of broader community goals, such as mixed land use, proximity to residential areas, access to transport and especially public rapid transit corridors, and the use of "green technologies" and "green construction" in the design of employment sites and buildings.

Physical Infrastructure

Physical infrastructure is a defining feature of the urban landscape, comparable to the urban form in its degree of influence on the structuring of cities. The overall outcome sought in identifying future infrastructure networks needs: *is to provide for sustainable, healthy and resilient infrastructure types — transportation, water and waste-water, energy, communications, security — necessary for the orderly development of cities and for their economic competitiveness, through the balancing of the maximum use of existing infrastructure networks, including their rehabilitation, with the development of new infrastructure geared to specific growth-areas, such as transit-oriented network development.*

Some of the key results targeted through the physical infrastructure component of cities include the following:

- planning and maintenance of infrastructure is based on the long view through a life-cycle perspective and approach, and the introduction of new standards reflecting changing climate conditions;

Supportive housing — housing that includes ongoing social services such as counselling or job training — is considered the most successful solution to the problem of homelessness ... [Also] increasing the amount of public funding directed to affordable housing is a critical piece of the larger strategy for solving homelessness ...

City of San Francisco report quoted in Vince Hoenigman (2003)

Employment land is important for many reasons. From a planning perspective, employment land is part of the balance of uses that municipalities plan to encourage thedevelopment of healthy and vibrant communities. From an economic development perspective, employment land accommodates a lot of jobs [45% of the total employment in the Greater Toronto Area]. And employment lands are not only important in suburban locations ... Not only does employment land matter to individual communities, from a broader perspective it is also a crucial factor in keeping our metropolitan and national economies healthy.

Antony Lorius (2004)

Les réseaux de transport constituent des éléments structurants de l'aménagement du territoire et, à l'inverse, l'aménagement du territoire influence de manière déterminante la demande en transport ... [L]es investissements en transport contribuent à orienter la croissance et à déterminer l'extension spatiale des métropoles, bien que d'autres facteurs soient également en cause pour expliquer comment s'organise une agglomération ... [U]n des outils les plus significatifs à cet égard demeure l'équilibre emplois-logements. Ainsi les temps de déplacement domicile-travail sont toujours plus courts pour les zones où les nombres d'emplois et de résidents sont mieux équilibrés ... [L]a solution aux problèmes de mobilité passe par une meilleure gestion de l'utilisation du sol ...

Adapted in part from R. Cervero and J. Landis Paul Lewis (1997)

- consideration and implementation of alternatives to traditional public funding include a role for the private sector when appropriate and on the basis of a demonstration that it coincides with the public interest;

- requirement for greenhouse gases reduction is recognized and accommodated;

- public investments are increasingly prioritized along or adjacent to public infrastructure corridors; and,

- infrastructure planning, development, maintenance and rehabilitation integrate broader community goals such as transport reduction measures, coordination between land use and transportation,[13] mixed land uses, adoption of "green technologies" and deployment of "green infrastructure", support for alternative energy and energy conservation, and protection of future infrastructure corridors.

Community Facilities

Community facilities, representing another component of the urban form, play a dual role in the life of cities — as a response to different local socio-economic and socio-cultural needs and as a source of identity for residents and communities as they interact with the outside. The overall outcome sought in establishing sustainable, healthy and resilient community facilities in cities: *is to provide a range of cultural, educational, health, recreational, meeting spaces, open spaces and green space endowments, responsive to residents and visitors needs and aspirations, through the balancing of more immediate, day-to-day community requirements with broader community interests, associated with the provision of services geared mainly but not exclusively to external clienteles.*

Some of the key results targeted through the community facilities component of cities include the following:

- the range of community facilities responsive to both local and external needs and aspirations;

- the presence of community facilities as an additional criteria to confirm either the timeliness or the prematurity of development projects, in addition to physical infrastructure criteria;

- community facilities express and reflect community values;

- planning and development of community facilities based on public discussions while shaping local identity and mirroring local diversity;

- community facilities help shape urban form and contribute to quality of life, of the environment, healthy living and lifestyles;

- community facilities contribute to community economic development, as key components of tourism infrastructure;

- planning, development and maintenance of community facilities integrating a life-cycle approach;

---

[13] See "Thinking Strategically about Transportation" at the end of the chapter.

- development of community facilities incorporating "green technologies" and "green construction"; and,

- community facilities as contributor to the safety and security of communities.

Natural Resource Areas

Resource areas, a sub-layer of the broader environmental layer, represent another major structuring element of cities, in addition to the urban form and the physical infrastructure. The overall outcome sought in identifying and designating sustainable, healthy and resilient natural areas in cities: *is to protect and preserve watersheds, agricultural lands, forests, wetlands and shorelines as guarantors of the community's environmental integrity and as a source of identity, through the balancing of their short-term use in response to community needs with their long-term stewardship, as bequests to future generations.*

Some of the key results targeted through the natural resources component of cities include the following:

- watersheds constitute a key territorial reference unit in the planning, development and governance of cities and regions;

- the ecological integrity of natural ecosystems is protected;

- role of natural areas is broadened through the consideration and integration of the "ecological services" concept — natural areas acting as a "green infrastructure" and contributing to biodiversity preservation;

- natural areas are protected from encroachment and development;

- surface and ground water supplies are legally protected;

- management and stewardship of natural resources integrate appropriate environmental assessment methods;

- prime agricultural lands are protected and their re-designation for urban uses strictly limited or prohibited;

- agricultural employment succession is a key consideration in communities' human resources planning and management;

- local food is provided and supplied to markets;

- land use buffers are identified and protected; and,

- public access to shorelines is allowed with ongoing monitoring of negative impacts.

Contrary to many predictions, there is little evidence that increased use of computer modems is dispersing population or economic activity. But other transformations are more of a threat ... [U]rban abandonment ... is very much underway in Canada ... In the face of these troubles, there is enormous doubt as to how government should respond ... [G]overnment must invest in the dignity of their cities ... [T]he cultural dimension of the urban experience is too often neglected by local authorities in Canada ... Nothing can be more democratic than investment in the public realm of a great city.

John Barber (1995)

[B]etter urban growth policies means less agricultural land lost to urbanization. Applying this type of framework as the foundation of effective growth management changes the pattern of urban growth from a greenfield-based view to a city-building philosophy that promotes efficient use of existing urban land and infrastructure to accommodate a greater amount of population growth.

Greater Toronto Area Agricultural Action Plan quoted in John Michailidis (2004)

Municipalities and the public are becoming increasingly aware that the health of our communities depends on access to vibrant natural areas. Beyond the well-known ecological benefits of urban nature such as wildlife habitat and biodiversity, the social and economic contributions are becoming better understood. By bringing people together, urban nature strengthens community ties and creates a sense of place. Naturalized landscapes also reduce landscape maintenance and storm-water treatment costs, thereby increasing adjacent property values and more.

Stewart Chisholm (2002)

PLACE FOR DIALOGUE, EXPERIENCE AND LEARNING

A key challenge for decision makers in Canada and elsewhere is to overcome inertia in governance structures and come up with tools and frameworks to help chart new paths for evolution and change. The first note proposes such a framework, enabling the consideration of transformative change through different lenses and with a different appreciation of the evolving realities of cities.

The urban form and the physical infrastructure constitute two defining drivers for the urban agenda. In the next two notes they are considered in greater detail, i.e., the heritage preservation and rehabilitation, and transportation planning and implementation, respectively.

Viewpoint:

Repositioning Strategies in Urbanism

An interesting challenge constantly confronting the professionals of urbanism is how they can address the changing realities — especially the transformative types — that affect all communities, in meaningful ways, leading to appropriate policy responses. When approaching these types of situations, a first level of inquiry generally consists of scanning of the local, regional and more global environment, providing both diagnostic and prognostic measures of the forces underlying community change and evolution. Moving to a deeper and more comprehensive level of analysis and synthesis usually follows, where urbanists provide an appreciation of the different layers of reality characteristic of communities, as well as their interfaces, with a focus on the integration of social, economic, political, temporal and geographical aspects with procedural aspects and considerations. With the recognition of the massive and unpredictable change that will confront society in the foreseeable future, the ability and capacity to propose "repositioning strategies" — the renewal and the necessary adaptation to visions, policies, plans and action programs in response to forces of transformation in communities — will be a key strength of the urbanist and a major contribution of his/her profession. Some illustrations based on my practice are offered below.

The creation in the early 1980s in the Saint-Jérôme Region of a new governance institution — the regional county municipality (RCM) — and the development of a first regional plan, meant significant changes were required for the nine local municipalities and their councils working together and planning a territory that they previously had

approached in almost total isolation. The controversies associated with the planning and development of the Mirabel Airport by the federal government, and the adoption and implementation of provincial legislation, seen as too normative and prescriptive, further compounded the difficulties to get elected officials, particularly the mayors, to espouse this alternative governance framework and obtain their commitment to make it work.

The main challenge when I initiated the preparation of the regional plan was to set in motion a number of initiatives that would enable the mayors to look at their work using different "lenses" than before and bring them to recognize new criteria of appreciation for the larger territory for which they collectively were now entrusted with planning and stewardship. In effect, the mayors had to evolve a totally new world-view to make possible this transition from one planning regime to another. Although, after four years, the outcome proved to be quite modest and territorial silos were still very much prevalent, the adoption of the first regional plan helped the introduction of innovative processes and practices that energized a shared working experience; triggered the creation of a base for a planning constituency in the RCM; and enabled tackling, at a regional level, such issues as transportation, economic development and waste management.

When I joined the National Capital Commission (NCC) in 1992, it had entered fully into what can be described as the "post 1950 Gréber Plan era". Several factors underscored this passage to a new period in the life of the organization including: the transition to a renewed mandate putting a greater emphasis on the national role of the NCC with a corresponding de-emphasis of the support provided to regional development; a budgetary and fiscal environment characterized by a definite retrenchment in contrast to the financial abundance of the 1960s and the 1970s; a new style of relationship with municipalities reflecting a focus on greater harmonization and coordination between "crown and town"; and, finally, a wholesale change in the public expectations of how the NCC should manage its affairs with increased demand for more openness and transparency.

This changing governance context led to a comprehensive rethinking of the planning framework of the NCC that included a revised vision of Canada's capital as it was getting ready to enter the 21st century. The plan for Canada's capital of 1988 and a revised version in 1999 included strategic orientations and policy statements that called for major changes in the approach to the planning and stewardship of three key areas of Canada's Capital Region (CCR): the Greenbelt, Gatineau Park and the Capital core area (corresponding to the downtowns of the cities of Ottawa and Gatineau). Over a ten-year period, I dedicated a great deal of my time and energy to the elaboration of three plans that involved strategically repositioning these special areas of the Capital region. These three repositioning strategies — although relating to different contexts, with distinct antecedents and proposing three separate paths of evolution — proved nevertheless to be unified in regard to their expected outcomes, creating the necessary synergy to the realization of a

vision for CCR in the 21st century, contributing to a new regional dynamic with new opportunities, and fostering the renewal of the NCC.

Providing enlightened, meaningful and practical responses to the incessant change that characterizes urban areas is far from straightforward and simple. In grappling with the phenomenon of change, its diverse contours in the context of cities, and its multi-faceted and multi-level implications, it is helpful to recognize that the response to changing situations and circumstances by all stakeholders requires on their part a shift in position and, at times, of interests that make previous paths of growth, progress or development partly or wholly inadequate, untenable and unsustainable. From the small adjustments of the land use configuration of a neighbourhood to a significant reorientation of the mandate of a public institution, or the introduction of innovative approaches in the delivery of public services, the management of change sets in motion the emergence of new realities, new contexts and new frameworks that can range from an improved *status quo* to a transformative reordering of structures and relationships. Repositioning strategies represent and invoke new perspectives, new perceptions and appreciations, and new processes and procedures in the planning, development, stewardship and governance of communities, small and large. They should be front and centre in channelling proactively and positively the evolution of our complex urban society and in making possible the necessary transition and adaptation to new societal practices and responses.

Leading Practices:

Heritage Rehabilitation — The Lachine Canal, Montreal

Honouring the memories and legacies of past generations of Canadians is equally as important to the achievement of sustainable, healthy and resilient cities and regions as is planning and preparing for future generations. Without an adequate understanding and appreciation of the experience, achievements and wisdom of our ancestors in developing Canada as an urban nation, it is very difficult to nurture the hindsight and foresight necessary to envision the future of our country and its urban areas with any sense of assuredness, confidence and hope.

Leveraging and capitalizing on past investments in physical infrastructure, facilities and other built forms, both small and large, is a critical ingredient to smart future progress, growth and prosperity. But incorporating heritage conservation in the long-term planning and development of cities is neither easy nor straightforward. It is part and parcel of the balancing and integrating acts involved in the practice of urbanism, between opposing or contradictory forces and factors, e.g., valuing the old versus the new, the short-term versus the long-term, the simple versus the complex, the core versus the periphery, the traditional versus the leading edge, the incremental versus the transformative.

An increasing number of Canadian cities are espousing heritage conservation and rehabilitation as priority considerations in charting the future course of their development in the 21st century. However, the legislative and organizational underpinnings to heritage interventions and strategies are often absent, e.g., knowledge base, technical expertise, fiscal and financial incentives, investment capital, creation of partnerships, regulatory designation, recognition and protection.

While there are many examples of successful heritage rehabilitation projects in Canada, few are of the scale, scope and level of complexity involved in the Lachine Canal. An important piece of legacy infrastructure of the 19th century industrialization of the City of Montreal, the canal and its surroundings had gone into general disuse by the first decades of the 20th century and, by the 1970s, reached an advanced state of disrepair and abandonment. As the building blocks for the city's next stage of development were being put in place, in the aftermath of the 1967 World's Fair and the 1976 Olympics, and its economy was making the transition from a secondary to a tertiary and even a quaternary-dominated economy, based on its world-city status and important tourism magnet — the possibilities represented by an eventual rehabilitation of the Lachine Canal became more obvious and promising.

It was a collaborative effort between different levels of government that allowed the project to move forward and to come to fruition. The leadership role played by the public sector helped also to put in place the necessary conditions to unlock private sector investment and re-investment in lands and/or buildings alongside the canal. This case study will review the key factors that have made the Lachine Canal rehabilitation the vibrant area that it has become in the City of Montreal.

Achievements

Within the broader Metropolitan Montreal context, the recognition that the Lachine Canal represented a key piece of strategic regional infrastructure capable of helping bridge the past and the future of the community, served as an early impetus to the identification and the prioritization of this heritage rehabilitation project. The true strategic value and significance of the Lachine Canal can best be appreciated when combined with the ongoing redevelopment of Old Montreal, the Old Port and the Islands Park, as the largest waterfront revitalization project in North America.

The rehabilitation of the Lachine Canal is premised on the following vision and objectives: to act as the westward extension of the Old Port; to maintain the industrial character of the area while fostering a greater mix of land uses and urban activities; to serve as catalyst for the revitalization of Montreal southwest, bringing new life to this working class neighbourhood and improving the quality of life of its residents, while limiting as much as possible gentrification; to protect and strengthen the heritage character and fabric of the Lachine Canal and its surrounding buildings, especially in regard to its significance to the development of Montreal; to create a tourist destination and places for recreational activities; and, to act as a spine to a network of public spaces.

The project is a collaborative effort of the federal government (Parks Canada) and the City of Montreal, with important participation from the private sector. The first improvements were carried out between 1990 and 1992, involving mainly the restoration of two locks and the removal of fill in the canal. The official announcement of the Lachine Canal rehabilitation project was made in 1997 and the canal was reopened to small craft navigation in 2002. Through the implementation of the rehabilitation project, the Lachine Canal underwent the following physical, functional and/or operational changes: environmental characterization and monitoring; wall restoration; archaeological characterization and excavation; raising of three bridges to permit navigation; restoration of five other locks; introduction of new landscaping; and, provision of interpretation and visitor facilities and services.

The project has helped to reconnect the Lachine Canal to the larger city through the following undertakings: interpretation of the industrial heritage of the area; reorganization of the Atwater Market via an extension to the canal edge; conversion of industrial heritage buildings to contemporary mixed uses, such as the Redpath Sugar Refinery; decontamination of brownfield sites; and, development of recreational activities, including tour boating. More than $300 million has been invested so far as a result of the Lachine Canal rehabilitation project, $100 million by the public sector and $200 million through private-sector investment.

Limitations

Some of the constraints or downsides associated with the project include: a governance framework that did not provide for an optimal coordination of all partners and stakeholders as would be expected of a project of this scale and magnitude; competing objectives in the implementation of the project did not enable the level and extent of heritage preservation that was required in order to fulfill this core objective, in particular of heritage buildings in the eastern sector of the canal; the socio-economic conditions of the surrounding neighbourhoods and of their residents did register some improvements but the objective of maintaining the majority of the working class population in the area was not met, some gentrification having set in; and, significant investments have been made in and around the Lachine Canal, however, the prioritization of some of these investments and the resulting land use and urban activities have not been based on sufficient and adequate analyses and justification.

What Was Learned

Strategically linking several development or redevelopment areas can create catalytic and synergistic effects that amplify overall community benefits while helping to minimize economic and financial risks, making the whole much bigger than the sum of the parts. Extending the socio-economic and socio-cultural life of buildings, giving new life to older structures through appropriate policies, guidelines and standards, contributes not only to perceptual changes but also to upgrading the broader environment, making it more meaningful, a source of identity and, at the same time, replacing vicious circles with virtuous circles in terms of response to community heritage and legacy.

Achieving success in the rehabilitation of heritage structures and assets depends on meeting a number of requirements: the critical nature of adequate and timely investments for the preservation of heritage resources, through a life-cycle approach; the role of incentives and disincentives in ensuring expected behavioural responses and effective decision making in regard to heritage resources, such as optimal municipal zoning and appropriate fiscal treatment; the combination of old and new in rehabilitation strategies and interventions can help create unusual, unexpected and even surprising mixes of uses and activities that can draw people; the importance of strategic communications and public relations to substitute a shared image of an heritage area, capable of attracting investment and residents, to a state of affairs characterized by pervasive negative perceptions; and, ensuring the concordance between heritage designation programs and the identification of uses for heritage resources that will foster their sustainability, health and resiliency.

Sources: Mark London (1998, 2003), Parks Canada (2008).

Viewpoint:

Thinking Strategically about Transportation

It is, initially, through my involvement in the elaboration of community improvement plans and the implementation of streetscape improvement projects, and later, and perhaps more significantly, through leadership roles in regional and multi-stakeholders transportation planning undertakings, that I truly started to reflect on the right place for transportation in the work of the professionals of urbanism and the need to adopt radically different approaches to transportation planning. The predominance of transportation in many critical dimensions of our society — the consumption of predominantly non-renewable energy resources, its incidence on lifestyles, its influence on the physical organization of communities, the dominance of private motor vehicles in the supply of transportation modes, its financial costs, and its contribution to the production of greenhouse gases — confirm the necessity to step back and to advance a new transportation world-view, one that is anchored in connecting rather than separating transportation and surrounding land uses and urban activities. Some of my professional experiences illustrate this search for a new transportation world-view.

In 1990, in the course of a substantial review of its official plan, the City of Ottawa was contemplating important shifts in several policy areas, including the central business district, the environment and transportation. In this latter area, the placement of roads in their broader context, including the response to the needs of pedestrians, was being particularly emphasized. The budgeting of significant capital budgets for streetscape improvements in and around the downtown area was a clear demonstration of the renewed attention given to the interface between transportation and the built realm. Through several projects, I was able to contribute to the revitalization of many streets and neighbourhoods while also expanding and broadening the sense of place attached to the experience of streets and sidewalks in those areas. The attention paid to community identity, the safety and security of pedestrians, the greening of streets right-of-way, the resolution of long standing problems and conflicts, and the quality of the design of the streetscape improvements contributed to the enhancement of the quality of life of residents and marked the beginning/emergence of a new prioritization in transportation modes, with a preference accorded to public transit, and walking and cycling over private motor vehicles.

In spite of a long and relatively successful tradition of long range planning, Canada's Capital Region's (CCR) track record in transportation is mixed. Some success stories can be noted — the preservation of green corridors and old rail corridors which were subsequently integrated in the planning of public transit networks; the public transit system of the City of Ottawa (the Transitway) which has won national and international acclaim; a sustained multi-stakeholders investment in transportation data gathering, analyses and modelling through the TRANS Committee; and a positive collaborative relationship between the transit operators, OC Transpo and the Société de transport de l'Outaouais. However, an examination of transportation planning in CCR over time reveals many weaknesses, including the absence of proper coordination and integration between land use planning and transportation planning, and the limited collaboration between the two sides of the Ottawa River in the planning of major transportation infrastructure, especially in regard to inter-provincial crossings and linkages between highway networks.

Since the mid 1990s, several transportation planning initiatives have tried to overcome these poor results. The need for a more strategic approach to transportation planning became quite apparent in the context of the 1994 Inter-provincial Bridges Study. The fact that the study was realized strictly at an administrative level, with no political oversight and approval mechanism, meant that it could not ultimately substitute ongoing collaboration for the divisiveness in inter-provincial transportation planning in CCR. A subsequent study completed in 2000, under the aegis of key political champions, proved to be more successful in delineating the strategic requirements for an inter-provincial transportation network in the region.

From my perspective, the development and approval of the strategic transportation initiative (STI) by the NCC in 2005 really created the groundwork for a more strategic approach to transportation in the Capital region. Capitalizing on the past leadership role of the NCC and the future opportunities suggested by the 2006 review of the NCC mandate by the federal government, the implementation of the STI provides the NCC the necessary leverage to play a catalytic role in transportation and provide a menu of strategies — including a strategic transportation network and a strategic funding mechanism — to ensure an integrated approach to decision making in matters of transportation in CCR.

It almost goes without saying that transportation must be given central consideration in the renewal of Canada's urban policies and action planning, as the country progresses and advances in the 21st century. Notwithstanding the inertia that has characterized the approach to transportation in Canada and other countries — especially the difficulties experienced in getting real "lift off" of the public transit modal share — it is dawning on an increasingly larger proportion of stakeholders in cities, and also the general public, that a "reframing of transportation" is a requirement if our society is to rise up to such ambitious goals as sustainable, healthy and resilient living milieus. A world-view centred on "mobility" must be substituted by one focusing on "accessibility and complementarity"; that recognizes and captures the underlying connections and linkages in how people conduct their lives and activities; that fosters a transition from multiple points of origin and destination to a nodal structure of the land use/ transportation nexus; and one that can deliver reductions in travel time, energy consumption, infrastructure costs and the overall footprint of cities.

A new approach to transportation will ultimately depend on new models of collaboration between all Canadians with, as a central mechanism, financial and non-financial incentives to help guide and attain new perceptions and behaviours in cities. Thinking strategically about transportation is a call to move from patchwork reflection on the land use/transportation interface to a higher level of coordination and resolution, resulting in more coherent and integrated urban/ regional plans and solutions.

Halifax

The moral development of a civilization is measured by the breadth of its sense of community.

Anatol Rapoport quoted in Thomas Homer-Dixon (2000)

CHAPTER 5
WINDOW ON THE FUTURE OF CANADIAN CITIES

Canada has every right to be proud of its cities. When Corporate Resources Group ... based in Geneva, ranked 118 cities according to 42 measures of quality of life in 1995, Canada was the only country with more than three cities in the top 20: Vancouver ... Toronto ... Montréal ... and Calgary ... Other international rankings of cities have come to similar conclusions ... The main reason Canada's major cities do so well, and their great strength, is that they are big enough to be lively and interesting, and yet small enough to avoid the severe congestion, pollution and general unmanageability associated with the world's biggest urban centers. A second reason is that Canada's biggest cities still have healthy downtowns.

David Foot and Daniel Stoffman (1996)

This chapter will provide a window on Canadian cities from a continental and, in some instances, global perspective in order to understand and capture their strengths and weaknesses, which, in turn, will further contribute to the identification of crucial pillars for the development of Canada's urban agenda.

CANADIAN CITIES IN THEIR INTERNATIONAL CONTEXT

For many years during the 1990s, Canadians basked in the appreciation and knowledge of the high standing of their country and many of their cities in international rankings sponsored by the United Nations or private sector research consultancies. As an example, Canada ranked first for a few years in a row in the late 1990s on the UN Human Development Index.

These results, largely publicized in the media, were not only a source of pride and celebration by many Canadians, but also an important wellspring of political capital for politicians at different levels of government.

While this type of information can be a great boost to the morale and the ego, it is nevertheless important to inquire about its meaningfulness and, more crucially, ponder its usefulness from a policy standpoint for Canada and its cities.

The fact that Canada, in subsequent years, registered a downward shift in some rankings, ranging between fourth and eighth on the UN Human Development Index in the early 2000s, gave an indication that something was amiss north of the 49th parallel and served as a wake-up call for Canadians.

However, at a more fundamental level, these results were also indicative of the limits of such rankings as a source of understanding of the nuances of what constitute the strengths and weaknesses of Canada from a global comparative basis. In establishing benchmarks for the urban agenda, it is clear that high level, coarse measurements of Canada's standing will not do and that there exists a need for different lenses and indicators in order to get a more precise sense of the situation faced by Canadians in a continental and worldwide context.

The praise heaped on Canadians year after year in the 1990s, and even in more recent times, could have had a certain numbing effect on the capacity to appreciate the situation of Canada and its cities as they entered the 21st century. Too much praise can create an attitude of overconfidence and even indifference that blinds and that is not conducive to an appropriate level of engagement. This is particularly so when contemplating the changing policy direction and priority setting required by the problems and challenges that are besetting and will beset Canada and its cities in coming years and decades.

The recognition that Canada and its cities have to evolve and be governed in the context of an increasingly globalized and urbanized world makes international comparative analyses important and crucial for policy debate and public communications. They do help position and ground Canadians' understanding of their performance as people in an interdependent world and help pinpoint areas where they need to improve and do better. Ultimately, an ability to compare can provide a significant hedge in terms of building a capacity to compete.

Answering the question "Are Canadian cities special cities?" must involve not only considerations about their distinctive character at continental and global levels, but also help direct the development of policy insights and options in the context of Canada's urban agenda.

Although this question has not necessarily received a great deal of attention — urban analyses having focused predominantly at the national and regional levels — some independent scholarly and journalistic work in Canada and abroad has indeed contributed to shedding some light on and enabling an improved appreciation of the situation of Canadian cities in relation to their counterparts in the United States and elsewhere in the developed world.[14]

Based on the above research results — and using as criteria for comparison and evaluation key goals and principles of contemporary urbanism and environmentalism, e.g., sustainability, health, resiliency, human scale, efficient use of land and infrastructure, diversity, valuing and preserving ecosystems and built heritage, accessibility, social harmony, participation, etc. — three threads of inquiry can further inform our knowledge of the situation of Canadian cities:

1. What are some of the dimensions that provide cities with a comparative advantage — their strengths?

2. What are some of the dimensions that represent vulnerabilities in regard to their future competitiveness and the competitiveness of Canada — their weaknesses?

3. How can the identification of these areas of strength and weakness contribute to the discussion of possible pillars for orienting the urban future of Canada?

Before launching into this discussion, it is useful to review the defining characteristics of the Canadian *oekoumène*, some of which were noted previously:

• hugging the 49th parallel, in close proximity to the United States, with significant ramifications in time for the east-west versus north-south (national versus continental) patterns of exchange and trading relations;

In many respects, almost all our major urban centres are a synthesis of American and European urbanism — sprawling and car-oriented on the one hand yet cosmopolitan and vital on the other. In the coming decades of the 21st century Canadian cities will experience an epic tug of war between these different halves of their split personalities.

Juri Pill quoted in John Lorinc (2006)

Evidence points to much greater stability in the Canadian central city and metropolitan area — Canadian central cities unlike those in the US have on average been growing over the past decade

Michael A. Goldberg and John Mercer (1986)

---

[14] Including Jeb Brugman (2009), Richard Florida (2008), Frances Frisken (1994), Harvey M. Kitchen (2002), John Lorinc (2006), Michael A. Goldberg and John Mercer (1986), Nathalie Brender *et al.* (2007), Ian Skelton (2003) and Stephen V. Ward (2002).

[The] Canadian urban form ... is considerably denser and more compact than its American counterparts.

Adapted from Michael A. Goldberg and John Mercer (1986)

Despite their country's colder climate, Canadians are three times as likely as Americans to hop on a bicycle to go to work ... [T]he greater use of bicycles in Canada [is attributed] to the higher urban densities and greater frequency of mixed-use development ... and several other factors, such as lower incomes; higher costs of owning, driving, and parking a car in Canada; safer cycling conditions; more plentiful bike facilities; and more extensive training.

New Urban News (2006)

[T]here are more than four times as many lanes of freeway available to the average American metropolitan resident compared with the analogous Canadian ... Americans own and operate 50% more automobiles ... [P]atronage of public transit facilities on [a] per capita basis is two-and-a-half [times] higher in Canada's urban regions.

Adapted from Michael A. Goldberg and John Mercer (1986)

- dispersed population, with its mobility and infrastructure requirements;

- diverse, multicultural population;

- few large cities, totaling an important share of Canada's population, making it an overwhelmingly urban nation, with consequences in regard to Canadian productivity and the need for strategic investments;

- northern climate, with energy and life-cycle cost implications;

- rich in natural resources, with implications for the structuring of the Canadian human settlement pattern and economy; and,

- historical imperative for Canadians to define and develop in recognition of their particular geography a special pattern of relationship, a distinctive culture and flexible governance.

AREAS OF STRENGTH

The areas in which Canadian cities exhibit some form of comparative advantage in relation to cities in other developed countries (for our purpose: United States and the European Union) can be referenced according to the following typology: urban form, mobility, community character, environment, security and governance.

It must be noted that in some instances, the comparative advantage enjoyed by Canadian cities can be described as absolute in relation to other cities. But, in other cases, it is only true in relation to cities in the United States and not so in relation to European cities or vice versa.

Urban Form

Although Canadian cities are afflicted with an inflated physical footprint, typical of their North American situation, they are nevertheless recognized as being somewhat more compact than their American counterparts. They are also characterized by a higher average density while showing a greater prevalence of mixed land uses. The suburban pattern of development in Canada is acknowledged as more ordered in terms of its overall evolution and as providing a higher quality of life. In relation to European cities and their smaller, more compact territorial footprint, Canadian cities lag significantly behind all the above measures of urban form.

Mobility

Also reflecting again their North American situation, Canadian cities have been planned and developed around the personal automobile as the dominant mode of mobility for more than fifty years, and this pattern will likely continue for the foreseeable future. However, alternative modes of transportation, especially the use of public transit and of bicycles, have witnessed a higher rate of adoption by Canadians over the recent decades — not to the same degree as by Europeans but much more so than by the Americans. The higher cost of owning and operating a car in Canada, in relation to the United States, can explain this difference in behaviour to a certain extent. The greater preference for alternative modes to the car — reflecting better public transit options among other factors — is a positive evolution. It bodes well for the future of Canadian cities when considering some of the trends and challenges foreseen over the coming decades, including the diminishing supply of oil, increasing cost of energy, greater focus on healthy living, and the greater diversity of the population.

Community Character

This is a dimension for which Canadian cities are deemed to benefit from an absolute comparative advantage. Every year, people from all over the world come to Canada to understand and, possibly replicate, the policies and approaches that define and enable our unique blend of community character and cohesion. More specifically, they scrutinize some of the aspects that account for Canada's success, including its incredible diversity, the less polarized nature of Canadian cities, their greater humanity in terms of how people look after each other, the fact that they are less segregated, less differentiated and that affluence is more equally distributed and finally, that over time, central areas in Canadian cities have remained somewhat more stable than their American counterparts, in particular by retaining a greater share of their population. Despite this favourable overall performance in terms of community character, Canadian cities have begun to see an erosion related to their absolute comparative advantage in recent years. As such, Canadians should not be indifferent nor complacent about this negative transformation.

Environment

Evaluating, in an objective manner, the environmental performance of any country, especially one with the size of Canada and its complex *oekoumène*, as previously described, is indeed a daunting task. The debate surrounding the Kyoto Accord on climate change and the apparent failure so far by Canadians to make their mark in addressing this global challenge illustrates the difficulties posed by environmental planning, benchmarking and monitoring. By all accounts, Canada is not failing to confront its environmental responsibilities. But neither in the early 21st century is it providing the strong leadership that it was reputed to exhibit in all those surveys and rankings throughout the 1990s. At a macro-environmental level, one of the key achievements by Canada is the creation of a unique network of national parks all across the country, representing and preserving the different Canadian ecosystems. Another area of achievement, although not of the same significance, is its planning and development of a human settlement system in the context of a northern climate. At the urban level, Canadian cities have played an important role in establishing links between the health of people and an environment of quality through the successful, but unfortunately ephemeral, Healthy Communities Program. Canadian cities are also recognized as providing an overall higher quality of the environment, in particular, being cleaner than their American and European counterparts.

In 2004, KPMG, an international accounting services firm, ranked Canada as the world's most cost-competitive country in which to conduct business, ahead of all other G-7 nations ... Why? Because [Canadian cities] are safe, convenient, welcoming, affordable, and lively ... Canada's major cities would seem to be a good news story.

John Lorinc (2006)

Canada's hub cities have a huge social and environmental advantage over almost all their US counterparts ... they never hollowed out in response to social strife, inner-city violence, and poor schools. There is no stigma associated with downtown living ... The gravitational pull of Canadian downtowns ... has functioned as a counterweight to the outward momentum of sprawl-style development, which has shifted hundred of thousands of good jobs to edge-city employment districts.

John Lorinc (2006)

Security

Canadians have evolved over their short history as a people — a unique culture — that emphasizes as a fundamental characteristic, open, positive and peaceful relations between groups and communities. This particular and distinctive set of values has not only influenced, to a significant degree, Canada's approach to international relations, but also the organization and design of its cities and how people live within them. In as much as community cohesion was recognized as a dominant strength of Canadian cities, their safety and security constitute clear corollary achievements that distinguish them from some cities in the United States and Europe. With the complexity inherent in the integration of people coming from all over the world, this orderly and safe environment of Canadian cities has been increasingly put to the test, as some social conflicts have manifested themselves lately, especially in larger cities.

Governance

How Canadians approach the governance of their cities is another area where they benefit in some respects from a comparative advantage in relation to American and European cities. Through innovative approaches at the level of metropolitan areas and regions, Canada has positioned the governance of its cities at a middle ground between the very decentralized approach in the United States and the more centralized approach characteristic of some European countries. The less fragmented governance of cities in Canada combined with

a preponderant role of the public sector — more similar to European cities than to American cities — has contributed to the establishment of stricter land-use laws, which positively influence the evolution of the urban form as previously noted. Although the greater focus on controls is often seen as inhibiting market forces and thus reducing the overall competitiveness of Canadians cities, from a long-term planning and development perspective, such a strong framework will help facilitate and set the stage for policies enabling greater urban sustainability, health and resiliency in Canada. However, as we will see below, in order to capitalize to the fullest on the areas of comparative advantage, Canada will have to broaden its policy tool kit and enhance the competitiveness of its cities.

AREAS OF WEAKNESS

The areas in which Canadian cities are proving to be more vulnerable in terms of their long-term sustainability, health and resiliency prospects, in relation to cities in other developed countries, can be distinguished on the basis of a similar typology as for the areas of comparative advantage: urban form, community character, environment and governance.

Urban Form

Similarly to American cities, Canadian cities have developed after World War II on the basis of the suburban model with its associated sprawl and other land-use and transportation inefficiencies. At the beginning of the 21st century, one of the many challenges related to this pattern of development is how it can be regenerated through a better use of existing infrastructure and a push toward more land-use intensification. Some cities have begun to take action to reverse to a certain extent this dominant development model but much more remains to be done. Capitalizing on existing strengths is clearly the way to go, but a great deal of leadership from all sectors of Canadian society will be needed to provide the necessary innovation, give the appropriate traction and invigorate it with the needed momentum. Canadian cities in the course of that improvement process could learn from European cities to a certain degree, taking cues especially in such areas as the land use and transportation integration.

Community Character

Despite the fact that Canadian cities are often looked upon as role models in regard to their social characteristics, they have, like their American and European counterparts, to confront difficult community issues, some emerging but some more ingrained in their urban fabric. Fundamentally, the social problems found in Canadian cities are linked, to a large extent, to the difficulties of providing the necessary conditions for some people to harmoniously integrate into Canadian society, be they some recently arrived immigrants, people of Aboriginal ancestry, and homeless people or people facing other shelter challenges. The absence of coordination between the different stakeholders and, especially the levels of government, is often cited as the root cause for many of these integration problems. They are exemplified by the failure to address, in a holistic way, the supply

of affordable housing and to manage the social consequences of urban regeneration and gentrification, especially in areas of cities that have historically played a key role in ensuring the accommodation needs of residents facing a personal transition or crisis.

Environment

The environmental world-view of Canadians is still very much influenced by and anchored in the 19th and 20th centuries environmental legacy and not really adapted to the fast changing circumstances of the 21st century. Largely based on the industrialism and mass consumption paradigms — not unlike what also prevails in the United States, Europe and other developed countries — the desired shift to greater urban sustainability, health and resiliency, based on life-cycle, green development and "cradle to cradle" thinking, is still very much in its infancy. Considering the behavioural adjustments that such a shift will require and the failure, so far, by the different levels of government to provide the necessary incentive systems to direct and steer such an evolution and change, Canada is clearly putting itself at risk in regard to what change is required and the costs that will have to be supported. Putting greater emphasis on the integration of environmental concerns in the planning of cities — and especially improving their performance in regard to the protection of natural ecosystems, management of waste, the improvement of the quality of the public realm and more emphasis on urban design — would be ways to begin to address this environmental vulnerability.

While Canadian cities have less poverty and show lower levels of crime [compared to US cities], recent changes to Canada's social, education, health and other safety net programs may lead to a greater degree of convergence between the two countries in the future.

John Lorinc (2006)

[T]roubling social fissures were becoming glaringly apparent in all of Canada's largest cities ... The 1990s saw a mounting housing shortage, falling high school graduation rates, and an emerging homeless crisis. Recent immigrants — the vast majority of whom settle in big cities — have faced an ever tougher time establishing themselves, finding suitable housing, and securing work in the professions in which they are trained. In Western Canadian cities, many Aboriginals live in highly distressed, crime-ridden communities that have assumed the character of American ghettos ... Sprawl has gobbled up vast tracts of arable land, fostering energy-gorging suburban cities that grapple with grid lock, bad air and an evidence of obesity.

John Lorinc (2006)

Canada ... has the world's third-largest ecological footprint ...

John Lorinc (2006)

[C]anada's federal electoral system [is] weighted heavily in favour of less populous rural and small town ridings ... Parliament itself is skewed against urban issues.

John Lorinc (2006)

Governance

Inefficiencies and dysfunction in governance put Canada at risk in the short- to medium-term if no corrective actions are taken. The emergence of multi-faceted and distributed leadership across the different sectors of Canadian society hinges to a significant extent on moving to an enhanced governance model.

The lack of attention given to large cities in terms of their requirements to be more competitive in an urbanized and globalized world is particularly troubling and a source of preoccupation. The chronic incapacity of the different levels of government to cooperate in the elaboration and implementation of a cohesive and integrated urban policy is another area that is of concern and demands concerted attention. Through better alignment of micro- and macroeconomic policies, Canadian cities could reap the benefits of improved overall productivity and targeted strategic investments in creativity and innovation. Transformation of the fiscal regime, including greater power for municipalities to raise their own revenues, would help create some of the incentive systems needed to alter the behaviour of Canadians in such areas as personal mobility, energy consumption and recycling, among many others. Another area where change is warranted is in the distribution of the Canadian population — recognizing that it is predominantly urban — and the electoral districts which are currently more favourable to rural areas.

PILLARS OF THE URBAN AGENDA

In order to broaden and enhance the areas of comparative advantage that Canadian cities enjoy and to mitigate and reduce the areas of vulnerability that put them at risk, the elaboration of a consolidated and integrated urban agenda, involving all the key stakeholders and ordinary Canadians, stands out as a key short-term priority. Based on the previous findings in this and earlier chapters and on the work of other authors as documented in the references,[15] it is possible to circumscribe a set of ideas in a preliminary way that could act as pillars for Canada's urban agenda. Five such pillars will be briefly outlined below in the form of statements of principle.

Canadian Urban Policy — Putting the People of Canada First

Considering the rich legacy of Canada and its cities in the creation of diverse communities with strong social links and character;

Considering the many changes and transformations witnessed by Canadian cities over the last decades and those forecasted for the coming decades, with their implications for sustained community cohesion; and,

Considering the inherent complexity and lack of coordination in the elaboration and implementation of urban policies, with their consequencial impact on the level of commitment and engagement by Canadians in the future of their cities;

---

[15] In particular, Nathalie Brender *et al.* (2007), External Advisory Committee on Cities and Communities (2006) and Prime Minister's Caucus Task Force on Urban Issues (2002).

Consequently, as a first principle, the development of urban policies in Canada should clarify the roles of all stakeholders and recognize that the people of Canada need to strongly adhere to and be involved in the policy process, and, furthermore, that Canadians must constitute the fundamental reference point in all future urban policy work.

Canadian Urban Federalism — Toward a New Balance

Considering the importance of cities for the future of Canada and its competitiveness within an urbanizing and globalizing world;

Considering the key role played by the different levels of government in ensuring that the essential conditions are in place to enable Canadian cities to succeed as sustainable and resilient places; and,

Considering that the roles and responsibilities of cities are not formally recognized in Canada's overall governance framework and as a result, Canadian cities are severely handicapped in responding to the needs and aspirations of Canadians;

Consequently, as a first principle, the development of an urban agenda should coincide with a strengthening of Canada's federalism, whereby the roles and responsibilities of Canadian cities are clarified in relation to the senior levels of government, and new relationships are set in motion from which a new balance of power between the levels of government can emerge.

Canadian Urban System — Major Cities as Top of Mind

Considering the special role of major cities in Canada's urban system as vectors for investment and innovation within the broader Canadian economy;

Considering the particular governance requirements of major cities in Canada to level the competitive playing field with major cities in the United States and other developed countries, especially in order to create the urban context and environment favourable to the attraction and retention of the creative people critical to their success; and,

Considering that the contribution of major cities in Canada in terms of their relative weight in the overall Canadian society is not recognized and prioritized to the extent that it should be by senior levels of government, with negative implications for their ability to sustain and enhance their competitiveness, attraction and livability;

Consequently, as a first principle, the development of an urban agenda should prioritize the provision to major cities in Canada an appropriate weight in the governance of the country, as well as the tools and resources that they need to fully assume their leadership role in ensuring the long-term orderly development of Canada, and the well-being and prosperity of Canadians.

Addressing Urban Problems — Thinking Outside of the Box

Considering that the identification of solutions to complex urban problems and new directions can benefit from original and fresh insight and ideas by people not committed and invested in the *status quo*;

Considering that ramping up Canadian productivity constitutes a key challenge for the coming years and that re-energized cities, with the appropriate leadership, governance, tool kit, infrastructure and resources, could make a difference in filling the productivity gap; and,

Considering that one of the key conditions for improving productivity in Canada is to provide the necessary reward systems that will make possible the emergence of greater innovation and creativity;

Consequently, as a first principle, the development of an urban agenda should recognize, as a key policy orientation, the value accorded to experimentation and unusual approaches and solutions, through appropriate recognition, facilitation and celebration.

Activating the Urban Agenda — Solutions Made in Canada

Considering that a key aspect of the implementation of an urban agenda should be the deployment of a change management strategy in order to facilitate and ease transitions to the new urban governance by Canadians;

Considering the tradition in the governance of Canadian cities for a greater role by the public sector and a somewhat lesser role by the private and not-for-profit sectors; and,

Considering that a key factor of success for the realization of an urban agenda will consist of broadening the involvement of Canadians in the governance of their cities;

Consequently, as a first principle, the development of an urban agenda should provide for an appropriate role for the public, private and not-for-profit sectors, based on a balance between regulatory, fiscal, market and value-based incentives that could enable the necessary adjustments or changes in behaviours by Canadians and ensure their alignment with the expected urban outcomes.

Diagram 2 shows the further development of the content introduced previously in Part I, adding the elements that have been discussed in Part II. The vertical lines at the bottom of the diagram illustrate the seven drivers of the urban agenda that were presented and discussed in chapter 4. Above the seven drivers, the urban reality component has been rounded off with the addition of the strengths and weaknesses of Canadian cities. Also proposed in chapter 5 were the five pillars to support the evolution of Canada's urban agenda. The final addition to the diagram references the notions of dialogue, experience and learning as a metaphor for the urban agenda, further strengthening the evolution by Canadians of a world-view for their urban areas.

Diagram 2
Schematic of the Development of the Urban Agenda, Part II

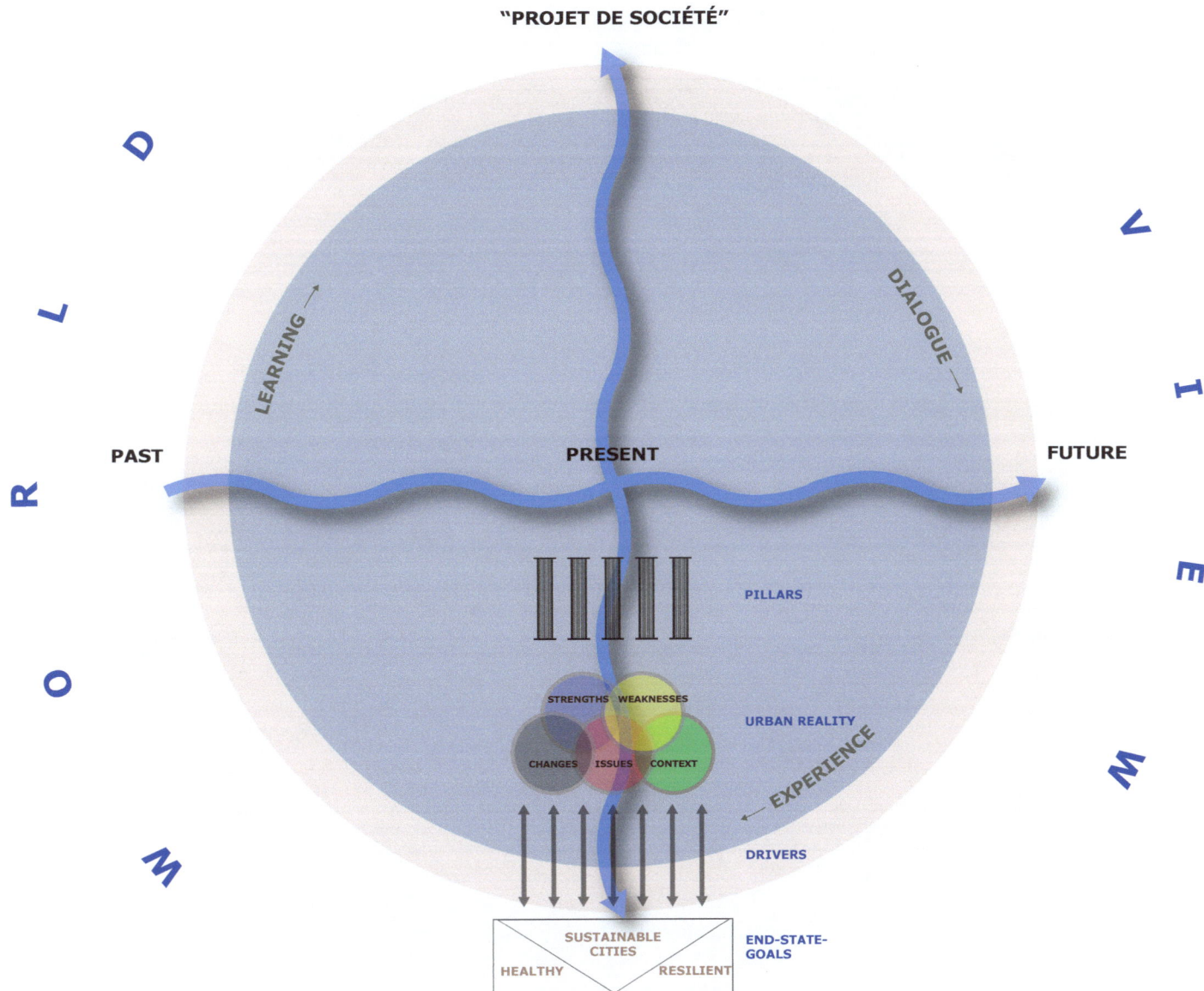

"PROJET DE SOCIÉTÉ"

WORLDVIEW

LEARNING

DIALOGUE

PAST

PRESENT

FUTURE

PILLARS

STRENGTHS   WEAKNESSES

URBAN REALITY

EXPERIENCE

CHANGES   ISSUES   CONTEXT

DRIVERS

SUSTAINABLE CITIES

END-STATE-GOALS

HEALTHY   RESILIENT

PLACE FOR DIALOGUE, EXPERIENCE AND LEARNING

Another way to answer the question "Are Canadian cities special cities?" is to make the transition from the general to the specific. Consideration can be given to how certain Canadian cities have fared when measured against key criteria of sustainability, health and resiliency. The following notes examine the performance of Vancouver and Ottawa-Gatineau (Canada's Capital Region).

Leading Practices:

The Vancouver Experience

One of the most, if not *the* most, important aspirations as we move forward with Canada's urban agenda is to put in place the conditions for a successful transition to sustainable, healthy and resilient cities and regions, this over the short-, medium- and long-term. Some of the conditions deemed essential for the achievement of these goals include: the integrated and holistic management of growth and declining pressures in cities and regions; the comprehensive, cross-sector and intergovernmental perspective and approach to urban and regional planning, development and governance policy making; the recognition of stakeholders and citizens interests, needs and aspirations and the harnessing of their collective energy in the planning, development and governance of cities and regions; the convergence and bridging of economic prosperity, community well-being and environmental integrity; the clear definition of roles and responsibilities, rules of engagement and framing of participatory processes in the planning, development and governance of cities and regions; and, the creation and maintenance of a quality of life and sense of place in the planning, development and governance of cities and regions.

The City of Vancouver and its metropolitan region (Metro Vancouver) have achieved, over the last quarter century, an impressive transformation that, in many ways, heralds the leadership of the largest city-region in British Columbia in matters of sustainability, health and resiliency. The harmonization of municipal planning processes, regional policy directions and provincial objectives, innovative public engagement activities, and an effective and efficient development decision-making process help define what has made the City of

Vancouver and its region different, and in many respects *avant-garde*. This achievement has been recognized and celebrated both at national and international levels, through many prizes and awards. The Vancouver experience does represent an example worthy of examination, reflection and emulation.

Achievements

Metro Vancouver (previously the Greater Vancouver Regional District) has created, over several decades, and in an incremental/cumulative fashion, a regional planning framework that has allowed the making of a more "liveable region". Key decisions included: the absence of an inner-city highway network; the development of a regional public transportation system: the Sky Train; the distribution of employment across the region, with its implications for the transportation/land use interface; the preservation of agricultural lands and natural areas: the Green Zone; and, more recently, the conduct of a successful, award-winning 100-year planning process, with a focus on the sustainable and resilient region.

The City of Vancouver, through the preparation of the CityPlan, used innovative and award-winning approaches for the involvement of the public in the planning process. Key characteristics included: harnessing public ideas and energies to the resolution of long-standing problems, through such forums or media as kitchen-table circles, ideas books, ideas fairs, citizen tool kits; increasing public ownership of planning policies through direct input in their elaboration; getting people to talk face-to-face in a non-confrontational way; reaching out to groups that previously did not get involved in the planning process;

exposing citizens to inevitable conflicts and the need for trade-offs; providing greater awareness of the dangers and risks associated with not-in-my-backyard (NIMBY) thinking; and, explaining and clarifying key areas of challenge for the City of Vancouver.

Another forward-looking move by the City of Vancouver was the establishment of an innovative review and decision-making process for the approval of all major development projects — what is known as the Vancouver model. Key characteristics include: principle-based; inclusive and transparent; clear lines of responsibility in the making of development decisions; professionally-driven, with no direct political involvement; clear design requirements and an incentive framework to foster quality results; and, inclusive of a peer-review component. Some of the outcomes and results include: more lively, safe and attractive streets; more diverse architecture; greater mixed uses in the downtown, with clear priority accorded to residential development; enhanced quality of street design; active ground-floor uses that help animate the streets; attention to the transition from the public to the private realms; range of building densities; enhanced urban forest; protection of important view corridors; integration of micro-climate considerations; and contribution by developers of community facilities and amenities.

Limitations

Some of the limitations associated with the Vancouver experience include: loss of affordable housing in the process of transformation of the downtown; re-enforcement of deeper social, economic and political divisions and sense of exclusion on the part of some citizens as a result of the strong focus on the aesthetics of development;

greater civic indifference to problems of poverty in certain areas of the city; time required for the delivery of tangible results to communities following the approval of the CityPlan; and, continued expansion of the physical footprint of Metro Vancouver, with concomitant problems of sprawl and inefficient distribution of development densities.

What Was Learned

The key learning points are: in moving forward with the sustainability, health and resiliency agenda, the critical importance of political and professional leadership; the need for close collaboration between public and private sector professionals of urbanism in advancing and realizing visions for cities and regions; fostering the creation of a community culture that places high value on quality urban design through the planning process; the opportunity to leverage private investment toward the provision of civic infrastructure and facilities with development incentives and the transfer of development rights; importance of appropriate and flexible regulatory/legislative frameworks that can enable independent delegated approval authority to professional staff as well as facilitate development review innovations; balancing, through the development approval process contextual considerations such as the provision of incentives to facilitate a variety of development forms; to help define and balance the roles and responsibilities as well as interests of stakeholders through comprehensive and exhaustive review processes; and, the use of peer-review to foster professional work of a higher standard leading to greater performance and outcomes.

Sources: Larry Beasley (2003, 2004a, 2004b), Paul Bedford (2006b), City of Vancouver (1995, 2008), Ann McAffee (1995), John Punter (2003), Metro Vancouver (1996, 2005).

Leading Practices:

Planning for Future Generations — Canada's Capital Region

All urbanists seek, through their practice, to enable and facilitate the successful bridging of the short-term and the long-term planning and development of the communities in which they carry professional mandates. Fundamentally, realizing sustainable, healthy and resilient cities and regions is very much about vision, charting the long view of any community, and the ability and capacity to implement this "image of the future" over several generations.

Capitals of federal states like the United States, Australia and Canada are examples of the successful implementation of transformative vision over a long period of time, with, as a starting point, a master plan for a new city (Washington and Canberra) or an existing one (Ottawa). Because of the special character of capital cities — as the symbol and role model of their respective country, and the requirement for a layering of their roles as urban areas as well as their international, national and local dimensions — it is easy to grasp and understand their ability and capacity to meet such high standards. But the examination of the experience of capital cities can also be instructive in regards to the governance systems that were created to enable the structured, consistent and efficient implementation of their inaugural vision over time. This case study will examine the lessons learned from Canada's Capital Region (CCR), an excellent illustration of planning for future generations.

Achievements

A vision for Canada's Capital first emerged in the early years of the 20th century and served as a foundation for all subsequent planning and development activities, spanning more than a hundred years.

In identifying the rich and diverse natural endowment of Canada's Capital Region — in spite of the dominant industrial landscape that characterized Ottawa and its region at the time — the vision set in motion a number of key decisions that accounted largely for the contemporary recognition of Canada's Capital Region as a "green capital". During the last century, the vision fostered the preservation of the Gatineau Hills (which became Gatineau Park), the protection of shorelines and green corridors, and the creation of several urban parks as well as the Greenbelt on the Ontario side of CCR. It led also to the adoption of a dominant approach to the siting of most federal institutions, called "pavilion in the landscape". All these decisions and actions took place in the context of the evolution of a major metropolitan area, creating in the process a dual context — the "capital realm" and the "civic realm". Although subtle in terms of its early articulation and meaning — the integration of the natural environment as a key building block for the development of CCR — it proved also very much prescient in regard to some of the ideas that would frame the capital building agenda in the last decades of the 20th century, e.g., preservation of ecosystems and sustainability.

A key characteristic of the vision has been its dynamic nature, evolving as the country and its capital were evolving. In the 1980s, it was reformulated to superimpose symbolic dimensions to the previously prevailing environmental/physical aspects. Through this evolution, the vision proved instrumental in leading the capital to its next stage of evolution: as a means to explain Canada to Canadians and to the outside world, as a valued cultural destination, and as a stage for national celebrations, e.g., Canada Day and Winterlude. As Canada and the National Capital continue their evolution in the 21st century, with the challenges and the opportunities involved, the vision would also continue to evolve. From the natural environment as a keystone to its symbolic focus, the vision should point out and illuminate the next stage of evolution of the capital, possibly from symbol to model for future generations of Canadians.

In the early years of the 20th century, as the task of planning and building a national capital for Canada was shifting into higher gear, the creation of a special institution — a capital commission — was deemed the appropriate governance mechanism to undertake and realize this important but also complex work. Considering the special circumstances under which Canada's capital was being established — superimposed as it was on a fledgling but existing city, Ottawa — the adoption of such a model was seen as providing the necessary power, authority and capacity to achieve the efficient and effective balance and integration of interests between the capital and civic realms. An alternative governance model to the capital commission was the subject of a great deal of scrutiny up to the 1970s: the federal district (similar to Washington, D.C.). While it did offer many appealing possibilities — especially from a holistic decision-making perspective — it presented too many unmitigatable problems to prove acceptable and sustainable in the political environment of CCR, e.g., its clear lack of alignment with the prevailing intergovernmental practices of Canada's federalism. Looking to the 21st century and the changing requirements for the planning and building of CCR, the capital commission appears to remain the optimal governance model in terms of its ability and capacity to realize the vision, and its flexibility in allowing the necessary evolution and adaptation to emerging conditions and circumstances.

Despite the existence of a consensus for the development of a representative national capital for Canadians, supported by visionary leaders and organizations, a very challenging regional and national context — e.g., two world wars, economic depression, lack of political support and limited planning expertise at the local level — resulted in a limited number of implementation activities in the first half of the 20th century. The growth and the optimism characteristic of the post-World War II period provided the necessary national and regional impetus for the transformation of Canada's Capital Region from an industry-based region to a modern green capital region. The National Capital Commission (NCC) led the way in carrying out this unique and significant transformational work, based on the 1950 Gréber Plan. Key achievements included: railway relocation away from the centre; decentralization of federal employment in specialized nodes; construction of parkways; creation of a greenbelt, green corridors and urban parks; expansion of Gatineau Park; and, provision of public access to rivers' shorelines and improvement to the water quality of the Ottawa River.

After the 1970s, the NCC continued its implementation efforts but shifted its level of intervention from a regional development role to the national perspective of the capital. Key recent NCC achievements include: development of Confederation Boulevard, the ceremonial route in the Capital core area; siting of major institutions and commemorative monuments; protection of significant views to national symbols; control of land-use change and the quality of urban design through regulatory approval processes; stewardship of the green capital; and organization and staging of national celebrations.

Based on the experience of the NCC in implementing the capital vision and capital plans, the following key requirements for successful implementation activities can be identified: the crucial importance of political leadership in the creation and nurturing of a constituency for the planning, development and governance of the capital; ownership of large areas of land; the availability of long-term financial resources; good economic conditions; organizational competency and credibility; the availability of skilled staff; sound fiscal management; superior project management capacity; and, patience. Through its work, the NCC created not only a capital that is a source of identity and pride for Canadians, characterized by a high quality environment and a high quality lifestyle, but also a significant legacy for current and future generations of Canadians.

Limitations

From a comparative vantage point (nationally and internationally), the planning, development and governance of Canada's Capital Region is generally seen as a success story. However, the emphasis placed on the positive attributes of the national capital has had the unintended consequence of masking a certain number of weaknesses. If left unattended, these weaknesses could pose a significant threat to the legacy of the 20th century capital builders. Some of the key issues when looking at the future of the CCR include: the continued development and nurturing of a capital constituency, which has not been receiving the necessary degree of attention since the 1980s, especially from political leaders; the need to ramp up the communication efforts in the planning, development and governance of CCR, something that the NCC has struggled with in the last decade; the need to put the financial and fiscal foundation of the ongoing building and stewardship of CCR on stronger footing, following several decades of cutbacks; the need to consolidate and solidify the collaboration between the capital and civic realms, to foster the creation of the partnerships required for the continued evolution of

CCR as a model for the rest of Canada; and, the need to raise the level of coordination between the Quebec and Ontario sides of CCR, to overcome a long-standing problem and to make the Ottawa River a source of unity rather than of division.

What Was Learned

Ensuring the successful continuation of the making of a sustainable, healthy and resilient capital for Canada will require a number of key elements: leadership at all levels of government and in other sectors of the Canadian society, in order to ensure the effective, efficient, flexible and adaptable planning, development and governance of CCR; commitment and engagement of numerous political champions for the ongoing development and maintenance of a multi-party political constituency for the national capital; need to continue to evolve a transcending vision for CCR, one that simultaneously can be a reflection of the essence of the country, a source of meaning, and that can capture the major thrust of its ongoing evolution; role of the NCC in leading the planning, development and governance of CCR by balancing local and national interests as well as short-term and long-term orientations; development of a framework to manage in a comprehensible, holistic and integrated manner the intergovernmental relations by promoting and fostering the creation and maintenance of networks and forums of dialogue and collaboration; and, the importance of putting innovation and creativity at the forefront of the planning, development and governance of CCR by facilitating learning opportunities, including those from other capitals at the national and international levels.

Sources: Andrew Cohen (2007), David L.A. Gordon (2001, 2005, 2006), National Capital Commission (1999b), Panel on the NCC Mandate Review (2006).

PART III: WHAT DO WE NEED TO DO ABOUT IT?

Across Canada, people are awakening to urbanism, quality of life, the value of our cities and the imperative to make them flourish ... [W]e have a solid history of workable, caring cities ...However, we face big problems and people want real, effective answers. ... Let us commit to rebuild the "city by design".

Larry Beasley (2004a)

Calgary

Post-capitalist society requires a unifying force. It requires a leadership group which can focus local, particular, separate traditions onto a common and shared commitment to values, a common concept of excellence and of mutual respect.

Peter Drucker (1993)

CHAPTER 6
START WITH A VISION ...

SETTING THE STAGE

By their essence, visions should clearly articulate a future linked with the past and woven into the fabric, traditions and cultures of a country or a community. At the same time, they should signify a break from that past and propose a path for necessary change that, while sensitive to their current situation, can build upon, expand and improve, and, in certain instances, transform the country's or the community's future.

Unfortunately, of late in Canada, the word "vision" has been given many meanings, has often not been used appropriately, and has even been abused. This difficulty in articulating sound, meaningful, inspiring and lasting visions for the country and its citizens reflects some of the conflicts in values and interests that characterize Canadian society at the beginning of the 21st century.

It also accounts to a certain extent for the difficulties encountered in achieving important and needed change in key areas, such as intergovernmental relations and decisions related to health, fiscal and environmental matters.

In order to tackle the lack of an overall shared perspective for the future of Canada, to start the elaboration of a shared vision and the identification of key policy directions for the country and its cities, several considerations need to be put on the table to inform such an important process:

- the need to look at issues in terms of their relationships to each other, or connections, rather than in isolation;

- the need to consider and to bring into balance many additional demands for resources with a finite supply of public funds;

- the need to consider present but also future generations of Canadians;

- the need for greater collaboration and consensus building; and,

- the need for the inception of new institutions and national or community symbols.

An essential requirement for the launch of a visioning and policy-making process such as the one above — or the urban agenda — is to instil in Canadians, their leaders, and their public, private, and volunteer sectors a recognition of the importance and value of a shared appreciation of the future of Canada, including the future of its cities and regions.

Two related questions are raised as a result. Is the achievement of a shared perspective of the future of Canada — a "common vision" — a realistic expectation? If so, what would be the prerequisites?

The answer to the first question can be affirmative as long as one of the first principles stated in the previous chapter — the fundamental reference point in the governance of the country must be the Canadian citizenry — is clearly enunciated, understood by Canadians, their leaders and their organizations, and embraced by all over time. The Canadian citizen as a reference point obviously alters in a major way the traditional and dominant tri-level government-centred model, inducing a democratization of the relationships between citizens, the civil society and the different levels of government. Moreover, such a shift would allow moving away from often fruitless jurisdictional and political power plays and gamesmanship that have perennially frustrated and, at times, enraged Canadians.

For Canada and its institutions, this would constitute a transformation of the first order. However, in light of the recent history of the country, the tensions that exist between levels of government, and the demands by Canadians and the civil society for more responsive government, this transformation can be seen very much in line with the natural evolution of Canadian governance. Furthermore, at its most basic and pragmatic level, this perspective recognizes that politicians, whether at the municipal, provincial or federal levels, are all elected by the same voters.

The citizen-centred perspective is not and should not be construed as an ideological sleight either from the right or the left of the political spectrum. It should, to the contrary, be envisaged and conceived as both a challenge and an opportunity to enhance the effectiveness and efficiency of government and as a key contributor to a sustainable, healthy and resilient Canada as well as to its cities and communities.

The prerequisites to the development of a shared perspective — answering the second question — can be categorized in three distinct but related sets of consideration: values, synergy and decision making.

Values

As previously argued, a transformation of Canadian society and its cities must be considered, decided, and realized on the basis of the generally recognized and admired Canadian values of:

- peace, e.g., our preferred approach in resolving conflicts;
- respect, e.g., of differences in our diverse society;
- freedom, e.g., to affirm one's identity;
- helping others, e.g., underpinning the establishment of our social programs;
- integrity, e.g., how we expect our businesses and political organizations to manage their transactions;
- fairness, e.g., how we want decisions made and conflicts resolved; and,
- cooperation, e.g., defining trait of how we see our relations with the world community.

These values have always served Canada well and are aligned with the proposed focus on a seamless approach to the response to the needs and aspirations of Canadians.

Synergy

A synergy between Canadians, their leaders and their governments will be key to the achievement of a common

Canadians want seamless government where the organizing principle is around the citizen or their business, not the department or ministry or individual program.

Michelle D'Auray *et al.* (2003)

In terms of urban experience, no citizen is more or less important than any other, so harnessing the potential of the many has far more clout than inspired top-down direction. In such a way, wide-spread, passionate participation in a vision which is shared by the participants gains its own, self-fulfilling momentum ...

Charles Landry (2006)

The new reality of power is that to share power is not an abdication of responsibility but the only feasible and responsible means by which leaders can possibly achieve everything they want for their communities. By sharing power, cities can achieve far more for their citizens ... Cities need leaders at different levels and spheres, as urban success depends on the successful results of a myriad set of initiatives. As long as there is a sense of [a] clear unfolding urban story, based on a set of explicit principles, self-activated leaders can funnel and focus energy so complexity is reduced.

Charles Landry (2006)

More and more work gets done by horizontal process, or it does not get done. More and more decisions are made with wider and wider consultations, or they don't stick ... In the ... knowledge environment we have to rethink the very nature of rule, power, and authority ... Collegial not command structures become the more natural basis for organization. Not "command and control" but "conferring and networking" become the mandatory modes for getting things done.

Harland Cleveland quoted in Gareth Morgan (1989)

vision for the future of Canada and its cities. This will require the pooling of efforts and resources, and also the ability and capacity to build and sustain consensus. Some of the key ingredients to successful synergy are:

• sharing information;

• fostering creativity and ingenuity;

• sharing and benefiting from the exchange of leading practices;

• improving collaboration and conflict resolution in relationship building and decision making; and,

• being authentic, truthful and passionate about our stands, beliefs and positions on issues and problems.

Decision Making

The third set of conditions and factors of success is of particular importance since it is through sound decision-making processes that values are channeled through society, and that synergy can really take place. Five particular considerations, among others, are proposed to help deliver successful decision making:

• inspired, inspiring and widely shared leadership;

• inclusive, participatory and coordinated approach to the identification of common interests and decision making;

• a long-term view supporting short-term decisions;

• flexibility — an ability to adapt and to change course as required; and,

• sustaining the momentum of change through the building of ongoing support for decisions and actions.

Ultimately, a common vision of the future of Canada and for the future of Canada will rest on how successfully the principle — the fundamental reference point in the governance of the country being the Canadian citizenry — as well as its prerequisites are manifested in the institutional structure of the country.

The clear articulation of distinctions and complementarities between roles and responsibilities and areas of jurisdiction for the different levels of government will be an important factor in achieving a common vision of and for Canada, and by extension, of and for its cities.

This evolution toward a common vision will also have to reflect a shift from a command and control approach to governance to an adaptation and partnership approach. In the future, "integration, integration, integration" will be to successful governance what "location, location, location" is to successful real estate.

In the tradition of Canadian pragmatism and incremental perspective and approach, the development of a common vision will build on existing foundations, will be progressive and not revolutionary, and will neither seek nor represent a perfect or absolute solution to the current fragile state of consensus on the future of Canada by Canadians.

The next section puts forward a vision statement. It is intended both as an illustration of the application of the principle and prerequisites set out above, and as a personal statement reflecting my views and aspirations for the evolution of Canada, inclusive of its cities and regions.

MY VISION FOR CANADA

Canada is and will continue to be a special country, within its North American context and also within the concert of nations. As a federal state, Canada will strive to give a stronger voice and be respectful of the identity and specificity of its regions and provinces. Canada will build and sustain a society that puts its citizens first and foremost in its governance and decision making. Canada will give high priority to the development of sustainable, healthy and resilient cities and regions as foundations for its social and cultural cohesion and inclusiveness, its economic prosperity, its open and democratic institutions, and its quality of life and environment. Canadians, for their part, will cherish their belonging to a special country in the following ways:

We, Canadians, look at present times and also our future in the 21st century and beyond, with optimism and confidence.

We are proud of our individual and collective achievements, and we are committed to continuing to build and improve this country, oftentimes admired and emulated by other countries.

We embrace, respect and protect our individual rights and freedoms; however, their manifestation and expression are set and viewed within the broader life of our communities, which are more than the sum of the needs and aspirations of individual citizens.

We aspire to a sustainable way of life, in its social, economic, institutional, environmental, physical, and temporal dimensions and ramifications, for the present but also, and especially, for future generations.

We value our diversity — the foundation of our country and its identity — and we are committed to sustaining that diversity through the continuous welcoming of new Canadians; we wish to ensure the preservation of some of the cultural traits of those new Canadians as part of and in balance with the continuing evolution of Canadian society, with its particular values, traditions and overall culture.

We appreciate the earlier and essential contribution of our Aboriginal people and their communities in the discovery and settlement of our country; although complex and lengthy in its time requirements, the formal recognition and confirmation of their ancestral social, cultural and territorial rights and prerogatives is something that we are committed and dedicated to now and in the future — this in the context of the broader evolution of Canada.

We are city dwellers in the majority, our inner cities, suburbs and towns being increasingly where we dream our futures, where we respond to our basic needs and our aspirations, where we strive to develop sustainable, healthy and resilient communities; we also make it possible for our governments to realize over time these futures while also ensuring that the requirements of non-urban areas, whether rural, resources, natural or wilderness, are also sustained.

We are trading people: our past, present and future prosperity are tied to our ability to trade in resources, manufactured goods and services within and outside Canada; as committed traders, we conduct and will continue to conduct our business openly, fairly, equitably, and within the bounds of proper and enforceable reciprocal arrangements and trading relations.

Les infrastructures de transport, qui envahissent les berges, et le réseau autoroutier, qui fracturent la trame urbaine, devront faire place à la réappropriation de l'espace riverain et de l'espace urbain, dans une perspective de développement durable [pour que les Montréalais puissent profiter de l'emplacement exceptionnel de leur ville en bordure du fleuve].

La réappropriation de l'espace riverain — Redonner le fleuve aux Montréalais leur permettra de jouir d'un plan d'eau pleinement accessible pour y pratiquer toute une gamme d'activités récréo-touristiques, aussi bien sur les berges que sur le fleuve.

La réappropriation de l'espace urbain — La reconstruction des secteurs déstructurés par la présence des autoroutes permettra de retisser la trame urbaine, de développer l'habitat urbain et de créer un milieu de vie animé.

Le développement urbain durable — Concevoir l'avenir du havre dans une perspective de développement durable, c'est favoriser la mixité des fonctions urbaines en assurant leur cohabitation harmonieuse et privilégier l'habitat urbain en favorisant la mixité sociale.

Société du Havre de Montréal (2004)

We value our health, the health of our communities, organizations and leaders; we strive to achieve a healthy Canada through appropriate lifestyles, a priority accorded to preventive medicine, and the provision of necessary investments for the caring of the sick and disabled — this based on a truly and sustained collaborative approach between all Canadians and their institutions.

We are proud of our traditions and achievements in global relations and outreach through the actions of individual Canadians on the world stage, the contribution of our volunteer agencies, and our participation in international organizations and institutions, and we remain committed to achieving an equitable worldwide sharing of resources and development through appropriate and sustained support and investment.

We constantly seek to improve how we govern ourselves and our country, based on our values, traditions, history and vision of the future of Canada; we want to ensure that our basic needs and aspirations are attended to, provided for, and remain the focus of attention through appropriate decision-making institutions and forums, participation of users and beneficiaries, collaborative arrangements between government levels, the allocation of the necessary tool kits and resources to cities in order that they be able to fully exercise their responsibilities, and the provision of public goods and services delivered effectively, efficiently and seamlessly.

We look at the future of Canadian society through short- and long-term lenses, conscious of the constant change of generations, the enrichment that their coming together represents; the relations between generations provide for the preservation of past memories and legacies, and the fundamental requirement to bequeath to future generations a country in a respectful, equitable and sustainable manner.

We recognize and value the importance of learning, education, creativity, ingenuity and innovation, within an evolving knowledge-based world and society, as guarantors of our cohesion, diversity, prosperity, quality of life and of the environment, as well as our capacity and ability to rise to the many challenges and many opportunities that Canada will face and benefit from in the future.

We are a secular society, with a clear separation between church and state; while we agree that this separation must be maintained, we also aspire to bridge these two realms, our individual spirituality acting as a fountainhead for our shared values and our commitment to each others well-being.

We are conscious of the role and importance of security and safety for the orderly, peaceful and sustainable evolution of our world, country and communities; this is a fundamental requirement to the good functioning of democratic institutions as well as the protection of people, property and state. This will be achieved through the use of appropriate security and safety infrastructure and institutions, but also, and importantly, through a commitment to open, fair and equitable relations with other countries, and participation in the international community through activities, organizations and institutions, as well as through investments in people and their societies.

PLACE FOR DIALOGUE, EXPERIENCE AND LEARNING

A "grand vision" is really at the core of urbanism; it echoes and defines the aspirations of a community for its long-term future. Visioning is fundamentally an expression of the preferred path (or paths) that citizens elect to give themselves as a guide for how they want to chart and fashion their evolution. The more explicit the vision, the better it can connect with the heart, mind and soul of the people. Its meaningfulness is often tied to the identification of significant change (breakpoints) in the existence of a society. The process of visioning can really be exhilarating but behind the allegories, myths and symbols of the vision statement are hidden many challenges, including the difficulty in achieving shared meaning; the failure to elicit the rise and sustenance of a leadership group to power its realization; the lack of attention to communication and explanation of the vision; the absence of nurturing and follow-up by communities, among others. Through the following examples, I explore the different aspects and the different meanings that the "grand vision" has represented in my work.

Viewpoint:

Reframing the "Grand Vision"

The dramatic demise of Robert Campeau's namesake company in the 1980s constitutes quite clearly a case of a "grand vision run amok" — a systemic failure of vision, leadership, resource decisions and governance structure. My time with the company preceded many years of Mr. Campeau's continental and even global aspirations and, ultimately, failure. I would characterize the latter part of the 1970s as a period during which steps were being taken to consolidate the "grand vision" from a "regional-based company with some national exposure" to evolving the organization as a "national brand but with points of entry in the U.S. market". Although the link between my work and the evolving vision was not evident to me at the time, the focus placed on bringing to the company a more sophisticated approach to market R & D across Canada is indicative of greater national ambitions. Within a very small but highly collaborative team, involving real estate, marketing, planning and computer specialists, we were able to develop a synthetic profile of different Canadian markets that could indeed support an aggressive national-based expansion program in the housing and commercial sectors.

When I arrived in the Saint-Jérôme region in the early 1980s, I found an area with great inherent qualities, especially its people and its natural environment. But I also soon discovered a region lacking an overarching vision, exhibiting conflicting political direction, and also reflecting a distinct disinterest in establishing for itself a coherent strategic position within its broader socio-economic environment. The absence of vision, leadership, and strategic foresight in resources

prioritization and an appropriate governance structure was recognized and lamented often, but very little was actually done to address and overcome these limitations and inhibitions to the evolution of the area. As Director of Planning for the City of Saint-Jérôme, I dedicated a lot of time and effort to the development of a "grand vision" for its downtown, on the basis of the recognition of the many untapped possibilities that the synergy of its many stakeholders, institutions, natural and heritage assets, and development sites could offer. This investment of energy did not pay off while I was still working for the city. However, afterwards in the 1990s, the emergence of a new leadership group, advocating a new and refreshing "grand vision" for the city, led to important transformative changes, that enabled the Saint-Jérôme region to assume a more active and dynamic presence in the evolution of the lower Laurentians. I would like to think that I helped in some way in planting the seeds for this change.

The grand vision for Canada's Capital Region (CCR) constitutes a good example of a "transcending vision", not only spanning several generations of people in time but also many epochs and stages in regard to its physical development footprint. This vision reflected many explicit choices, translating a deep appreciation of the symbolic importance and meaning of the capital by Canadians. A distinctive trait of the grand vision is its "organic" perspective of the evolution of the urban form of Canada's capital, a marked difference from the more traditional "monumental" character of the planning and building of capital cities. In the Canadian way, the grand vision for CCR has not been achieved with great exuberance; rather it has evolved with a great deal of subtlety and flexibility, which allowed that it be adequately grounded, thus ensuring its enduring character. Initial attempts at reframing the grand vision reflected a preoccupation with the broadening of the geographical reach of CCR, especially its spanning of both sides of the Ottawa River. A more recent reframing was more concerned with broadening the national reach of the capital, elevating its symbolic importance and significance.

As Director of Planning for the National Capital Commission (NCC), I have been intimately associated with this more recent iteration of the grand vision, my work having been geared to the creation of this "greater reach" for CCR, through an emphasis on "relationship building" and a focus on the "experiential dimension" of the physical planning and development of the Capital region. The most recent push in reframing the grand vision calls for improved alignment between the planning and development of CCR, and the realities and challenges that Canadians will be facing in the 21st century. The new vision will need to capture the priority for Canadians to achieve a more sustainable, healthy and resilient sort of development and the possible role of the capital as a source of inspiration and example.

In view of the evolving Canadian society, and especially the significant changes that affect and will affect its cities, there exists a clear requirement to recast the grand vision in the work and the professional practice of urbanists. To carry deep meaning and to energize Canada's transition into a future that will certainly be very different from its past, the grand vision should espouse a larger contour of the Canadian reality and align with a more encompassing storyline about what lies ahead for the country and what it will mean for its people. Reframing the grand vision is really about renewing and even challenging the grand narrative that has shaped all dimensions of our contemporary world, in Canada and elsewhere. Some of the key assumptions or premises of this grand narrative — the supremacy of human society over the natural environment, the growth model based on ever-increasing material consumption, the living-in-the-present mindset and the little attention paid to the needs of future generations, the absence of measurement of the inherent risks associated with our past and current civilization's drive and reach, and the relative inertia in how people elect to govern their mutual relationships and transactions — no longer constitute a viable path and viable underpinnings for the longer term sustainability, health and resiliency of the country and its cities. I associate realizing a new grand vision with a change in world-views at the grassroots level, advanced and facilitated by a new breed of leaders that can leverage the support of a wide range of contacts and networks, a variety of tools (educational, legal, fiscal, environmental, scientific) and a belief that transformative change is to be fundamentally rooted in human initiatives instead of being based on a "technological quick-fix".

Leading Practices:

Visioning in a Contemporary Context — Hamilton Vision 2020

At the beginning of the 21st century, in rapidly changing and increasingly more complex national and global environments, the importance and value for cities and regions to achieve a broad-based consensus on a shared image of their future is generally acknowledged and recognized. But the realization of such common visions and more importantly, ensuring their implementation over the short-, medium- and long-term, are fraught with numerous difficulties and challenges. Over the recent years, the transformation of urban areas as a result of socio-economic, governance, environmental and technological changes, has made visioning processes even more difficult and challenging to initiate and bring to fruition.

In July 1992, the Council of the Regional Municipality of Hamilton-Wentworth (now the City of Hamilton) approved Vision 2020, following an extensive community engagement process. During the following year, an implementation strategy was developed and put in place, including mechanisms for the review and the renewal of the vision. Since its inception, Hamilton Vision 2020 has garnered a great deal of attention across Canada and internationally, even winning several prestigious awards. Its success reflects not only the comprehensiveness of its process and content, but also and more significantly, its resilience under the dramatic changes that have engulfed the Hamilton region as it was entering the new millennium. Hamilton Vision 2020 is worthy of examination as an urbanism leading practice, with its many benefits but also its potential pitfalls.

Achievements

In the late 1980s and early 1990s, a changing national and global economic environment meant for the Council of the Regional Municipality of Hamilton-Wentworth more difficult and challenging policy and budgetary choices, and the need to consider alternative decision-making frameworks and criteria. In a vanguard decision for the time, regional council shifted its decision-making processes toward the just emerging "sustainable development path", which emphasized an integrated approach to society's environmental, socio-cultural and economic dimensions. In adopting this new decision-making framework, the Hamilton-Wentworth Region also acknowledged the limit of strict governmental action and the importance of approaching the changing regional reality through a much broader community effort. In order to achieve the necessary cross-sector and behavioural changes, the active involvement of all stakeholders and the public was seen as an essential requirement. Hamilton Vision 2020 emerged from this governance transformation as an innovative vehicle for the creation of the necessary community engagement and participation. A task force was established and conducted an extensive public engagement process that involved several participatory mechanisms, including town hall meetings, focus group discussions, a vision working group, an implementation team, community forums and sustainable community days.

Written as a "story of the future", Hamilton Vision 2020 sought to paint a picture of the Hamilton Region in 2020, this as vividly and realistically as possible, e.g., visioning a quality of life, valued landscapes, urban and rural communities co-existing in harmony, people efficiently getting around, priority to residents' livelihood, and promoting stakeholders' participation. When regional council approved Vision 2020, it identified for each of its theme areas' specific goals, strategies and action plans. The development of monitoring mechanisms was also seen as very important to establish and maintain council and staff accountability for the vision to the public. Measurable performance indicators were developed to enable the ongoing assessment of the implementation of the vision and more precisely, whether priority goals were being realized and behavioural changes were actually taking place.

The national and international recognition received by Hamilton Vision 2020, and the high level political and public engagement that it fostered over the years in the Hamilton region, reflect a number of decisions and undertakings by regional leaders: the direct incorporation of over a third of the task force recommendations into the 1995 regional official plan; the creation of a senior staff coordination committee charged with the implementation of the vision from an inter-departmental and intergovernmental perspective and approach; the requirement that all reports to council include a sustainable development section; the production of sustainability reports on an annual basis; the development and implementation of a regional economic development strategy; the development of an integrated transportation master plan; the organization of annual sustainable community days and youth forums; the introduction of an urban accessibility program designed to allow persons that are physically challenged to navigate the urban environment as easily and conveniently as the rest of the population; and, the approval

of other sustainability measures related to water and waste-water management, green fleet transportation, downtown heating district, climate change adaptation and mitigation, and planning with a focus on public health.

Since 1992, the City of Hamilton and its region have witnessed momentous transformations, among others — demographic changes, a shift from heavy industry to value-added manufacturing based on a cluster approach, and the amalgamation of several municipalities into the new City of Hamilton on January 1, 2001. Some of these transformations (demographic and economic) proved to be well synchronized with the overall direction set by Hamilton Vision 2020. However, municipal amalgamation has involved some adjustments in regard to the follow-up process given to the vision; some observers even suggested that city council, through these changes, has fundamentally subverted the overall intent of the vision.

Limitations

The limitations of Hamilton Vision 2020 can be cross-referenced, for the most part, to the emergent political environment following the creation of the amalgamated City of Hamilton. Some of these limitations include mixed performance results in implementing aspects of the vision; some of the dimensions of the vision proved insufficiently jurisdiction-specific, failing as a result to address, in meaningful ways, important public concerns; the new governance framework introduced by the new City of Hamilton Council is seen as moving away from the community engagement opportunities that underpinned Hamilton Vision 2020; this governance framework has also not been embraced by some stakeholders, because of a perceived lack of clarity in how it is translating past commitments contained in Hamilton Vision 2020; and, some of the recent developments in Hamilton have been shown to be performing less well according to sustainability criteria in comparison to the performance of older neighbourhoods, re-enforcing the perception of a loss of commitment on the part of the city toward the tenets of Hamilton Vision 2020.

What Was Learned

Visioning initiatives and processes, in a day and age where public engagement is increasingly seen as an incontrovertible requirement of responsive and, ultimately, successful governance, offer opportunities to involve and inspire the public, to create the necessary conditions for inclusiveness. Visions, to connect with people and be capable of bridging the immediate and the future, must provide more than generalities and be, instead, truly meaningful, showing the way in which the hard issues that affect and confront people in their day-to-day can be addressed, while at the same time providing signposts for the emergence of confidence and hope. They must make possible leveraging the power of shared images to help understand the present and picture the future, creating in the process the necessary energy to bring people forward, not in isolation but in a united front, as a community. Visions, while promoting and nurturing bottom up processes involving the usual stakeholders and also, hopefully, some members of the silent majority need to be able to foster sustained community leadership, a constituency of support, enable continuity in processes while ensuring that the longer term goals always remain on the "radar". Finally, visions must balance prescription and "going with the flow", helping leaders and followers to find comfort in ambiguity, confidence in moving beyond certainty, and promoting such values as spontaneity, creativity and risk taking.

Sources: Jill Grant and Jaime Orser Smith (2006), City of Hamilton (2008), Don McClean and Bob Korol (2004), Bill Pearce (1998), Sinisa Tomic (2003).

Vancouver

A vision without action is just a dream; an action without vision just passes the time; a vision with an action changes the world.

Nelson Mandela quoted in CIDA Sustainable Development Strategy 2001-2003 (2001)

CHAPTER 7

FIVE THEMES FOR ACTION

[C]ities in the next century will experience a greater frequency and diversity of shocks than has ever been experienced before, except in terms of war. Planning for the long term is planning for surprise … [S]ix major external forces [will] transform [the] built environment over the century ahead [technological change, climate change, globalization, demographics, resource scarcities, and changes in world view]. Most of these forces will experience an increasing rate of change.

City of Ottawa (2004)

FROM VISION TO ACTION

The three goals of sustainable, healthy and resilient communities have become the increasingly favoured "path of change" to the planning, development and governance of cities as well as the way forward to best experience them over time, in Canada and in other countries. These goals are providing a sound foundation for charting the future course of Canada's urban agenda.

However, their realization has been confronted with many obstacles, whether for long-range decisions or in the day-to-day activities of municipalities, other levels of government, and in other sectors. Philosophical and ideological differences have been sources of difficulty. But the rapidity of change, the inertia of large institutions, and the cumulative effects of phenomena, such as the dominance of the private automobile as a principal mode of transportation, combined with over-consumption of non-renewable resources, indebtedness of individuals and organizations, national and global resource inequality, and lack of long-term perspective, among others, have also posed significant challenges to a transition to sustainable, healthy and resilient cities and regions.

This transition was never meant to be effortless or without consequences. To the contrary, to move from vision to action will require the application of a number of "levers of change", including discipline, a voluntary approach to change, a commitment to new behaviours and ways of doing things, patience, and the acceptance of errors as a source of learning along the way.

To overcome the angst, cynicism and skepticism often on display when referring to a sustainable, healthy and resilient future, and to bring some form of closure to the question of their validity, it is important to be clear as to what should underpin the elaboration and implementation of the urban agenda — the action plan for a "projet de société".

The approach to the development of an action plan needs to pass critical tests if it is to develop any traction in urban and regional milieus, and build the necessary momentum to ensure some form of continuity. Any proposal should be: issue-driven; principle-driven; reality-driven and, priority-driven.

Issue-driven

For any action plan to be meaningful and actionable, it should, at a first level, be seen to address and provide balanced responses to social, cultural, economic, political, institutional, environmental and spatial/physical community issues as well as their interplay, and this for short-, medium- and/or long-term durations and horizons.

Principle-driven

Moving along the continuum of "vision to action", a second set of considerations needs to be integrated and built-into any proposed measures and interventions: first-order principles and complementary principles.

The first-order principles correspond to the previously identified "pillars" for Canada's urban agenda:

- making Canadians the fundamental reference point in Canada's governance;

- strengthening the role of cities in Canada's federalism;

- providing an appropriate weight to major cities in the governance of the country;

- valuing experimental and unusual processes and solutions; and,

- balancing regulatory, fiscal, market and community-based mechanisms.

An ensemble of complementary principles to the first-order principles can help to further anchor the philosophical underpinnings of the "projet de société":

- proximity/subsidiarity — to ensure that decisions regarding the meeting of needs and aspirations of Canadians are made as closely as possible to those affected by them;

- openness — to enable citizens to witness how decisions affecting them are made, including access to relevant information as well as decision-making processes;

- triple bottom line — to consider the environmental and social outcomes as of equal importance to the financial/economic results;

- accountability — to provide for regular reporting by decision makers on their activities and results;

- redundancy — to provide alternative means, including alternative physical infrastructure, as a way to reduce the effects of unforeseen events and manage risks associated with future uncertainties; and,

- flexibility — to ensure an adequate, adaptable and changing approach to decisions and actions, in response to unforeseen circumstances.

Reality-driven

More intangible and context-sensitive, the reality test is as crucial in ensuring ultimate ability and capacity to fulfill the hopes, aspirations and needs of Canadians through the elaboration and implementation of an urban agenda. To pass the reality test, any proposal should meet the following criteria:

- be socially acceptable — around which a majority of people can rally;

- be politically defensible — reflecting a balance of interests; and,

- be technically feasible — can be realized within a predictable timeframe and budget.[16]

Sustainable development does not define a particular path for development, but focuses on what would enhance the quality of life. It requires the capacity to adapt to constantly changing conditions, as well as the flexibility to work with uncertainty, and with differences in local conditions and in public expectations shaped by culture, values and experience. Above all it is participatory, ensuring that local communities and individuals have substantive input into designing and implementing development programs and projects. Only when local people have a sense of ownership and personal investment in their own development will they have a stake in ensuring its long-term sustainability.

Canadian International Development Agency (2001)

---

16 See Panel on the NCC Mandate Review (2006).

Any system with an ability to self-organize must have a degree of "redundancy", a kind of excess capacity that can create room for innovation and development to occur. Without redundancy, systems are fixed and completely static.

Gareth Morgan (1998)

Priority-driven

And finally, the content of the action plan should reflect an order and be priority-driven. The following priority action areas are in alignment with policy directions previously identified for the urban agenda. They are seen as key requirements for the urban agenda to deliver any promised results:

- connections — to look at issues in terms of their relationships rather than in isolation;

- resources — to help balance the supply and demand of limited public resources;

- generations — to consider the needs and aspirations of current and future generations and different cultures in decision making;

- collaboration — to build greater consensus, or at a minimum, a climate and conditions for the resolution of differences in intergovernmental relations and public debate; and,

- institutions — to create new institutions and symbols in response to the evolving needs of Canada and its cities and regions.

INTRODUCING THE ACTION PLAN FOR CANADA'S URBAN AGENDA

The priority action areas outlined above will serve as the five themes for action for the urban agenda. The following fourteen possible action items are put forward — grouped by theme — and will be detailed in the remainder of Part III of this book.

1. Connections

- ▸ land use and transportation — working at the interface;

- ▸ urban development and the environment — ensuring integration;

- ▸ citizenship in cities — expanding scope and meaning; and,

- ▸ professional work in cities — valuing inter-disciplinary collaboration.

2. Resources

- ▸ life-cycle perspective and approach — aligning the short- and longer term;

- ▸ alternative management strategies — looking at options to vary our choices; and,

- ▸ ubiquitous creativity and ingenuity — embedding in all facets of organizational life.

3. Generations

▸ relations between generations and cultures — thinking present and future.

4. Collaboration

▸ intergovernmental relations — expanding tripartite decision-making;

▸ communities of practice — creating different work and networks; and,

▸ cities and their surrounding regions — reaching out, sharing in.

5. Institutions

▸ citizen houses — creating new symbols;

▸ citizen forums — harnessing social energy toward political ends; and,

▸ ceremonies and celebrations — multiplying the occasions.

This constitutes an action-plan package in the context of Canada's urban agenda.

Fredericton

[I]f planning means anything it means seeing not only the immediate but the more distant consequences of action. If we understand the more distant consequences of our actions, both in our relation to non-human nature and to other humans, then we will understand that we can survive only by cooperation and trust.

Hans Blumenfeld (1983)

CHAPTER 8
URBAN AGENDA: CONNECTIONS

General planning in the 20th century can be summed up in one word: isolation.

Philip N. Loheed and
Brandy H.M. Brooks (2006)

[T]he [organization] that once saw itself as ... separate ... now recognizes itself as ... part of a complex web of inter-organizational relations and must modify its managerial philosophies and systems to take this into account ... The development of effective inter-organizational relations and mindsets that are able to sustain and develop patterns of mutual dependence become as important as the design and operation of specific activities.

Gareth Morgan (1988)

Separation was the defining characteristic of the industrial era, both with regard to the make-up of society and its institutions, and the physical structure of cities. The hierarchical nature of jobs and work in organizations, and the required isolation between different land uses in municipal plans and by-laws, regardless of their relative compatibility, are just two of the many possible examples of this dominance of and focus on separation in the 19th and 20th centuries.

This tendency to separate continues to be an important trait of the Canadian society and its cities at the beginning of the 21st century. In some instances, it remains justified, considering the nature of certain activities or the requirement to reduce or mitigate negative effects. However, the information age has put an onus on greater coordination and integration in the lives of people and businesses, and in the organization of space and time.

Rapidity of change, constantly changing activities and organizations and, more particularly, the capacity of technology, such as computing, the Internet and social media, to provide a separation-free approach to the delivery of results and services, account for and explain to a large extent this movement towards greater integration.

Integration or alternatively, connection, is not strictly something that can be observed; it also reflects a new way of thinking and acting by different groups and spheres of the Canadian society. It represents a major shift in people's perspective of society and life in society, and will demand, over the coming years, a corresponding adjustment on the part of organizations and institutions in order that they become more responsive to the needs and aspirations of Canadians.

From division and separation, integration and connection are becoming more and more top of mind, resulting in less hierarchical organizations, with work based on teams and partnerships, and work procedures conducted simultaneously or in parallel. Connection and cohesion in the organization and working of society are increasingly given preference over disjointed approaches.

In the context of Canada's urban agenda, the following areas of connection warrant closer examination and evaluation: land use and transportation; urban development and the environment; citizenship in cities; and professional work in cities.

LAND USE AND TRANSPORTATION

The separation between land uses — such as between residential and work/commercial areas — is the outcome of an approach to city planning and development that treated mobility and accessibility as an end in itself rather than a means to efficient, productive and sustainable land use.

The separate approach to land use and transportation planning has meant more travel in urban areas, with many negative consequences, including the dominance of the car, the loss of time, inefficient use of non-renewable energy sources, financial costs, a larger urban footprint, an urban form with much less variety, and higher greenhouse gases (GHG) emissions.

A more integrated approach to the planning and development of cities, whereby land use and transportation infrastructure are seen as complementary and synergistic, can foster the emergence of truly sustainable, healthy and resilient communities, either through a gradual transformation of existing ones or the development of new communities.

The key actions supporting the transformation and/ or renewal of the interface between land use and transportation in cities include the following:

• A more integrated approach to planning, where local and regional authorities join forces in mapping out a comprehensive sustainable, healthy and resilient development strategy, e.g., intensification, mixed uses, better and more effective use of existing infrastructure capacity, more efficient use of energy sources, improved quality of the public realm and the design of buildings, and healthier lifestyles and enhanced quality of life.

• A clear recognition of the key demographic drivers influencing the need for greater coordination between land use and transportation, especially an aging and more diverse population. On the latter aspect, there is empirical evidence showing newcomers having a greater rate of transit use than Canadian-born.

• An approach to municipal investment that over time helps achieve the prioritizing of transportation modes in urban areas based on the policy ordering of: 1. public transit, 2. walking, 3. cycling, and 4. private vehicles.

• Emphasis on linking the socio-economic, cultural, environmental and spatial dimensions of the land-use/transportation nexus through a green mobility framework, e.g., intermodal perspective and approach; transportation demand management strategies; reduction in the average traveling distance between home and work: promotion of alternative modes to the car, etc.

• A system of fiscal and regulatory incentives that can foster the creation of transit-oriented developments (TOD).

Improving the connections between land use and transportation would require on the part of Canadians changes in behaviour for sure: however, with the right incentive structure, such behavioural adjustments could proactively help lead the way to addressing some of the future problems and challenges to confront Canadian cities.

[L]es villes sont le champ de bataille privilégié de la lutte aux gaz à effet de serre.

Pierre Bergeron (2005)

While the Science Council recognizes that the automobile as an urban vehicle has served us well during the past half century or so, it also realizes that entirely inadequate support has been given to public transit authorities. This has resulted in severe imbalances in most urban areas of the country, characterized both by inadequate facilities for mass transit and by an undue influence on the city of the automobile and its associated problems ...

Science Council (1971)

One of the most interesting and promising aspects of mixed land use is its ability to create, on relatively small areas of land, environments that have many of the characteristics usually associated with urbanity: the proximity of activities, the increased educational and cultural opportunities, and the possibility of choice in one's contacts and associations.

Dimitri Procos (1976)

URBAN DEVELOPMENT AND THE ENVIRONMENT

As noted previously, the environment is often perceived as a distinct and separate dimension in urban planning and development processes. It is, at times, considered an afterthought, rather than an essential component within a larger set of planning elements.

To illustrate the poor integration between the environment and urban planning and development, environmental assessments and their associated mitigation measures constitute appropriate cases in point, being frequently sources of anxiety and conflict in the context of development projects. The consideration of these mitigation measures is, in many instances, realized in a piecemeal manner instead of being envisaged as contributing to the overall aim, quality and success of projects.

However, in recent years, an alternative perspective and approach to the environment — one more integrated into urban planning and development, founded on ecological principles and knowledge as well as values and ethics — has emerged. Through such concepts and methods as watershed planning, ecological cycles, natural linkages and buffers, the "4R" (reduce, recover, recycle, reuse), "biomimicry" and "cradle to cradle", this renewed approach conveys appropriately the multifaceted character and strength of the environment.

While added complexity in urban planning and development may be an end result, the many tangible benefits and positive outcomes that flow from such an approach make this greater complexity less of a preoccupation.

A holistic and integrated approach to the environment — of which the land use and transportation connection previously discussed above is a key contributor — constitutes a preferred path to a sustainable urban future.

In steering Canadian cities toward this preferred path, the following links between urban development and the environment are recognized as some of the essential elements of successful urban planning and development practices and processes:

- Natural areas, e.g., wetlands, are integral to a communities' environmental structure, identity, and uniqueness, substituting, in some instances, for man-made physical infrastructure in the natural processing and filtering of storm water.

- Fauna and flora, e.g., plant, animal and insect life, although often over-looked, do constitute key contributors to the ecological cycles and processes of communities, through the protection of rare and endangered species and the control of invasive species.

- Cultivated agricultural lands, when protected from urban development, can provide for and contribute to communities' and regions' food self-sufficiency.

- Waste management, when made to rely less on landfill, can support the reduction, recycling, and the reuse of "waste".

- Green construction is an alternative method to traditional construction, which minimizes the use of energy and water, provides for the recycling of water and waste-water, among other features, in the operations of buildings, and saves money.

- Infill construction, in the context of an urban intensification strategy, makes better use of land and infrastructure, and decreases the need for greenfield development.[17]

- Brownfields, consisting of the rehabilitation of contaminated sites, reduce both the need for greenfield sites and the footprint of cities while contributing to a more optimal use of urban land and infrastructure.

green spaces, can foster an urban form characterized by its human scale, its distinctive character, reflective of the communities' identity, and supportive of safer and more secure cities.

Alone or in combination, these urban development and environment connections not only promote and help achieve sustainable urban development in the long-

A major investment in new environmental technologies could generate significant new opportunities for Canada's prosperity and competitiveness in the long term.

External Advisory Committee on Cities and Communities (2006)

INTERNATIONAL COUNCIL FOR LOCAL ENVIRONMENTAL INITIATIVES (ICLEI) — LOCAL GOVERNMENTS FOR SUSTAINABILITY

http://www.iclei.org

ICLEI is a high-energy, membership-driven association of local governments working together to tackle global problems by starting locally. Over 1,900 cities, towns, counties, and their associations worldwide comprise ICLEI's growing membership. ICLEI works with these and hundreds of other local governments through international performance-based, results-oriented campaigns and programs. ICLEI provides technical, consulting, training and information services to build capacity, share knowledge, and support local government in the implementation of sustainable development at the local level. ICLEI's basic premise is that locally-designed initiatives can provide an effective and cost-efficient way to achieve local, national and global sustainability objectives. A fundamental component of ICLEI's performance-based campaign model is the milestone process. Each campaign incorporates a five-milestone structure that participating local governments work through: establish

a baseline; set a target; develop a local action plan; implement the local action plan; and, measure results. ICLEI influences international negotiations by raising the collective voice of local governments on the international sustainability stage, through the United Nations, other forums and the media. Through the Resilient Communities and Cities Initiative, ICLEI is working with local governments to reduce the impact of disasters on their communities by increasing their community's resilience. Through ICLEI's Biodiversity Program, it is working with local authorities to retain the relationship between people and nature. ICLEI's Water Campaign engages local government to shift to an integrated approach to local water management. ICLEI's Climate Resilient Cities and Adaptation Initiative is developing local capacity to identify and reduce the vulnerabilities associated with climate change, and adapt infrastructure and internal risk management systems in preparation for climate change.

---

[17] See "Addressing Contemporary Urban Development Challenges — Profiling the Work of Avi Friedman" at the end of the chapter.

Cities are places where varied publics can come together to co-create a civic realm — a precondition for a confident civic society to uphold rules and justice. This is where citizenship is more important than ethnic group, clan, tribe, religion, party or cadre allegiance. Cultures and societies which place such an emphasis on citizenship are likely to be more resilient, flexible and ultimately prosperous than those that are divided along lines of blood or traditional allegiances.

Charles Landry (2006)

Meaningful civic engagement has to be built on dialogue, exchange, different ideas and a full appreciation that with each choice also come consequences. This is a serious gap as many community groups today do not think about the consequences of their actions or the choices they make.

Paul Bedford (2006b)

term, but also help cities, in the short- and medium-term, achieve significant savings.

CITIZENSHIP IN CITIES

Canadian cities could become much more responsive to the needs and aspirations of their citizens if they were able to enhance the coordination and integration of the work, involvement and contribution of the many people, organizations and institutions participating in the delivery of urban programs, projects, and public goods and services.

A more complete, fulfilling, and, ultimately, successful interplay between people and institutions within cities — such as education and learning, health promotion and care, welcoming and integration of new Canadians, enhancing the life of people of Aboriginal ancestry, and facilitating access for the accessibility challenged, among others — will require a broader and deeper awareness and understanding of what city and civic life means for their citizens.

The concept of "citizenship" in its more traditional sense — expressing the values, culture, way-of-life, rights and responsibilities of Canadians — does not and cannot capture the complex and intricate web of knowledge, relationships and involvement required of Canadians. A more encompassing model of citizenship is needed in order for Canadians to successfully navigate the many aspects of their day-to-day life in cities, and achieve a fulfilling life with its many conflicting demands, and exciting possibilities.

An expanded meaning of citizenship in cities would need to reflect more specifically the many linkages that exist or should exist between education and the broader public domain. This could be achieved through modified curricula, new networks and forums, and coaching and mentoring. Only through this greater integration can the awareness and knowledge base required of Canadians for their meaningful involvement in the life of cities be promoted, harnessed, and, ultimately, enhanced. The role of community leaders in fostering this expanded meaning of citizenship needs to be emphasized, particularly in providing the platforms and templates for people of all ages to participate in the life of their communities and, as a result, achieve a higher sense of belonging.

Similarly, other possible new or expanded links between people and the broader public domain, within an improved understanding of citizenship in cities, could encompass:

• Healthy communities — a broader positioning of health in and for the life of people, including its curative and preventive dimensions, could have wide ranging positive ramifications for lifestyles and the wider evolution of cities. One of the aims could be to achieve a better balance between personal and work lives through closer residential and employment locations, use of alternative modes of mobility to the car, and acceptance and adoption of greater diversity and intensity of land use, among other means.

• Life-long learning communities — a more diverse agenda and reach of civic and cultural activities could foster the emergence of a more aware and enlightened citizenry in cities. Broad-based learning opportunities, extending in the different spheres and dimensions of people's life, could help enhance their understanding and appreciation of, as well as their involvement in, the different aspects of life in society, e.g., consumption decisions, democratic participation, charitable work and donations.

• Meaningful communities — an enriched urban environment through such means as interpretation of sites and buildings, and commemoration of people, events and achievements, could contribute to a layering of meanings in the experience of cities by people. New urban monuments, symbols and signs could help also to improve communication, accessibility and discovery of the different parts of cities, while, as a result, helping enhance people's ability to participate in and influence the urban development process.

• Supportive communities — a greater accent on the dedication of time by citizens to volunteer and participate in charitable endeavours could help promote and extend goodwill between various groups and cultures in cities. Other benefits that could accrue from such supportive activities include the establishment of formal and informal relationships between citizens, provision of timely assistance to those with special or in dire need, and resolution of differences and conflicts.

Renewing the perspective of citizenship in cities, while contributing to the emergence of a different world-view, could also create a more engaged and committed citizenry toward the wider commonwealth of their communities.

PROFESSIONAL WORK IN CITIES

Many professions contribute to urbanism — architecture, urban design, landscape architecture, urban and regional planning, engineering, law, accounting, administration, real estate, public safety and security, among many others. They are actively involved and make important, if not critical, contributions to the planning, development and governance of Canada's cities and regions.

Canadian professionals are mandated and guided by professional bodies — mainly provincially based — that are among the best in the world, and often copied and emulated by other countries.

In consideration of the significance of their role in charting the future of Canada's urban areas, it is of interest and also worthwhile, to identify possible areas where professional work could be improved in support of Canada's urban agenda.

The complex nature of activities and projects in cities and the decisions on which they are based and carried out now seldom involve a single professional discipline, but instead require the contribution of many disciplines. A great deal of attention has been given to the improvement of collaboration between professional disciplines — called multi-disciplinary collaboration — yet too often the results of professional work still reflect a lack of coordination and integration.

Successful countries in the global era will develop the social capacities of people and communities to live in states of mutual trust and to contribute to innovations.

Peter Clutterbuck and Marvyn Novick (2003)

The link between the prevalence of diabetes, obesity, cardiovascular and respiratory disease, air pollution, depression and the physical environment is clear. Introducing public-health impact costs into decisions on land use and transportation policies would start to ensure provision for the the long-term health of people in our environment.

Dan Leeming, Diane Riley and Dena Warmar (2006)

[C]ity-making is the overarching activity that draws on a wide variety of disciplines, soft and hard ... Mostly people will need to work in interdisciplinary teams, as only occasionally is one individual able to grasp the overarching picture.

Charles Landry (2006)

There is a renewed focus on place making — on drawing on history and heritage to create great places that foster a sense of community. It's about creating places that inspire, places with character, places that draw people through a powerful sense of identity. This trend is reflected in a willingness on behalf of architects, urban designers, urban planners, and developers to rely less on habit as their guide, to break from the conventional, and to experiment. The result is more architecturally compelling, more dense, more complex design that integrate land uses.

Richard M. Rosan (2004)

If the connected approach to the improvement of Canadian cities is to occur, a more interdisciplinary approach must overlay the multi-disciplinary one. Its major aim should be the development of integrated solutions and recommendations rather than the disciplinary breakdown often observed. In the urban development process, the environmental assessment of plans and projects, the planning and development of mixed uses, and the redevelopment of brownfields, are examples of undertakings that demand an interdisciplinary approach.

Professional work in Canada would also benefit from the creation and maintenance of new networks of professionals — such as federal, provincial and municipal professionals — to maximize the use of their skills in guiding urban change and addressing issues related to succession in the different professions. Improved and more systematic use of project and portfolio management in urban undertakings and the stewardship of public assets will also improve integration of professional work in Canadian cities.

In achieving more interdisciplinary focus and results, Canadian professionals would enhance their role in guiding cities, elevate the awareness for citizens of both short- as well as long-term considerations in the urban planning and development processes, improve their ability to balance different interests and put the public's interest at the forefront of the urban agenda, and finally put themselves in a better position to speak to and influence power.[18]

PLACE FOR DIALOGUE, EXPERIENCE AND LEARNING

Three notes complement this chapter. The first one, related to the urban development and the environment policy area, examines proposals geared to addressing contemporary urban development challenges. The other two, relate to the work of professionals in cities, and consider the relationships between the professions and power as well as possible approaches to enhance inter-professional exchanges.

---

[18] See "Speaking Truth to Power and Making Inter-Professional Exchange Happen" at the end of the chapter.

Leading Practices:

Addressing Contemporary Urban Development Challenges — Profiling the Work of Avi Friedman

Of the many factors that are rendering the realization of sustainable, healthy and resilient Canadian cities more rather than less challenging, two in particular have perhaps not received the level of attention and scrutiny consistent with their relative importance to the urban agenda: how to address the problems that are increasingly making the suburbs out of step with the conditions and requirements underpinning the broader evolution of urban areas in the 21st century, and, more significantly, how to bridge the development and redevelopment of central cities and suburbs in such a way as to make urban areas integrated instead of disconnected and dysfunctional as is often the case; and, how to ensure that all citizens have equitable access to the necessities that provide for their well-being and quality of life, in particular, the supply of affordable housing.

Achieving sustainable, healthy and resilient cities in Canada and other parts of the world will clearly demand a renewed perspective of urban areas: that they be looked at through new lenses, and, in many instances, on the basis of approaches that will be far removed from the "beaten path". Professor Avi Friedman, Director of the Affordable Homes Program at the McGill University, School of Architecture, has personified, through his work as a teacher, as a researcher and as a consultant, this quest for a new world-view on the resolution of some of the most deep-seated problems affecting cities at the beginning of a new millennium. In a meticulous, pragmatic, collaborative, and most of the time, leading-edge manner, Dr. Friedman has put forward many ideas for the sustainable resolution of the divide between central cities and suburbs. Perhaps his advocacy for and dedication in finding solutions to the affordability gap that confronts an increasingly

large number of citizens in cities best epitomizes his contribution to scholarship and policy guidance in the field of urbanism. Through his multi-faceted initiatives and innovations, solid foundations have been laid in moving forward proactively on key dimensions of Canada's urban agenda.

Achievements

Avi Friedman's contention is that suburbs are not sustainable as an urban form. Because of the social, economic, technological and environmental transformations that have marked urban areas in the late 20th century, and will characterize them as the 21st century unfolds, they no longer respond to the reality, needs and aspirations of people. At the same time, suburbs will clearly not be disappearing as a form of human settlement; they will continue to be developed because some of their inherent characteristics (scale, layout, privacy, open spaces) will continue to appeal to people. The challenge posed by the future evolution of suburbs is to evolve a design process that will permit, over time, their sustainable joining with central cities, with the aim of making the resulting urban areas "whole".

Key aspects of the proposed design process include that: it must balance respect for the existing character of suburbs while allowing for modifications that will make them sustainable, healthy and resilient; it must be rooted in common sense, be simple, practical and flexible; it must involve citizens in order to create the necessary awareness to the limitations of the suburban way of life, to provide them with options that enable the finding of their comfort zone, and to elicit on their part responsiveness to change instead of a reactive response, e.g., NIMBY response. It must contribute an urban form that, while not transformed, is less segregated, reflects a gradient from centre to periphery, introduces a greater mix of land uses, somewhat raises densities, with the recognition that each suburb has its particular requirements, that involve the determination of an appropriate threshold of change. The design process must also bring, as a result, some reduction of sprawl, increase cities' tax base, optimize the use of infrastructure, foster greater use of existing facilities and green spaces, provide for healthier living, and create opportunities for making alternative modes of transportation to the car more relevant and attractive, especially public transit.

Three distinct design processes have been developed and tested by Dr. Friedman and his many collaborators, addressing three different types of urban context: the re-planning of an existing suburb to add a new layer of suburban growth to the existing, well-established layer; the design of residential infill within an established neighbourhood to integrate the new development seamlessly within the existing context; and, the planning of a new suburban community to challenge the convention whereby a fully detailed master plan is prepared for the whole site, despite the fact that the realization of such a project may take a very long time, thus limiting its adaptability to the changing demands of the market.

For Avi Friedman, there exists a widening gap between the evolving needs of society and people, and the type and nature of response to those needs as found in urban areas. As an illustration, cities have become less and less accessible to many of their citizens socially, economically, politically, technologically and/or environmentally. The lack of residential affordability experienced by many of the less fortunate expresses perhaps most vividly and acutely this problem of accessibility and also disenfranchisement. In the search for solutions, it is imperative not to consider the issue of residential affordability as an unsolvable and unmanageable problem. Instead, it has to be

considered and approached as a golden opportunity to address and respond creatively to unfulfilled needs, with their positive socio-economic implications and ramifications. A life-cycle perspective and approach — in regard to the range and variety of needs experienced by people, and the different stages of evolution and transformation that cities and buildings go through, for both over their entire lifespan — is suggested as the most realistic and feasible way to bring into better alignment solutions to affordability problems with the achievement of sustainable, healthy and resilient urban areas.

Any proposal geared to the resolution of the affordability gap in cities should meet, at a minimum, the following criteria: it must truly resonate with people, find grounding at social, intuitive and psychological levels in order for physical solutions to be appreciated as in tune with needs and to be acceptable; it must support a goal of longevity and quality in construction for any residential development, including those deemed affordable, to foster the necessary flexibility and adaptability in responding over the long-term to the changing needs of occupants; it must facilitate the emergence of non-traditional practices in the design and construction of housing, with careful attention to monetary implications of all decisions, both in pre- and post-construction — in the latter case to lower as much as possible occupancy and maintenance costs; and, it must be championed by the right leadership group, that will advance the necessary regulatory changes, and introduce fiscal and financial incentives, from which creative and innovative practices can emerge and be implemented.

From Dr. Friedman's perspective, the ability, capacity and willingness to explore and experiment with the shaping of new ways of urban living, will likely create the necessary conditions to make urban areas whole — linking central cities and suburbs through the use of gradients and thresholds of change, and resolving the affordability gap in the provision of a home to the less fortunate. Accommodating and facilitating new ways of urban living is seen as particularly important in enabling transition and adaptation to changing circumstances that the future will inevitably bring to Canadian cities. From the ability and capacity to manage constant change seamlessly and efficiently will rise a more positive and proactive perspective and approach to challenging situations and problems.

The combination of regulatory and market mechanisms and responses should frame the search for creativity and innovation in how to house Canadians in the 21st century. As a way to demonstrate this thought process, informing a new outlook on urban issues and translating the resulting insights into creative and innovative solutions, Avi Friedman was the originator of two successful and award winning residential ventures: the Grow Home, with planning for future indoor expansion constituting the central intent and focus; and the Next Home, a three story structure designed to demonstrate how flexibility and transformation can be used to achieve affordability, including the option extended to buyers of purchasing the type and quantity of "housing" that they need and can afford.

Limitations

The breadth and depth of coverage in the work of Avi Friedman leaves very little unsaid or unexplored in addressing key urban development challenges, such as the future of suburbs and resolving the residential affordability gap. Two areas could perhaps have benefited from greater depth — universal accessibility and the rehabilitation of brownfields in the context of strategies for urban regeneration. Both topics have been addressed but more intensive treatment would have resulted in a more balanced perspective and outlook of their relative importance in regard to the challenges and issues facing urban Canada.

What Was Learned

In order to plan, design and build sustainable, healthy and resilient neighbourhoods and cities, we need to have a good understanding of the past to prepare and set the stage for a successful future. By grasping at what has made the suburbs the success that they are, but also recognizing their limitations as we move forward in the 21st century, we can unlock possible pathways of evolution that will enable the development and redevelopment of integrated urban areas — making them whole through their connection with central cities. Development decisions should be informed by the particularities of a project's context rather than as a result of arbitrary and limited agendas. A new system of checks and balances is needed to make both regulations and markets responsive to creativity and innovation in resolving accessibility issues in neighbourhoods and cities, especially the residential affordability gap. Necessary conditions for public and private investments — such as fiscal and financial incentives — must be put in place.

Neighbourhoods and land uses are built at a time, "into history", and as such, a life-cycle perspective and approach must inform and guide their planning, design and construction. Integral to the planning, design and construction processes of neighbourhoods and cities is the requirement to account for change, renewal and transformation as key evolutionary constraints and opportunities.

Sources: Avi Friedman (1996, 1998, 2002, 2003, 2005, 2007).

Viewpoint:

Speaking Truth to Power

On few occasions, I have made proposals or recommendations concerning projects or initiatives that contradicted or were at odds with the official orientation, position and/or preferences. Professional, ethical and/or legal considerations motivated such courses of action.

Despite the fact that Campeau Corporation was having discussions with a major department store in the planning of a traditional community shopping centre in the west-end of Ottawa, in a market analysis memorandum to the vice president of Development, I made the case that the west-end market was not propitious for such a project. I recommended instead an alternate approach, geared to a niche model. Ultimately, a traditional community shopping centre was built but it never fulfilled the return on investment sought by a succession of owners. At a later date, interestingly, it was transformed into a specialized centre.

When I returned to the City of Saint-Jérôme in 1988 as Director of the Planning Department, I was confronted with many development projects in contravention of the existing municipal plan and by-laws having been erected or constructed without the necessary authorizations or permits. Over several months, I undertook a dialogue with the city manager and members of city council to further sensitize them to the seriousness of the situation and, in particular, of their obligation to support the department in the application of municipal regulations. In the absence of a clear signal from city council in how it wished to manage these non-conforming projects, I issued a strongly worded letter to the city manager indicating my unwillingness to

continue to operate within such an unacceptable professional working environment, pointing out the necessity for me to protect, first and foremost, the public interest, and that any association on my part, even outside my immediate span of control, with any illegal acts was in breach of my professional code of conduct. Although I eventually received in writing an acknowledgement by the city manager of the inappropriateness of what had happened and that I had to exercise my responsibilities according to my professional ethics, it did not strengthen my confidence in the willingness of the city to follow an appropriate path for the development of its territory, and resulted in my decision the following year to leave the employment of the city.

In the context of vision initiatives and the implementation of plans, the National Capital Commission (NCC) put forward major proposals in high profile areas of the cities of Ottawa and Hull (now Gatineau). Some of these proposals either were not consistent with generally recognized principles underlying the long-term development of Canada's Capital Region and/or did not reflect the inherent environmental value of the areas where they would take place. As Director of Planning, in association with several professional colleagues, I expressed my concern in regard to the merit of the proposals. We also identified the risks that the NCC would be confronted with should these proposals be made public. The proposals were eventually advanced and the risks previously identified did materialize. The NCC had to withdraw the proposals and either replace them with proposals more contextually sensitive or abandon any further action altogether.

The realization of sustainable, healthy and resilient cities and regions will involve the balance of various and often divergent interests as well as the management of complex situations, involving a wide range of environmental, social, economic and political conditions. In such dynamic and volatile circumstances, urbanists and other professionals will find, at times, their advice and recommendations contrary to the position of decision makers. Because of the rapid rate of change and the challenges involved in bringing about renewal, adaptation and transformation in urban areas, such conflicts may become even more prevalent. In order to successfully "navigate these troubled waters", speaking truth to power will take on special importance and a whole new meaning for professionals. Their ability and capacity to operate in an environment characterized by trust, integrity and transparency will depend on direct and frank discussions and exchanges with the "constituency of power", especially in regard to differences of perspective and approach.

CHAPTER 8

Viewpoint:

Making Inter-Professional Exchanges Happen

One of the most interesting and also rewarding aspects of my work in urbanism consists of the collaboration between a wide-range of professionals through multi-disciplinary work groups. When such a collaborative environment operates at its best, the complicity that prevails between different professions really brings out the best in people and sets the stage for much better results and outcomes. On the other hand, if professionals are reluctant to engage their peers in open and transparent work spaces, opting instead to function in more distinct and separate work units, with limited connectivity and linkages, the exposure to failure of coordination and risks of delivering poor products and services rise commensurately. Although I have participated in projects involving the latter type of professional relations, fortunately the collaborative model has prevailed to a large extent throughout my career, and some of these experiences are reflected here.

The Neighbourhood Improvement Program (NIP) in Saint-Jérôme and the Community Improvement Projects (CIP) in Ottawa provided me with first hand experiences in inter-professional work groups. Through the coordination of various housing renewal projects and the development of several neighbourhood parks, NIP brought together various professionals, including engineers, landscape architects, architects, lawyers, bankers, building contractors, among others. CIP involved the assembly of a similar line up of professionals, mainly in the context of streetscape improvement projects. The close collaboration established with professional engineers and the translation of urban design concepts into projects, involving the transformation of the urban form, also represented key learning aspects of CIP. Interestingly, for many of the professionals involved in NIP and CIP, the inter-disciplinary environment in which they were called upon to work often represented a first experience in such working conditions. As project leader or coordinator, I was able to create dialogue opportunities among the various professionals, contributing in the process to a greater awareness of the merits of this collaboration, both from a technical and a human dimension.

Collaboration within a variety of administrative committees, steering committees and other work groups provided other opportunities for inter-professional exchanges.

The Administrative Committee on Planning and Transportation (ACPAT), the Joint Administrative Committee on Planning and Transportation (JACPAT) and the Central Area Transportation Strategy work group (CATS) are some of the coordination bodies in the Ottawa-Gatineau Metropolitan Area/Canada's Capital Region (CCR) that played an important role in ensuring that professionals coordinate their efforts toward the achievement of improved projects and better results. The existence of such committees was particularly important considering the complex administrative and jurisdictional character of Canada's Capital Region. Although most of these professional forums have folded over time, inter-professional collaboration remains a hallmark of how different organizations work together in CCR, with the difference being that a shift has taken place to more project specific work groups.

A third set of collaborative work environments fostered improved inter-professional dialogue and exchange at the National Capital Commission: through the development and enhancement of project management and portfolio management manuals and procedures. The identification of skills requirements, the clear definition of roles and responsibilities, the integration of work plans, the preparation of communication and risk management plans, among others, enabled professionals to better understand the prerequisites of multi-disciplinary work environments and to establish the appropriate conditions for the successful management of projects and the stewardship of real assets. My involvement in the determination of an asset portfolio management framework helped my comprehension of the interrelationships in the work of different professions in the context of distinct life-cycle phases and work processes. Overall, these experiences provided me with an improved knowledge of the contribution of the different professions in urbanism and a much better appreciation of the importance of professional synergy toward achieving sustainable, healthy and resilient cities.

Based on my recent experience in inter-professional collaboration, I can assert that great strides have been achieved in strengthening the integration of professional work in projects. The abhorred professional silos are, from my perspective, increasingly something from the past. The quality of professional work in Canada should be recognized to a greater extent and be the subject of much more celebration. Notwithstanding this progress in the conduct of professional work, the evolution of Canada's society and the projected changes in how cities and regions are planned, developed and governed over the coming decades, will require professionals to "raise the stakes" in regard to interdisciplinary collaboration; more specifically they will have to modify their world-view of where their respective profession fits within the bigger professional picture. Another perspective needs to emerge through the formalization of each profession's body of knowledge and the identification of the relationships/linkages/connections with other professions in the context of achieving sustainable, healthy and resilient cities and regions. Ensuring a transition by professionals to a new frontier should become a priority, in which how they relate to each other and their contribution to society is approached more holistically — the linkages between professions assuming as much if not more importance than the specificities of each profession.

Edmonton

To raise new questions, new possibilities, to regard old problems from a new angle, requires creative imagination and marks real advance in science.

Albert Einstein quoted in Gareth Morgan (1993)

CHAPTER 9

URBAN AGENDA: RESOURCES

[T]he effective functioning of economic systems, including whole metropolitan areas, requires peaceful interactions among constituent parts and a willingness to observe the rules of the game that transcend pure market relationships. Maintenance of this framework cannot depend solely on relationships in which all participants clearly gain. It must also include activities that in the short-run harm some participants ... To sustain this vital and psychological framework, people must be willing to accept short-run setbacks as a price for longer-run gains. They will be far more willing to do so if they have a strong sense of solidarity with the entire system ...

Anthony Downs (1994)

The challenges and opportunities that will face Canada and its cities will make many new claims on already stretched and overburdened treasuries.

Existing or emerging changes — such as public sector debt and its repayment; the aging of the population with its labour market, fiscal, and financial ramifications; and climate as well as other environmental uncertainties, problems and crises — taken individually or, perhaps more significantly, considered together, will require new perspectives and approaches to resources, whether they be human, natural, financial, material, technological, or even time.

To bring into balance the supply of resources — either through new resources, their reallocation, or their improved management — with the demand side, will definitely not mean business as usual for governments at all levels. Through demand management strategies, the perceptions, expectations and behaviours of Canadians will need to be altered for this balancing act to happen.

An obvious area of scrutiny and focus will be improvement to the ability and capacity to create wealth in Canada. As an initial consideration, Canadians must think of the creation of wealth with a more positive and enlightened perspective. Greater value accorded to the entrepreneurial spirit and world-view, enhanced

productivity, expanded fiscal and financial incentives as well as other measures to enhance competitiveness, more efficient and effective public goods and services delivery, and more diversified and broader trade regimes and relations, could increase significantly the resource base of Canada through more wealth creation.

Whatever improvements are made in the management of scarce public resources, it is evident that the dialogue and decision making about resources requires a "reality check". The somewhat disjointed, short-term accent, and often acrimonious approach to resource allocation should make way for a more disciplined, rigorous approach, based on the longer view. Some of the levers for this renewed approach would include new models of resource generation and distribution, more emphasis on consensual methods and dispute resolution processes, recognition of the need for informed trade-offs between different interests, and a strong focus on the creation of a distributed leadership culture, in the country at large and in the cities more specifically. Other conditions necessary to the adoption of the long view in society and in decision making will also be discussed later in this chapter.

Resource decisions will also demand finely tuned approaches to priority setting, ideally based on specific and firm outcomes and results — on a per capita basis or as a percentage of GDP — in areas such as health, education, environment, cities, security, research and development, arts and culture, international aid, etc. They could be monitored and enforced through clear and well-communicated performance accountability regimes for public and elected officials.

When considering more particularly resources of cities and their management, a need exists for greater clarity and stability in defining roles and responsibilities of municipalities that reflect financial, fiscal and operational capacity criteria. A key outcome should be the provision of sustainable funding for cities, involving a broader range of sources of income.

With the aim of furthering and expanding the debate on municipal funding and the identification of new resource options for cities, the following three suggested areas are proposed for consideration: life-cycle perspective and approach; alternative management strategies; and ubiquitous creativity and ingenuity.

LIFE-CYCLE PERSPECTIVE AND APPROACH

Integration across many areas of intervention is required to underpin the development of sustainable, healthy and resilient communities. In the case of cities, one such mechanism is a more compact urban form, that can generate many benefits in terms of land use, transportation, infrastructure networks, reduced energy consumption, urban design, and the protection of natural areas, among others.

Another integration mechanism is the life-cycle perspective and approach. Examples of cycles in a community setting are many, including the personal life-cycle, the ecological cycle, the economic cycle, the housing market and stock market cycles, the product and project life-cycles, and the electoral cycle.

Although these cycles exhibit different characteristics depending on their nature, they also have some common denominators that make them useful and powerful integration mechanisms. Three can be identified:

1. perspective of time — integrating the short- and the long-term, the notion of beginning, end and, in some instances, new beginnings;

2. perspective of change — notions of scope and scale, transition and transformation, qualitative and quantitative dimensions; and,

3. perspective of learning — learning curve, gradual or rapid, ability and capacity to move from simplicity to complexity, etc.

Cities which aspire to a sustainable, healthy and resilient future must be able to reconcile the short- and long-term in how human, financial, physical, environmental and technological resources are used. How well municipal governments in Canada perform this difficult and complex balancing act is a key consideration and a key priority for the urban agenda.

An important consideration must be the recognition that the management of resources in Canadian cities and regions will become even more challenging in the

[F]ailure to address long-term risk factors sufficiently early may force future governments to adopt policies whose costs to the population living at that time will far exceed those borne by the same country's taxpayers today ... [I]f they neglect the long term, governments will miss the chance to consider a structured approach by which present policies can facilitate the achievement of long-term fiscal policy outcome that is both sustainable and equitable in sharing risks across generations ... There is a risk that, by failing to act far enough in advance on those issues that it can anticipate, the state's capacity to respond to other, less predictable problems, or to pursue appropriate macroeconomic policies, will be weakened. Finally ... [i]t is relatively easy, from a political perspective, to adjust policies that have erred on the conservative side, by reducing taxes or increasing expenditures. In contrast, fiscal over-optimism is far harder to correct, requiring politically difficult tax increases and expenditures contraction ...

Peter Heller (2003)

Additional resources come from collaboration because, if people and organizations follow jointly agreed ends, more value can be created and greater impact achieved without wasting time and resources by contradicting each other.

Charles Landry (2006)

The cycle of life is a definite psychological reality. It consists of discrete stages, each one fraught with its own difficulties, each one with its own special advantages. Growth from one stage to another is not inevitable, and, in fact, it will not happen unless the community contains a balanced life-cycle … [H]owever … if the balance of settings which allow normal growth through the life-cycle has been breaking down, contact with the entire life-cycle is less and less available to each person, at each moment in time … To re-create a community of balanced life-cycles requires … that the idea takes its place as a principal guide in the development of communities … Each community must find ways of taking stock of its own relative behavior in this respect, and then define a growth process which will move it in the right direction.

Christopher Alexander (1977)

future. Their ability to manage change and acquire new skills in the management of all types of resources will make an enormous difference in how successful they are in achieving sustainable, healthy and resilient urban development. Ultimately, a higher level of sophistication will be required in the planning and monitoring of resource use and expenditures over time.

The life-cycle perspective and approach can provide technical but also strategic support for investment decisions, to ensure the best use of municipal resources, both in the short- and long-term. Because of the need to address many priorities, life-cycle management can especially yield significant efficiencies in the development and maintenance of, and re-investment in, municipal infrastructure.

Additional areas in which some municipalities, other levels of government and private sector enterprises have successfully harnessed the many advantages and benefits of a life-cycle world-view comprise green procurement, more efficient waste management and recycling, energy efficiencies and savings, greener urbanism and other environmental leading practices.

INTERUNIVERSITY RESEARCH CENTRE FOR THE LIFE-CYCLE OF PRODUCTS, PROCESSES AND SERVICES (CIRAIG)

http://www.ciraig.org

The CIRAIG was founded in 2001 under the leadership of l'École Polytechnique, in collaboration with l'Université de Montréal and HEC Montréal. Since its foundation, seven other universities have also become active members: l'Université Laval, l'Université du Québec à Montréal, l'Université du Québec à Trois-Rivières, l'Université du Québec en Abitibi-Témiscamingue, l'Université du Québec à Chicoutimi, l'Université Sherbrooke and l'École de Technologie Supérieure. The CIRAIG's mission is to generate, integrate and interpret relevant knowledge in the fields of life-cycle assessment and products, processes and services management in order to support industries and governments in their transition towards sustainable development. The CIRAIG is an official partner of the United Nations Environment Program Life Cycle Initiative. At each life-cycle stage, there is resource and energy consumption and social, economic and environmental impacts created. Life-cycle thinking aims to minimize the negative impacts while avoiding the transfer of problems from one life-cycle stage to another. Life-cycle assessment consists of four distinct phases: goal and scope definition; inventory of all the inputs and outputs related to the product system; assessment of the potential impacts associated with these inputs and outputs; and, interpretation of the inventory data and impact assessment results related to the goal and scope of the study. Life-cycle assessment has become an important tool for the environmental impact assessment of products and materials, and businesses are increasingly relying on it for their decision making. The information obtained from life-cycle assessment can also influence environmental policies and regulations.

In combination with more sustainable, healthy and resilient urban planning and development and compact urban forms, life-cycle management can help improve equity between generations by avoiding new debt, by extending the useful life of municipal assets, ensuring their better use, improving their maintenance, while achieving significant cost savings over the longer term.

A commitment to and a disciplined and rigorous application of the life-cycle perspective and approach could generate much improved resource management by cities over the coming decades, and a corresponding reduction in resource allocation conflicts. What is required in the short-term is a shift in thinking and an acknowledgement that, while more investment may be needed upfront, significant savings will accrue over time.

ALTERNATIVE MANAGEMENT STRATEGIES

Improved strategic management practices such as priority setting, efficiency and effectiveness in work and business processes, and enhanced performance measurement and accountability can and will contribute to improved use of limited public resources. However, holding off and resisting improvements in how public goods and services are delivered, in both quantity and quality, will not provide the necessary responses to the upcoming shifts in reality for Canadians. Neither will it ensure that the emerging and different needs of communities are adequately and properly met.

The consideration of alternative ways of doing things should be embedded in the work and decision making of all governments and institutions. Better use of resources must go hand in hand with seeking and securing better results and better value for money. More rigorous management strategies, including the scrutiny of different options and policies, will require administrative foresight and political courage that is not always prevalent or on display now.

The use of alternative approaches does not call for a complete reversal and transformation of current governmental and institutional practice in Canada. Some of these approaches already exist but, and this is the key message here, not to the extent possible and necessary. What is sought is a more proactive scanning of different ways to realize projects and deliver public goods and services. A new perspective must be developed to look freshly at problems, consider alternative solutions, and decide on the right solution, at the right time, with cost savings, and ultimately, with a more sustainable use of resources.

Past investments, local and regional strengths, and recognized competitive advantages must obviously underpin this new perspective. The success of alternative approaches also hinges on integrating the key principle that should guide Canada's urban agenda — a people-centred perspective to activities, the delivery of public goods and services, and the provision of civic infrastructure. Three examples will help demonstrate the benefits of using different management strategies.

Life-cycle thinking sees the birth, fulfillment and decline process as natural, and stand as a warning to complacency and rigid routines. It gives a sense of evolutionary direction ... This does not mean everything has to change continuously, only that there is continual assessment. Some things will stay the same ... Yet over the long-term most things will have changed.

Charles Landry (2000)

If there is one area where we need to think outside of the box, it is how governments can better organize their approach to program delivery.

Thomas J. Courchene and Donald J. Savoie (2003)

For the average citizen in the population ... it would make sense for the different levels of government to share services centres that deliver services.

Mike De Souza (2006)

Citizen-centred services lead to a more co-operative or collaborative form of federalism.

John Milloy and Maryantonnett Flumian (2006)

[I]t is useful to think of e-government as the way in which governments use Information and Communication Technologies (ICTs) to (1) improve services delivery to citizens; (2) collect, manage, use, share and protect information as a public resource; and (3) enhance their relationship with citizens through more meaningful engagement ... The three dimensions of e-government ... are not only relevant in an Aboriginal context but the opportunities offered by the new technology may in some respect be a particularly useful tool in creating opportunities for Aboriginal people to catch up with the rest of the population. ICTs hold the potential to break down the barriers of geography and scale to address critical cultural, economic and social needs ...

Richard Jock *et al.* (2004)

Online Delivery of Services

The delivery of services through the Internet whenever and wherever people need them, in urban and rural areas, epitomizes fully the benefits of alternative ways of conducting government and institutional business.

The online model, while building on Canada's high rate of Internet use by households, promises also to revolutionize how Canadians and their governments and institutions interact in the exercise of democracy and in the use of public resources. While some progress has been made in achieving e-government, so far it has been mainly through a disjointed rather than integrated approach to services via single websites or 'portals'.

The online delivery of services could play a significant, even dominant role, in ensuring that Canada's urban agenda is a success. As such, it is incumbent on all levels of government and the institutions that serve Canadians, with perhaps a leadership role taken by cities as the closest to citizens, to pursue this integration of public services.

The obstacles to such an integrated approach are not technological in nature nor reflective of a lack of knowledge and competency on the part of Canadians. Rather, they correspond to the unfolding of a triple jeopardy: failure of coordination; insufficient investment; and, most significantly, absence of political will. A new governance framework, bringing all levels of government closer in terms of their common mission of services to Canadians, constitutes an essential condition to bringing online delivery of services to a new level of integration, performance and results.

Shared Facilities

Most investment by different levels of government and institutions in public facilities is generally based on specific needs rather than the coordination of services in shared facilities. Certain facilities, because of mandate restrictions and other specific requirements, can only serve a single user. However, in many other instances, synergy, efficiency, effectiveness and cost savings could be achieved by the creation of multi-user facilities, e.g., creating parks in school yards, sharing of parking spaces by different user groups, using parking spaces for alternative uses, mixing the use of public office and meeting space according to different time schedules.

This alternative approach, while reinforcing a focus on the needs of citizens instead of operational requirements of governments and institutions, would also contribute to a more effective and greater mix of land use and a reduced separation of urban activities.

In order to facilitate the transition to a multi-use worldview for public facilities, a new test should be established in their planning and development, whereby the standard of reference would be shared facilities and the exception, single use facilities, on the basis of appropriate justification and the proof of non-feasibility.

Regulatory and Market Mechanisms

The introduction of a partial or total market response, e.g., public-private partnerships, pricing mechanisms of public resources, to meet public needs in many fields such as infrastructure, real estate, asset maintenance, information technology, training, health and recreation, among others, has been the object of heated and passionate debate as to its desirability as well as its ultimate cost effectiveness.

This debate is both healthy and necessary because of the requirement to consider the public interest as a key determinant in involving the private sector and market-based price signals in the delivery of public goods and services. Other important principles must also be adhered to in such decisions: openness, equity, accessibility, fairness, security, inclusion of present as well as future costs to society.

At the same time, this type of debate, when conducted in negative, adversarial and ideological overtones, illustrates a tendency to artificially, arbitrarily and even dogmatically separate what could be achieved fruitfully and inclusively in the public interest.

Based on the careful consideration of the benefits and costs of harnessing the best attributes of the public and the private sectors, a better use of limited public resources and the attainment of superior results become real possibilities, while also achieving diversity, timeliness and quality.

These three examples represent only a fraction of the many alternative approaches available to support the better use of public resources by municipalities and other levels of government, either in the generation of new sources of funding or the improved management of existing resources.[19]

Other approaches include "greening initiatives and strategies" as well as the selective introduction of "polluters pay" principles and schemes. Capitalizing on the experience and leading practices in alternative delivery of activities, public goods and infrastructure, is of the utmost importance to expanding on the number, types and areas where this approach is adopted and used.

UBIQUITOUS CREATIVITY AND INGENUITY

Creativity and ingenuity have been, over the last few years, literally and figuratively, the "talk of the town". In almost every sector of society, the critical importance and role of creativity and ingenuity for the success of urban areas has been promoted, highlighted, and heralded — through books and other publications, conferences, hiring practices, strategic marketing campaigns, among other means.

The recognition of the contribution of creativity and ingenuity to the well-being and prosperity of cities, regions and countries is nothing really new. The level of attention devoted to creativity and ingenuity, and more particularly, the conflicting appreciation of their status in Canada and other countries — some identifying the attainment of an unparalleled threshold of achievement, others arguing the existence of a troubling gap — are definitely new phenomena.

[A]n educational facility should be used as a centre for student learning and as a support network that serves as the core of community activities, providing opportunities for students, parents and citizens. By offering their facilities for more than just learning, community-based schools can help municipalities not only to increase the level of education, but also to redevelop communities, foster tighter bonds among families, and ultimately, to bring the community together.

David G. Roberts and
Michael Sobel (2004)

---

[19] See "Breaking Down Work Silos" at the end of the chapter.

A key challenge ... is how to make the transition to a sustainable energy future ... Countries that lead the way in this transition will have a huge economic headstart on countries that lag behind ... The question ... is how Canadians can come up with the innovations that will allow the country to succeed ... Regulation is one tool. Another is what is known as Ecological Fiscal Reform ... The principles underlying EFR are ... based on an understanding that taxes and government spending have a tremendous effect on the way the economy works ... and that the way to maximize this impact is to make sure that tax and spending policies work together. EFR ... involves a strategy where the way the government spends, and the way it imposes taxes, create a unified set of incentives, both positive and negative, to support its goals ... By giving the right set of price signals, government enables the optimal allocation of resources to achieve environmental and economic policy objectives at lower cost ...

Eugene Nyberg (2004)

In relatively simple terms, creativity and ingenuity have always acted both as agents of change and as part of the tool kit used to respond to changing circumstances.

In the past, with a slower and more subdued pace of change, creativity and ingenuity were not given a special status, rather they were perceived as integral to the evolution of cities and regions, embedded in the ongoing search and identification of opportunities and solution to problems. But the pace, scale, scope and effects of change having been significantly enlarged in the closing decades of the 20th century, creativity and ingenuity have increasingly been given a higher standing, provided with a kind of premium role and a centre-stage position in addressing the challenges and problems confronting the planning, development and governance of Canadian cities and regions.

At the beginning of the 21st century, when considering the role of creativity and ingenuity in the management of change in Canada and its cities, and their contribution to the transition toward sustainability, health and resiliency, it is quite evident that their impact has been uneven across the dimensions of the Canadian society considered. It is instructive to observe in this regard the differentiated response represented by technological change and institutional change.

Technological change (information technologies, the Internet, etc.) has been so rapid, and so pervasive that it has emerged as a key force in the evolution and transformation of Canadian society and its cities. It has had significant and lasting repercussions in the day-to-day life and activities of most people, be it at home, at work, in their mobility and accessibility, in how they entertain, and in how they consume, among others.

Cumulatively, these socio-economic changes, largely but not exclusively induced by technological creativity and ingenuity, have required on the part of the citizens constant adjustment in their perceptions, behaviours and expectations, as they attempt to interpret, integrate and navigate the changing and shifting reality all around them.

It has also meant recognition that personal and professional improvement and life-long learning should be embraced if people are to successfully adapt and respond to the many new trends and changes in their lives and activities.

On the other hand, as many observers have recently noted, governance and institutional changes and innovations have lagged behind technological and socio-economic evolution, as demonstrated by the difficulty in properly aligning decision making and timely services delivery for Canadians.

Initially, this gap between technological and socio-economic transformation and institutional responses was more inconvenient than problematic. It has grown since to the point that a new perspective and approach to how governments and institutions deliver goods and services is requested.

Reconciling constant change in cities with their decision making and the delivery of goods and services is key for the urban agenda in Canada. As time advances, the requirement for both conceptual and practical solutions to changing conditions in cities will become even more pressing as the level, scale and scope of resources available becomes subject to more competing and conflicting demands.

The pertinence and benefits of creativity and ingenuity can be fully grasped in light of this complex and limited resource background. Because of the widely distributed pools of creativity and ingenuity in all communities — whether intellectual, cultural, artistic, technological, or organizational — the opportunity exists to approach many challenging aspects of the urban agenda in a more innovative manner and from a more sustainable, healthy and resilient perspective.

The difficulty encountered in instilling creativity and ingenuity in the governance of cities has often been beyond structural obstacles and inertia — how to tap creative and innovative ideas from the broader civic environment and channel them in the attainment of superior outcomes and results, e.g., mixing generations in work environment,

the opportunity provided to employees to reflect on how work is performed and to suggest improvements, work-teams asked to re-invent what they do and how they do it, the use of Internet and social media to scan out and seek out new ways of delivering services from end-users and beneficiaries, the introduction of new technological systems and governance structures as opportunities to transform work practices.

To overcome these limitations, the underlying aim of increasing creativity and ingenuity should involve valuing and integrating them into all sectors and all levels of organizations and institutions in cities — making creativity and ingenuity an inherent function of the operations of organizations rather than something that is highly valued but added on the top of the other organizational functions. Moving beyond talk of creativity and ingenuity, the conditions for such a transformation should include vision, leadership, flexibility, incentives, financial and human resources, acceptance of disruption, and trial and error, and commitment.

Municipalities could reap a multitude of benefits such as greater productivity, the ability to resolve complex problems, different ways to carry out business, reduced

A system that relies on a healthy mix of public and private funding will be more sustainable and successful than one that relies exclusively on either the state or the market.

John Lorinc (2006)

Creativity is applied imagination using intelligence and all kinds of mental attributes along the way in order to foster continuous learning ... It is thinking at the edge of one's competence, rather than the centre of it ... The creative impulse ebb and flow and depend on fortunate coincidences of circumstances, where creative individuals, an open institutional setting and various power brokers are in good alignment.

Charles Landry (2006)

Ingenuity — the ability to generate and implement practical ideas

Thomas Homer-Dixon (2003)

Capitalizing and harnessing the creative potential of local people has to be the defining core of any city's reinvigoration. Their applied creativity generates the wealth and solutions that will drive the city on.

Charles Landry (2006)

Creative places are able to overcome many obstacles as resilience is one of their key qualities. They know where they are going and have a vision that in broad terms is agreed to by key players. They take measured risks and push boundaries. They acknowledge that a creative place needs many leaders.

Charles Landry (2006)

costs, and better use of resources.[20] Another benefit would consist in enhanced competitiveness contributing both to the retention of creative and innovative people, and making cities more interesting and attractive to them. Improved people management, both young and older, is a prerequisite to the success of creativity and ingenuity in cities.

Ultimately, a more distributed creativity and ingenuity can increase the quality of work performed by people, resulting in a greater satisfaction with their work. This can lead to better overall performance by organizations and institutions, and in time, constitute a key ingredient in a successful transition to more sustainable, healthy and resilient cities.

PLACE FOR DIALOGUE, EXPERIENCE AND LEARNING

The following two notes are provided in response to the call for greater emphasis and use of alternative management strategies, and creativity and ingenuity in the planning, development and governance of cities and regions: "Breaking Down Work Silos" and "Creative Urbanism — Toronto Kings Areas".

---

[20] See "Creative Urbanism — Toronto Kings Areas" at the end of the chapter.

Viewpoint:

Breaking Down Work Silos

The inability or even failure of some organizations to operate in an integrated, wholesome manner — instead, exhibiting entrenched bureaucratic walls and barriers between groups and sections — is a great source of turmoil and a key explanation of their poor performance or, in extreme situations, of their disappearance altogether. Such work silos are found in both the public and private sectors. The root causes of these intra-organizational divisions and the chronic absence of coordination and cooperation are similar in both sectors — ingrained in the culture, because of a dominant top-down leadership style, policy based, result of poor organizational design, nature of work processes, existence of personal fiefdoms, rigid lines of communication, unbalanced allocation of resources and inappropriate mix of skills and competencies, among others. On the other hand, the consequences for the two sectors are different in nature — delivery of poorly executed, dysfunctional public services in contrast to the inability and incapacity to compete and supply services in a market responsive manner.

Organizations where work silos prevail over time are constantly bleeding, not retaining highly qualified and performing individuals, losing money or incurring higher per unit cost for the production of comparable goods and services, creating sources of conflict and at the end of the day, incapacitating the production of positive and constructive energy and synergy in their midst. I have not been spared the experience of work silos but as the following examples will show, I have tried to overcome some of their limitations and consequences through specific initiatives.

The existence of a streetscape improvement program funded through a capital account in the Planning Department, while certainly not unique in its kind among municipal planning departments in Canada, helped to breakdown work silos within the administration of the City of Ottawa. Involving cross-functional links with the Public Works and Engineering Department for project planning and delivery purposes, the streetscape improvement program brought together two groups of professionals that, in any other context, would likely erect barriers between themselves and their work. Personally, I learned a great deal through my regular interactions and exchanges with engineers. I was able to look at capital projects through different eyes, which helped me in my overall approach to the management of streetscape improvement projects as well as the establishment of other projects. Through a positive, win-win work environment, planners and engineers developed not only a more open-minded perspective of their collaboration and its merits, but also were able to share in the positive outcomes brought about as a result of their joint efforts.

I found the work culture at the National Capital Commission (NCC) more geared to collaboration than what was the case at the City of Ottawa during my two years there. While work silos were perhaps not as pervasive, they did exist, creating a definite drag within an otherwise highly committed and result-oriented staff. Because of successive organizational restructuring, accompanied by significant resource reductions, the focus of senior managers in the branches was to get their respective houses in order and breathe some relief into their work environments to compensate for painful changes and perceived losses. Through the attention dedicated to internal dynamic and *modus operandi*, inter-branch relations and cooperation paid a price and suffered as a consequence. In view of the particular exigency of my function as Director of Planning — my work is upstream to most of the activities conducted in the organization — very early on I became sensitized to the implications of such retrenchment and nesting by the different work units. Reflecting on the possible actions that could help at least alleviate these divisions and barriers, and perhaps over time, overcome them, I decided to orient my efforts on "horizontal" initiatives that could possibly deliver early relief and even modest success.

My first action was to provide consistent and visible support to the leader that was structuring and organizing the NCC directors group as an effective self-directed team. In light of the key role played by this group — at the interface between senior management and middle management (and at the confluence of the strategic and operational), enhancing and strengthening communication and collaboration between directors was clearly of high interest and importance for the transition to a new work environment and the elimination of silos.

The second initiative had to do with bridging the soft and hard sides of the mandate of the NCC. In the course of the preparation of the Capital Core Area Sector Plan, it became evident that the absence of coordination between the programming of "event space" (creating memorable experience for visitors and residents) and the planning of "physical space" (ensuring appropriate distribution of land uses, proper accessibility to sites and an urban design of high quality) was putting at risk the realization of the Core Area vision and related planning initiatives. In collaboration with colleagues in the Programming Branch, we redesigned the planning process, which yielded more balanced and integrated content for the plan.

The third and last initiative was to promote elevating on the corporate agenda the priority given to business processes re-engineering, in

particular those processes related to the management of projects and the management of portfolios. The eventual creation of work groups and steering committees — in which I took a leadership role — resulted not only in the renewal and even transformation of the perspective that the different work units had of their roles and responsibilities within the broader activity and delivery systems, but also in how afterward they conducted their activities as they became more conscious and receptive to the interrelationships that needed to guide the approach to their work.

It is important to place work silos in organizations in the right perspective. In as much as the factors accounting for their emergence and continued existence are many and variable from organization to organization, the preponderance of dysfunctional work environments is equally uneven and not always easy to detect and predict. Confusingly, there is a certain inertia and complacency when looking at how to tackle the issues head on and to put forward strategies to prevent the rise of silos or, at least, mitigate their impact and collateral damages. In many instances, one would look at the leadership cadre in organizations as a first line of attack on divided work culture. But unlocking the full potential of corporate synergies and collaborative relations among work units is not always straight forward, demanding instead systemic intervention, both top down and bottom up. Organizations should envisage work silos from a risk management point of view, by putting in place self-organization mechanisms that can provide the emergence of change agents as well as the distributed capacity for outside-of-the-box thinking when conditions warrant it.

To sum up, work silos are ingrained in the life and culture of organizations. Forestalling their appearance and diffusion must constitute a key pre-requisite to the quest for short-, medium- and long-term sustainability, health and resiliency.

Leading Practices:

Creative Urbanism — Toronto Kings Areas

Traditional urbanism tools, such as land use plans and zoning by-laws, have been on trial, from a variety of quarters, for many years. The reasons advanced for their poor reputation, especially in non-professional circles, centre mainly on the absence of flexibility — real or perceived — in managing the evolution of complex, unpredictable and constantly changing environments such as is the case with cities. The results obtained from their application in urban areas are often associated to "one-size-fits-all" approaches instead of conveying and reflecting a more positive appreciation, including "context sensitivity".

In the mid 1990s, the City of Toronto was facing challenging circumstances socially, economically and politically. While in the previous decades — the 1970s and the 1980s — the city was seen as having done many things right, including the development of quite a liveable urban environment; in subsequent years, it was giving the distinct impression that it was losing somewhat its way. Under the leadership of the mayor, supported by a group of thinkers and professionals, a number of ideas were advanced and formalized as ways and means to extract Toronto from this downturn and to recreate the necessary conditions to rekindle the interest of investors and ordinary people in making again the city the "talk-of-the-town" in matters of sound and creative urbanism. More specifically, the proposed strategies aimed to address, in a distinct but cohesive manner, the problems and opportunities of different sub-areas across the city as well as putting in place propitious tools to regenerate declining areas at the edge of the downtown area. The story of the Kings is a truly transformative undertaking in the life and times of the City of Toronto.

Achievements

Two premises underpinned the policy framework advanced by the mayor's group of experts: independent of the stage in the economic cycle — downturn or growth — the nature and effect of urban development varies in important ways between sub-areas of a major metropolitan area like Toronto; and, the social and economic dynamism of the city is not matched by the tools used by the urbanists, which are static by definition. The aim of the policy framework was to enable the urbanists to move away from this uniform perspective and approach to the control of development, through the elaboration and implementation of strategies adapted to the unique realities of different parts of the city, and also through the use of a variety of tools adapted to those different realities. The proposals entailed a three-prong approach to the regulation of development, what was called the "three lenses": for stable residential areas, traditional urbanism methods would prevail; for greenfield and brownfield areas, a combination of urban design and flexible land use methods could be drawn upon; and for declining areas, with an older stock of buildings, identified as "reinvestment areas", entirely new regulatory approaches would be put in place.

The third lense was conceived specifically to address the problems facing the Kings Areas in downtown Toronto — 500 acres, flanking the office core to the east (King-Parliament) and to the west (King-Spadina). Key characteristics and issues faced by the Kings Areas were: former industrial districts, with old warehouses, many with heritage value; the presence of several vacant lots and empty buildings; witnessed in previous years an "organic" change through the introduction of entertainment uses as well as the prevalence of many illegal use/squatting activities; and, property owners were demolishing sound buildings to reduce their tax burden instead of undertaking zoning changes, which were seen as too challenging and onerous.

The creation of reinvestment areas was aimed at building and strengthening past successes in the development of the downtown, in particular in ensuring its continued evolution as a rich and diverse area, with residential and mixed use throughout. The policy intent of reinvestment areas was to greatly ease the redevelopment of buildings and sites to make as many projects as possible "as-of-right", thus avoiding time consuming site specific applications. Reinvestment areas also responded to the observation that older land uses, often non-conforming, seemed to work much better, in terms of an urban experience, than what was coming out from traditional land-use plans and zoning by-laws. Conceptually, reinvestment areas represented a shift from the ephemeral city to a city that appreciates longevity, flexibility and adaptability, that is responsive to changing circumstances and a changing environment.

Some of the regulatory requirements established for the Kings Areas included: permitting almost any use or combination of uses, with the exception of a few toxic industries; deleting all numerical density controls (floor space ratios) and shifting the control of the size of development through built-form controls, such as height limits and setbacks; designing buildings to reinforce the existing built-form context with respect to height, massing, scale, setbacks, roof lines and architectural character; lowering parking standards to encourage more intensive use of lands and buildings; locating new buildings along front property lines to form edges to streets, parks and open spaces; designing building bases to reinforce the public realm to the adjacent streets, parks and open spaces; providing public uses at the base of new buildings; orienting buildings to protect light, air, views and privacy; and, designing new buildings to provide green spaces for the use of residents, visitors and area workers.

Reviews of the Kings Areas experiment were carried out in 2002 and 2006; they highlighted some of the results achieved in the King-Parliament and the King-Spadina areas. These two districts have emerged as highly desirable urban lifestyles communities; they have seen considerable new business development; employment activity in both areas has increased; residential development has been a focus of activity; conversion and retention of heritage buildings have taken place; and, transit usage by residents is high.

The innovative character of the Kings Areas/reinvestment areas can be summarized as follows: to let new types of neighbourhoods emerge, largely the play of market forces, tempered by a few rules about city form and scale; to facilitate an open-ended approach to the regulation and control of development, with the acceptance of the benefits but also the risks associated to processes of discovery and experimentation; to make the public realm the defining element in the development and redevelopment of this part of the City of Toronto; and, to foster the transfer of the approach to other municipalities in Ontario and Canada.

Limitations

The reviews of the Kings Areas experiment also uncovered aspects that either required further assessment or represented dimensions in need of improvement: improvements to parks and open spaces should be accorded high priority; unequal response to community needs was identified as a key concern by residents; achieving higher architectural standards should be an important aim for all future projects; new buildings' height often exceed the more traditional heights in the Kings Areas, with negative implications for their identity and overall fabric; in light of the high transit usage by residents, improvement to transit services would contribute to an increase in its modal share; the negative externalities associated to entertainment activities, especially noise, have a detrimental effect on the attraction of the Kings Areas as places of residence; and, housing affordability has been reduced — some gentrification has set in — making the areas less accessible to traditional residents such as working class people and immigrants.

What Was Learned

It is important for the practice of urbanism to focus on current realities and future opportunities instead of relating only past activities and uses. In a situation of urgency — like facing the effects of an economic downturn in places of transition such as the Kings Areas — the greater risk lies in not taking action. The most interesting urban areas are characterized by a dense fabric and a diverse mix of land uses, often the outcome of processes of discovery and experimentation instead of rigid development controls. Enabling the urbanists to take risks not only can yield clear value added in responding to development and redevelopment challenges and opportunities, but also can allow their creativity to "rise to the occasion", facilitating departure from traditional practices and experiencing the benefits of experimentation.

Sources: Paul Bedford (1997), Ken Greenberg and Frank Lewinberg (1996), Glenn Miller (1996), City of Toronto (2002, 2006).

St. John's

A sense of responsibility adequate for modern circumstances [depends] on cultivating a deeper sense of past and future, including the responsibility to generations yet unborn, and understanding the extraordinary facts of modern interdependence.

Geoffrey Vickers (1995)

CHAPTER 10
URBAN AGENDA: GENERATIONS

On associe souvent la vieillesse à l'image d'un adulte abîmé ... C'est une fausse réalité. Seulement 5% des personnes agées de 65 ans sont en foyer et de 10% à 12% souffrent d'incapacité. Il en reste donc 85% qui sont autonomes ... Les personnes âgées ont tendance à souder les générations entre elles, à agir comme piliers dans les familles. Elles ont un rôle de rassembleur ... Le vieillissement apporte maturité, maîtrise de soi, connaissances, expérience ...

Jonathan Trudel (2005c)

[R]etirement was a 19th-century invention that is becoming outmoded as the 20th century draws to a close ... Just as young workers should be able to ease their way into the workforce while being trained in their chosen occupations, so older workers should be able to ease their way out while retaining the dignity and sense of self worth that come with productive activity. A good worker doesn't suddenly lose his skills and knowledge at the age of 65 ... Sooner or later, demographics will impose a system of gradual retirement as an integral part of a flexible workforce ...

David Foot and Daniel Stoffman (1996)

Canada will witness a transition in the composition of its population over the coming decades. More numerous older Canadians combined with a greater number of immigrants and second generation Canadians will have significant ramifications for the future of Canada's cities and regions.

RELATIONS BETWEEN GENERATIONS AND CULTURES

In the demographic history of Canada and other countries, there has never been a generation like the "baby boom generation". As a result of its sheer and unprecedented size, it has had, and will continue to have for some time, a dominant influence on most of the dimensions of Canadian society — social, cultural, economic, political, technological and urban.

But for the next ten to twenty years, the fluctuating and evolving influence between the baby boom generation and the younger generations that followed in the latter decades of the 20th century — the "X and Y generations" — and the uncertain conditions that prevail, will constitute one of the most defining traits of Canadian society. This emerging generational shift will have many effects on Canada's socio-economic and political future.

Financial, fiscal and institutional considerations are often first highlighted and the object of closer scrutiny when analyzing this coming change in the influence between generations. Some of these considerations include: the increasing number of non-working Canadians in relation to the total working population; the pressures that such an imbalance could have on productivity, wealth creation, tax revenues, debt repayment and pension funding; and the challenges to be faced in enacting legislation to better balance the interests of different generations.

From the social, community and cultural perspectives, the picture that can be distilled from this emerging generational change is two pronged:

1. one of wealth transfer — in economic and financial terms and perhaps more importantly, in terms of community memory, knowledge and experience; and,

2. another of a more diverse and complex population — the need to increase immigration to compensate, at least partially and ideally fully, for the reduced natural growth of population, the special integration needs of second generation Canadians, and the growing non-working population, represented by the aging baby boom generation.

This evolving demographic profile of Canada, in combination with continental and global influences, will inevitably dictate the requirement for a renewed approach to the future evolution and development of Canada's population. Relations between generations and cultures should be at the forefront as a policy and program that emphasizes a more integrated approach to their coexistence.

In creating this dialogue between generations and cultures, three domains for action warrant closer attention and consideration: at work; in communities; and for immigration.

At Work

At the beginning of the 21st century, with a more complex and challenging economic and fiscal environment — including the rapidly changing organization of work and work force composition — the prevailing approaches to retirement are increasingly being questioned. Many advocate the elimination of compulsory retirement to provide more flexibility to workers in planning and managing their work lives, while also easing pressure on pension plans and their funding.

Looking at retirement options rather than a rigid set of rules is indeed a sensible and relevant approach. But this should be considered in the broader context of rites of passage and succession in the life of organizations and institutions.

While not all positions require a "succession plan", those critical to the culture and memory of organizations should be nurtured, in the same way that documents and other assets are carefully conserved.

In the current and future work environment, transitions between generations of workers may vary in complexity, being more difficult for those employers exposed to a faster pace of change.

Succession and rites of passage can contribute in important ways to the success of organizations — including municipalities — easing the process of entry by beginners, through orientation and coaching programs, with benefits for the "learning curve" and accelerating expected performance and productivity.[21] Similar gains can be derived through worker promotion, with senior executives playing the role of mentors, providing moral guidance and support.

Retirement, succession and transition are notions that make direct reference to the passage of time. One benefit of an intergenerational perspective in the work environment is the possibility for older generations to have a dialogue with younger people on the topic of time, the meaning of short- and long-term — beyond strict financial considerations — in reaching sustainable decisions. From an intercultural point of view, an important consideration is the level of attention given to work opportunities and civic involvement of second and third generations of Canadians.

[T]he Engineering Development Program [of the Ministry of Transportation of Ontario] was designed to address staffing challenges caused by demographics, attrition, issues of mobility, and competition with the private sector for skills, knowledgeable workers ... Qualified applicants to the EDP must have graduated within the last five years with a civil engineering degree ... The EDP exposes participants to a range of working environments in their respective regions and head office, including engineering, construction, operations and maintenance ... Recognizing that human resources planning is critical in order to have competent, skilled employees, the EDP is just one program that Operations Division is using to meet short and long term business needs. The EDP addresses a range of needs, including succession planning, recruitment, and development. The flexible nature of the program will allow it to evolve to support changing business initiatives.

Peter Makula (2004)

---

[21] See "Fostering Professional Succession" at the end of the chapter.

In Communities

In a fast-paced world, made possible by information and communication technologies, community identity, values and pride are increasingly blurred and even dissipated. Physical communities, represented by distinct neighborhoods, are competing as a source of reference and meaning in the day-to-day life of Canadians with communities of interest, informal or formal networks, coalitions or associations that are focused on ideas, political ideologies, or professional, artistic and technical work, among other themes.

While such a trend is an important force of change, community life is not imperiled *per se*. But its effect on cities, regions and countries is a source of preoccupation, especially when considering the importance of human ties, bonds, shared experiences and cultures in shaping sustainable, healthy and resilient communities.

Consequently, strengthening the relations between generations and cultures should be at the core of a new vision of citizenship in Canadian cities. At a minimum, greater value attached to relations between generations and cultures can help cement the ties and bonds between people. This can be achieved through the sharing of stories and memories, but also through the renewal of the process of community development, whether of a geographical kind or that of communities of interests.

More broadly, several "learning channels" for relations and communications between generations and cultures can contribute to more sustainable and resilient cities. They include partnering with local community schools and maximizing benefits from lifestyles preference — such as the proximity of a greater diversity of people, the learning of second or even third language, and experiences made possible by more mixed land use.

For Immigration

Canada has been very successful at integrating a large number of immigrants throughout its history. Immigration has helped in many ways to define and nurture the identity and the multicultural character of the country, and will continue to do so in the future.

However, immigration in the coming years should meet three tests if it is to contribute to a more prosperous, orderly, sustainable and resilient Canada:

1. larger numbers of immigrants must be successfully hosted and integrated into communities;

2. new Canadians should be supported and encouraged to make a positive contribution to the continuing evolution of Canada's society and its values; and,

3. integrating immigrants into communities must be anchored in their early transition into the work environment.

On a comparative basis, Canada has always been and remains one of the leaders in the western world in its approach to immigration. But when looking at the future changes and opportunities that the country will face, particularly the effect of an aging population, immigrants will be called upon to play a key role. It is conceivable that the integration of new Canadians could benefit from greater participation by older generations of Canadians in national and international networks of support.

The broadening of contacts by immigrants as they make the transition to a new life in Canada, especially through the work environment, could also benefit from improved intergenerational and intercultural relations in another way. Considering the difficulties and constraints faced by immigrants in obtaining fulfilling and remunerative employment, often as a result of their difficulty meeting professional and technical accreditation requirements, older generations of Canadians could perhaps help ease

It is not diversity or the magnitude of the immigration flow that concerns Canadians ... It is ... that the national whole should remain larger — should evoke a stronger sense of belonging and obligation among all here — than the sum of its multiple parts.

Richard Gwyn (2005)

The intercultural approach goes beyond equal opportunities and respect for existing cultural differences to the pluralist transformation of public space, institutions and civic culture. It does not recognize cultural boundaries as fixed but in a state of flux and remaking. An intercultural approach aims to facilitate dialogue, exchange and reciprocal understanding between people of different backgrounds.

Charles Landry (2006)

Intercultural life is a particular way of living with multiple cultures. In society and for the individual, it presupposes a certain type of relationship to cultures and a willingness to overcome the communication barriers stemming from the cultural differences in order to benefit from the treasures that each offers.

Gilles Verbrunt quoted in Marie-Linda Lord (2004)

TORONTO REGION IMMIGRANT EMPLOYMENT COUNCIL (TRIEC)

http://www.triec.ca

TRIEC is taking action on a key issue facing the Greater Toronto Region — the underutilization of skilled immigrant education, talent and experience. TRIEC's primary mission is to create and champion solutions to better integrate skilled immigrants into the Greater Toronto Region labour market. To achieve this mission, the council focuses on three objectives: to convene and collaborate with partners, creating opportunities for skilled immigrants to connect to the local labour market; to work with key stakeholders, particularly employers, building their awareness and capacity to better integrate skilled immigrants in the workforce; and, to work with all levels of government, enhancing coordination and effecting more responsive policy and programs for skilled immigrant employment. The Career Bridge Program responds to Canada's labour market demand for internationally-qualified professionals and to the aspirations of qualified immigrants eager to work

in their professional fields. A bridge between industry and immigrants, the program creates paid internship opportunities at a wide range of employers committed to providing relevant work experience to professional-level newcomers. TRIEC's successes have resulted in cities across Canada taking action in their own communities around immigrant employment solutions. ALLIES provides funding and supports cities in their efforts to learn from, adapt and implement successful approaches used by TRIEC. The Mentoring Partnership provides new immigrants in the City of Toronto and the regions of Halton, Peel and York with occupation-specific mentoring, opening networks and building relationships, leading to employment. Hireimmigrants.ca provides employers with interactive tools and resources to accelerate the integration of skilled immigrants into their organizations.

An intercultural education would instil the following six competences in young people:

- *Cultural competence — the ability to reflect upon one's own culture and the culture of others;*

- *Emotional and spiritual competence — the ability to be self-reflective, handle one's own emotions, empathize with others;*

- *Linguistic and communicative competence;*

- *Civic competence — the ability to understand and act upon rights and responsibilities and be socially and morally responsible;*

- *Creative competence; and,*

- *Sporting competence.*

Charles Landry (2006)

the transition of some of them through coaching and mentoring activities.

Additionally, better relations between generations and cultures could facilitate the cultural integration and mixing of new Canadians, providing them with exchanges and contacts beyond their own cultural or ethnic communities. Exposure to a broader spectrum of the Canadian society would enable immigrants to experience, in a direct but non-threatening manner, the Canadian way of life and help them to positively influence the shaping of citizenship in Canada and its cities.

In conclusion, through improved intergenerational and intercultural relations and communications, Canada would simply build up on its historical development path, maintain its status as a world role model in the successful coexistence of many cultures, enrich even more its society through the eyes, experience and diversity provided by new Canadians, and ensure that all the resources of the country — particularly its human resources — are put to efficient, effective and productive use. Essential provisos include the respect of Canada's defining characteristics — three founding cultures and two official languages are key examples; the implementation of measures to help reverse the declining birth rate, and a sensitivity to the country's national unity over the coming decades.

PLACE FOR DIALOGUE, EXPERIENCE AND LEARNING

Succession practices are key to successful intergenerational transition in organizations more particularly, and into the labour force generally. Within professional circles, succession planning is equally important and crucial for the longer term sustainability, health and resiliency of professions. The following note considers specific actions undertaken to facilitate and foster professional succession practices among urbanists in Quebec.

Fostering Professional Succession

Very early on in my career, "succession planning" took on a special meaning and significance for my work as an urbanist and also as an administrator of the Ordre des urbanistes du Québec (OUQ). The absence of formal and informal relationships between students in urbanism as well as young graduates and experienced members of the profession represented for me an important gap in the channels of communication between generations of urbanists.

The establishment by the OUQ of an information and exchange program geared to graduates and students in urbanism constituted a first attempt to connect different generations of urbanists and to plant the seeds for an intergenerational dialogue, that, if sustained and enhanced, could lead to a more holistic and integrated view of how the profession could evolve in time. Focused initially on exchange activities taking place on university campuses, the program later offered the opportunity for graduates and students to interact with professionals in their work environment. My vision for the program involved an eventual transition from informal exchanges to more formal relationships, including support for apprenticeships, coaching and even mentoring in urbanism. Although the information and exchange program was eventually discontinued, the recent creation by the OUQ of a program to facilitate access to the profession by students and graduates in

urbanism is an excellent initiative to foster professional succession. Obviously, greater relationships between generations of urbanists call for a commitment of time and the recognition that the pay-back period is not immediate but will come over the longer term. Personally, over subsequent years, I have maintained collaborative relationships with some of the urbanism programs in Quebec universities and mentored many urbanists as they prepared to become members of the profession.

As chair of the 2001 Annual Conference of the OUQ held in Gatineau, I was provided with another opportunity to advance the intergenerational dialogue among the professionals of urbanism. The theme of the conference was "Youth and Urbanism", and to my great satisfaction at the time, it contributed in no small measure to the opening of the profession to the younger generations of urbanists as well as to future urbanists. Both in its organization and its unfolding, the conference helped achieve many "firsts" for the OUQ. These included: the presence of several students of urbanism as contributors to the organization of the conference; the high number of students and graduates that took part in the conference; the contribution of many young professionals as speakers; the possibility offered to many politicians and media leaders to discuss in formal presentations the relevance of the theme of the conference for society; and finally, the communication in a "declaration" of commitments that the OUQ made to the young generations. Overall, the 2001 conference proved to be a resounding success, not only in demonstrating that it is possible and quite useful to move away from the "beaten path" in professional circles but also in its uncovering of the many benefits that can accrue from creating a place for the young in the practice of urbanism. Fulfilling the commitments made to the younger generations in the Declaration of 2001 is still a work in progress and will require continued efforts in the coming years.

Fostering professional succession must be envisaged as setting an ideal for how urbanists look at their profession, "raising the bar" in charting a future course for its evolution. When taking into account the coming demographic shift — transition of generations in society and also in professional circles — combined with the many forthcoming challenges to be faced by Canada and its

cities, it is important from my perspective to envision the practice of urbanism from different lenses, recognizing that expectations of professionals and the outcomes of their work will, in all likelihood, be very different from what was the case in the past. Fostering professional succession is clearly asking the professionals of urbanism to "push the envelope", stretch themselves, so that intergenerational dialogue and links become more formal and proactive instead of informal and reactive. The dialogue and the links between older and younger generations must be nurtured, with a special accent placed on the body of knowledge of the urbanists and how knowledge is transferred, how skills are made sustainable and resilient. Fostering professional succession has everything to do with the creation of the right conditions for intergenerational collaboration in the context of a complex, footloose, fast-paced, and often disjointed society and work environment of the future.

Regina

[W]e are now living in a new age, in an age where the stability of the world of Newton is giving way to the flux and relativity of Einstein. The challenge in this world is to develop capacities for self-organization rather than to "get organized", to develop organizing styles that can flow with change.

Gareth Morgan (1993)

CHAPTER 11

URBAN AGENDA: COLLABORATION

City-making is about making choices, applying values, using politics to turn values into policies and exerting power to get your way.

Charles Landry (2006)

Collaboration — a disciplined process of getting diverse thinking out on the table, seeing new connections, and co-creating innovative solutions to problems.

Len Bolger and Eddy Isaacs (2003)

Trust is the bedrock of collaboration. Without it, people will not collaborate or share knowledge.

Stephen Goldsmith and William D. Eggers (2004)

With the dominance of the different media in our life and their focus on "make and sell" news, the negative side of events and situations, from the individual to the global, are getting, it seems, the preferential treatment.

Adopting a simplistic perspective of reality and events, it is always possible to separate in a "black and white" fashion the bad and the conflictual from the good and the collaborative. But, as the great majority of Canadians will attest from their own lives, the nuances, the complexity, and the interrelationships that constitute reality in Canada and elsewhere, require a somewhat more sophisticated and robust approach to the relative contribution of both collaboration and conflicts in the evolution of society and cities.

In some instances, particularly where universal values and human rights are at stake and at risk to be compromised, and stark ideological differences threaten the survival of people and societies, open conflict can indeed have a role to play. They can transform a nation or nations positively in terms of vision and relationships, e.g., confronting and fighting fascism and other destructive ideologies.

In a societal context, past and present, where "collaboration" and "conflict" frame and create the relations and affairs between people, groups, organizations, governments and societies to an important extent, it is important to ask what has come from these distinct but related expressions of authority and power? And what judgment can we make as to their contribution and consequences for countries and cities?

Although "competition" is definitely another important vector influencing and determining relationships, germane mainly to the socio-economic/market sphere and to a lesser degree to the socio-political/regulatory sphere, it will not be examined in what follows.

Generally, it can be safely affirmed that collaboration provides superior results at all levels of society. Efforts invested in working out differences can create the right conditions for positive relations, ones that are based on common values, and that can foster trust and willingness to work together over the short-, medium- and even the long-term.

Unresolved conflicts, on the other hand, result in one or more parties partially or totally losing — contributing to poorer outcomes, with probable negative effects on relationships with other people, groups, organizations, governments and societies.

An overall assessment of Canada's track record in terms of collaboration and conflict reveals a collaborative thrust and focus. Obviously, as can be illustrated by some events in the past and the more contemporary history of the country, not all relations between people, groups, organizations, governments and institutions have been truly positive. A few have been characterized by conflict for protracted periods, as testified in continuing constitutional issues and regional differences. Nonetheless, in comparative terms, Canadians can be proud of their achievements — reflected in Canada's excellent image and reputation globally — as having been able to advance and sustain their national and regional interests in an orderly manner, without any major violent conflict.

Yet, looking at the future, the *status quo* in Canada's management of its affairs — its governance — will no longer suffice. Some change to improve "collaborative federalism" is required.

The traditional approach to decision making, from the top to the bottom of organizations, governments and institutions, with centralized structures and processes, is increasingly challenged. It is being substituted by a combination of top-down and bottom-up, centralized and decentralized, approaches. An ecological model for decision making, based on emergence, complex adaptive systems and self-organization, is worthy of consideration in charting a vision of governance in Canada.

A collaborative approach should orient this ecological model of governance, with the following premises as guiding lights:

- structures and processes geared as much as possible to power sharing;

- risk sharing in initiatives, projects and other undertakings; and,

- consensus building or alternative dispute resolution that can channel positive energy and focus on shared interests, with as a common denominator the needs and aspirations of Canadians.

The key results of any new approach to governance in Canada should include flexibility, responsiveness, adaptability, efficiency and value for money. Encouraging and fostering learning in collaboration between individuals, organizations, governments and institutions could help the gradual transition from the more simple to the more complex. This will include trial and error, and small victories through pilot projects and the application of "leading practices".

Three areas that could help further collaboration within the broader urban agenda are considered below: intergovernmental relations; "communities of practice"; and cities and their broader regions.

The development of partnership work between municipalities and provincial, territorial and federal governments for the city-region and neighborhood levels will create better places for Canada.

External Advisory Committee on Cities and Communities (2006)

[Self-organization] represents a decisive break with past management principles. The traditional bureaucratic approach developed through the fragmentation of work processes; different functions were allocated to different people. With [self-organization] integration is the rule. People are given multifunctional roles, thus creating the flexibility that allows self-organization to occur. This approach helps to make the most of an organization's human resources by encouraging employees to use their intelligence and abilities to full effect.

Gareth Morgan (1988)

INTERGOVERNMENTAL RELATIONS

At a conceptual level, because of the fundamental characteristics of Canada — its people, its geography, its economy — and the values that Canadians share — particularly openness to diversity, respect for differences, fairness through a balance of individual and collective interests — intergovernmental relations must not be considered and approached in a one-dimensional manner. Rather, they must be guided by Canada's complexity and the search for a more optimal governance framework.

Conflicting and deeply set ideological, political and administrative positions should give way to new perspectives and behaviours in intergovernmental relations. Only such a change can enable Canada and its governments to confront an increasingly more complicated and rapidly changing world, break from the past, and ensure the necessary transformation of the response to the needs and aspirations of Canadians.

Time being of the essence, the renewal of intergovernmental collaboration, in the context of the urban agenda, can be envisaged through two distinct but related lenses: governance structure and governance processes.

The place of cities at the intergovernmental table is the source of division in Canada, as noted before. The senior levels of government have maintained and continue to maintain that the *status quo* is the only possible avenue until the Constitution can be reopened and a new governance framework, more inclusive of cities, is established. Their perspective is guided more by political

choice than by a diagnosis of vulnerabilities, risks and, ultimately, a policy imperative.

Municipalities, for their part, have advocated for a long time a change of the intergovernmental pattern of relations in Canada — with or without constitutional change — in order to fully reflect the reality of Canada in an increasingly urbanized and globalized world. The current intergovernmental framework is considered anachronistic in the socio-political and socio-economic environment in which Canadian cities find themselves at the beginning of the 21st century.

It is quite evident that Canada's governance structure, when scrutinized against the five first principles of the urban agenda advanced earlier — making Canadians the fundamental reference point in Canada's governance; strengthening the role of cities in Canada's federalism; providing an appropriate weight to major cities in the governance of the country; valuing experimental and unusual processes and solutions; and, balancing regulatory, fiscal and market mechanisms — cannot be sustained by strict adherence to the *status quo*. It is in need of some form of renewal in order to be responsive to the new Canada and the new cities in emergence.

While the constitutional conundrum is real, it is worth reiterating that it should not impede how intergovernmental relations can be structured in order to improve the position of Canada in an urban world. New governance mechanisms within the prevailing constitutional environment must be imagined and made operational.[22]

... [C]omplex adaptive systems and self-organization ... [describe] the behaviors observed by scientists in several types of living systems. What these scientists noted is that living systems have an inherent capability to do exactly what needs to be done for [a] system to evolve and thrive in ways that could not have been foreseen ... For living systems to adapt so appropriately to their current situation there needs to be ... clarity ... But there also must be ... chaos ... Not enough chaos means not enough adaptive behavior. Without adaptive behavior, the implementation of ... initiatives often go sour.

Jim Alexander and Christopher Comeau (2008)

[N]etwork management is fostered by a ... sense of collective identity, managerial philosophies that recognize the importance of mutual dependence and collaboration and a collective sense of accountability and control ... Control in a network rests in the management of relations rather than in the management of discrete activities. Inter-organizational relations become as important as intra-organizational relations, and need to be developed at many levels ...The ability to develop mechanisms that promote mutual influence becomes more important than the ability to dominate.

Gareth Morgan (1988)

---

[22] See "Leading Intergovernmental Dialogue" at the end of the chapter.

A possible mechanism could involve the creation of the Alliance of the Confederation (AC), that would bring together all levels of government, including municipal representation — which could be determined by the Federation of Canadian Municipalities. The urban agenda would constitute its core program of action, determining a renewed outlook on the nature and priorities of intergovernmental relations.

The Alliance of the Confederation — complementing or even possibly replacing the Council of the Federation — would not interfere and put in jeopardy the exercise of the prevailing jurisdiction in Canada's governance structure. It would, instead, celebrate the complementarities and interdependence between levels of government, signify a shift toward a more urban federalism, and constitute a symbol of the reinvented Canadian federation.

The AC could meet annually or bi-annually, on the basis of a rotation between regions and major cities. The agenda of meetings could be structured around policy issues that require ongoing intergovernmental consultation, coordination and action planning, e.g., fiscal and financial considerations, immigration, infrastructure, environment, employment, R&D, guidelines and standards, inter-regional relations, international presence and commitment, etc.

Much more than a partnership, the AC should reflect an irreversible commitment to a new way of orienting and managing intergovernmental relations, one closer to the reality and needs of the Canadian people. It would ensure the harmonization of the intergovernmental collaboration necessary for the success of the urban agenda. In addition, it would mark the emergence of a new political culture, capable of addressing differences proactively and positively and resolving conflicts in a mature and responsible manner.

With the Alliance of the Confederation at the helm, the identification and development of governance processes that could nurture and render operational the new context of collaboration becomes essential. Leadership, vision, political courage, capacity for managing change, and an ability to enable a different sort of collaboration, must underpin the examination and implementation of collaborative mechanisms in an intergovernmental context.

Also, simplicity and a clear sense of priority need to characterize communications with Canadians, in order that they be, on one hand, able to relate their aspirations for change in intergovernmental relations with that which is actually proposed, and on the other hand, be willing to participate actively in this change.

In this sub-section as well as in the next, two examples of intergovernmental collaborative strategies will be described.

Intergovernmental agreements — whether bipartite, tripartite, public-private, or others — have been and, more importantly, can continue to be key mechanisms of collaboration within an expanded intergovernmental governance structure such as the Alliance of the Confederation. Through these agreements, intergovernmental collaboration can become more

It is a considerable challenge to bring the various departments of any one government or municipal administration together in a unified information program; it may appear almost impossible to seek the participation of all three levels of government in the setting up of integrated machinery to meet public needs in the information field. The fact remains, however, that the need for an integrated system for social communication is as essential and urgent as the need for a joint attack on many more obvious problems. The public, as consumer of necessary information, cannot be expected to wonder about a congeries of offices to seek out available information vital to its every day needs.

Science Council (1971)

The complexity of the diversity confronting urban communities demands more flexible and adaptive policy and support frameworks from provincial and federal governments. "One size fits all" does not accommodate the variety and degree of diversity with which urban communities are contending.

Peter Clutterbuck, Christa Freiles and Marvyn Novick (2005)

*A ... mechanism for intergovernmental cooperation is the establishment of formal or informal intergovernmental agreements ...
In their ... formal manifestation they may take the form of legally binding treaties ... More often ... they take the form of non-binding agreements ... [that] may relate to agreed processes for collaboration, agreed administrative arrangements or programs, or the delegation from one government to another of executive and administrative responsibilities in a particular sector.*

Ronald L. Watts (2003)

A major purpose of [intergovernmental] agreements has been to achieve substantive policy coordination in areas of overlap and to provide redistributive financing schemes ... Their general purpose has been "to rationalize the exercise of distinct but related competencies, avoid duplication and coordinate policy initiatives".

Ronald L. Watts (2003)

[I]ntegrated services takes us deep into how governments can work together. It is the new window on federalism.

John Milloy and
Maryantonnett Flumian (2006)

diversified, more predictable, more efficient and effective, and more responsive to the different realities of cities and regions across Canada.[23]

Some common considerations should characterize the nature of intergovernmental agreements and the process of development and implementation between the different levels of government and other stakeholders. Three key dimensions can be identified: scope, execution and integration.

Scope

Scope refers to the rationale for the development and implementation of intergovernmental agreements. Some of the questions that need to underpin its justification include:

What is the overall aim of the intergovernmental undertaking?

What specific accomplishments will characterize a successful outcome?

How does it build on previous initiatives?

What is the area under consideration?

Who should participate and be involved in the undertaking?

How is the undertaking to be funded?

How is it to be realized and what controls are to be put in place to ensure its success?

Execution

The execution of intergovernmental agreements should encompass three types of consideration: development; relationships; and outcomes.

The development of intergovernmental agreements can involve a diverse range of undertakings, e.g., social: housing, cultural, educational, recreational, health, etc.; economic: research, energy, fiscal and financial incentives and programs, etc.; and physical: urban form, heritage, infrastructure, transportation, green construction, natural environment, etc.

Intergovernmental agreements rely on pre-determined or to-be-determined working relationships between levels of government in the delivery of goods and services. These relationships can include online and front-line provision of services, use of shared facilities, and a combination of regulatory and market mechanisms. A life-cycle approach, and creativity and ingenuity agenda can also contribute to improved processes of collaboration in an intergovernmental context.

Finally, outcomes in intergovernmental agreements are expressed in measurable indicators of success. The inclusion of measurable indicators is particularly important in establishing levels of performance in terms of efficiency and effectiveness, value for money, sustainability and resiliency.

[23] See "Intergovernmental Collaboration — Western Canada Tripartite Agreements" at the end of the chapter.

Integration

In order to ensure enhanced intergovernmental collaboration in Canada and modify current practices, integration is probably the most critical of the three elements discussed here.

As previously argued in chapter 8, the success of the urban agenda — and this obviously includes intergovernmental relations — hinges on an integrated approach. Only through integration can such considerations as open decision making, ensuring value in public investments, and providing for accountability, fairness, equity and transparency be achieved.

Integration in intergovernmental relations should more specifically be concerned with some of the following aspects: socio-economic factors, political considerations, site-specific aspects, technological considerations, communications, resource allocation, decision-making processes and scheduling.

Effecting changes in intergovernmental relations through the development and application of joint agreements, while capitalizing on an area of experience and strength in Canada's governance structure, is also fraught with complexity, difficulties and challenges that must not be underestimated or neglected. However, an investment of political and administrative energy and goodwill in intergovernmental agreements constitutes an important element in a broader strategy to begin a transition towards a renewed governance approach in Canada, based on greater collaboration, characterized by power sharing,

risk sharing and consensus building, with, as an ultimate outcome, a more optimal response to Canadians' needs and aspirations.

Strong intergovernmental collaboration in Canada can be considered essential to the success of the urban agenda. Improvements in the governance structure — through the Alliance of the Confederation — and governance processes — through an expanded and more diverse use of intergovernmental agreements — offer the best prospects to foster sustained collaboration between levels of government. The rapidly changing environment for this collaboration requires more consistency, more flexibility, and better performance in relationships and decision making between levels of government.

COMMUNITIES OF PRACTICE

While an improved and enlarged use of intergovernmental agreements could enable a better fit between levels of government in areas of common or complementary interest, there is a requirement, nevertheless, for a mechanism to make such agreements feasible and sustainable over the long-term.

In the spirit of a citizen-centred perspective to governance, the approach should be primarily focused on policies, programs and activities, and only secondarily, based on jurisdiction. Improved collaboration in the intergovernmental context also means the integration of operations in and across organizations and institutions, as previously advocated.

Beyond the present cooperative focus on interoperable architecture for information sharing, a more ambitious exploration of collaborative and participative governance is also imperative. This latter realm … requires the formation of new citizen-centred business models based upon three key principles …

- *Participative service design … [stemming] from a growing emphasis on collective learning, public dialogue, and stakeholder engagement as enablers of service innovation and public satisfaction…*

- *Adaptive partnership … [requiring] … new planning, performance and risk management frameworks within each jurisdiction, and shared organizational and governance models across such boundaries … A specific Canadian challenge is aligning federal and provincial resources and delivery mechanisms with municipal authorities in ways that synergistically strengthen rather than fragment governance capacities at the local level …*

- *Networked and knowledge management … [requiring] … significant and shared investments in new skill sets and organizational competencies … [in particular] linking accountability to performance through … mechanisms capable of transcending jurisdictional boundaries.*

Adapted from Jeffrey Roy and John Langford (2008)

Communities of practice connect people from different organizations as well as across independent business units. In the process, they knit the whole system together around core knowledge requirements.

Etienne Wenger, Richard McDermott and William M. Snyder (2002)

[A] commitment [should be made] to establish roundtables, staffed by senior officials from each level of government, who will meet regularly to discuss the effectiveness [results and costs] of policies and programs [current and proposed], and identify opportunities for improvements and win-win-win solutions. These working groups could also be empowered to commission joint research, arrange seminars, facilitate intergovernmental staff secondment and exchanges, etc. The information exchanged through these mechanisms is to be fed into each government's budget, planning and operational decision-making processes.

Adapted from David Miller (2004)

Over the recent years, in Canada and in other countries, "communities of practice" have emerged as an innovative way to deliver results in many areas of endeavour. If further refined and broadened in terms of their scale and scope in the Canadian context, they could constitute a means for improved collaboration and integration.

What would be the key characteristics of communities of practice if they are to contribute to the redefinition of intergovernmental collaboration in Canada generally and in the context of the urban agenda more specifically? Four characteristics can be distinguished:

1. dedication to the long-term resolution of specific problems and opportunities;

2. provision of a pool of expertise, experience and skills;

3. continued deployment of human resources rather than the more usual project-based responses; and,

4. integration of appropriate succession and transition mechanisms.

On the strength of these basic characteristics, communities of practice in Canada would create new opportunities of collaboration between levels of government. This could contribute, simultaneously, to the formulation of governmental policy directions and priorities, the development of programs, and the delivery of services.

An Alliance of the Confederation could be the initial instigator of a limited number of communities of practice, to help define, in time, the scope, scale, range and conditions of their application.

Leadership in communities of practice would obviously have to reflect the lines of jurisdiction underpinning intergovernmental relations in Canada. The results achieved and the benefits derived from improved intergovernmental collaboration will help evolve, over time, communities of practice through the clarification of the roles and responsibilities of the federal, provincial and municipal levels of government in their initiation and nurturing.

Some of the areas that could benefit from the use of communities of practice include the further definition of the urban agenda as well as in the areas of social policies, environment, infrastructure, health, learning, creativity and ingenuity, relations between generations and cultures, between professionals, and in security matters.

Taking the urban agenda as an example, the creation of communities of practice would be based on dialogue between the federal and provincial governments, municipalities, professional associations, non-governmental organizations, and others as required. Under provincial leadership, the communities of practice could be deployed on a provincial or regional basis initially. It would be expected that over time, the outcome of these initial efforts would be reflected in programs and services delivered at the local or sub-regional levels.

Over the longer term, communities of practice would evolve as "networks within networks" of collaboration. As such, they could be expected to be more organic in their organization, structure and functioning. Rooted in flexible approaches, dictated by the present and future needs and aspirations of Canadians, they could make a direct and important contribution to the realization of sustainable, healthy and resilient cities in Canada.

CANADIAN CITIES AND THEIR SURROUNDING REGIONS

In Canada, central cities and their surrounding regions (that include suburban municipalities) do not, as a general course of action, engage in the types of close-knit collaboration that could and should exist. This is especially the case at a time when emerging socio-economic, cultural, and political challenges make the *status quo* in governance matters less and less an option.

While cities and their regions exchange services and consume common resources, the perspective of their relationship is often one of two distinct, separate realms. The dialogue regarding their respective responsibilities in the provision and sharing of resources in a fair, equitable and sustainable manner, can be characterized as often difficult, competitive and tense. The dictum "no taxation without representation" appears to reflect how institutions and citizens of both areas continue to wish their relations to be governed, even though the reality

JOINT TRANSPORTATION PLANNING COMMITTEE SERVING CANADA'S CAPITAL REGION (TRANS)

http://www.ncr-trans-rcn.ca

The TRANS Committee was established in 1979 to coordinate efforts between the major transportation planning agencies of Canada's Capital Region. TRANS is a neutral forum for the exchange of information on technical guidelines and leading practices. In addition, it manages transportation studies and collects data for transportation planning. The six members of TRANS span all three levels of government. They include the National Capital Commission, the Ministère des Transports du Québec, the Ministry of Transportation of Ontario, the City of Gatineau, the City of Ottawa and the Société de Transport de l'Outaouais. Funding

responsibilities are shared by the six member agencies. The proportion of contributions may vary for some projects. The TRANS Committee work extends over the entire Capital Region and includes three areas of focus: ongoing development and operation of a long-term transportation forecasting model; collection and management of data for transportation planning; and management of transportation studies. The TRANS library has an extensive collection of transportation reference materials, maps, reports and documents. It serves as a unique source of information on issues related to transportation planning.

To accomplish [its zero energy] goal — and make it viable for large-scale production — [the] Department of Energy is pairing research scientists at its National Renewable Energy Lab with its Building America program. [This program] is a public/private partnership that charters interdisciplinary teams made up of builders, engineers, architects, lenders, contractors, community planners, and others. To date, the program has involved nearly 600 individual industry partners. Working collaboratively, through the design and construction process, each team takes a whole-house approach to reducing energy use that encompasses all aspects of homes, from appliances to building materials. In the course of building a project, each Building America team installs promising new technologies, tracks energy savings, and evaluates financial costs and tradeoffs. Building America's industry partners benefit from their participation by staying in the vanguard of modern building technology and delivering projects with superior value to their buyers.

John Miller (2008)

If we view the world as a learning system, we can imagine a constellation of communities of practice — a "world wide web" of interwoven communities that focus on various civic practices at different levels, including district, municipal, regional national and global.

Etienne Wenger, Richard McDermott and William M. Snyder (2002)

A major governance issue concerns the lack of fit between jurisdictional boundaries and growth impact areas.

P.J. Smith (1995)

[T]he forces of urbanization have demonstrated that, for efficiency and quality of life, there is no substitute for the holistic planning of urban-centered regions.

Ira Robinson and Gerald Hodge (1998)

[U]rban versus rural is the most significant division facing the country … It's far more important than French and English, and far more important than East versus West.

Hugh Segal quoted in Charlie Gillis (2004)

has dramatically changed over the years and will continue to do so.

Because of the greater mobility of people and the many destinations associated with their daily activities, combined with the improved accessibility made possible by information, telecommunications and transportation technologies, the strict separation between places is less and less meaningful in the definition and designation of appropriate governance units.

In day-to-day life, cities and regions are not separate entities but rather a complex web of simultaneous relationships. The recognition of their deep-seated common interests, underpinned by a shared vision for a future that maybe uncertain but at the same time full of potentialities, offers the possibility to set aside entrenched attitudes, limited collaboration, and resistance over the sharing of limited resources between the two areas.

In order to appreciate the benefits of improved collaboration between cities and their regions, it is worth examining the reciprocal benefits that are enjoyed by both parties where and when joint exchanges, trading and consumption are regular practice.

- Benefits to the cities that can be provided by the broader regions — a sample:

  ▸ creation of a more autonomous food supply through the preservation of agricultural lands and operations;

  ▸ protection of natural areas (watersheds, wetlands, aquifers, etc.) that contribute to the safe and

continued supply of life essentials — such as quality water supply;

▸ provision of sites, facilities and infrastructure for recreation and tourism as well as other lifestyle related amenities and experiences; and

▸ contribution to growth management in urban areas through the decentralization of some residential development, employment and services to existing smaller centres at the periphery of central cities.

- Benefits to the regions that can be provided by central cities — a sample:

  ▸ supply of specialized personal services not available to residents in surrounding regions — such as health and retail;

  ▸ location of work opportunities beyond that which exists in and around smaller centres and in suburbs; and

  ▸ provision of facilities for entertainment as well as other life-style related amenities and experiences.

The identification, in specific terms, of the common interests and shared benefits between cities and their surrounding regions suggests a number of avenues towards structuring their possible future collaboration.

- Joint strategic planning — The establishment of joint planning committees and task groups, including communities of practice, could create conditions for collaborative efforts in more specific areas of common interests.

• Joint infrastructure programs — The complementarities of and reciprocity between cities and regions could justify the joint preparation of applications to infrastructure programs of senior levels of government, particularly for public transportation, environment, employment and other socio-economic development initiatives that could contribute to an enhanced quality of life and greater prosperity for cities and their regions.

• Joint agreements — The use of joint agreements for different types of projects — social, economic and physical in nature — and other undertakings, could enable the pooling of resources in the achievement of broader common regional objectives such as urban form, climate change, natural areas protection, health care services delivery, recreational and cultural facilities and activities, among others. The ability to attract and retain

ALLIANCE FOR REGIONAL STEWARDSHIP (ARS), USA

http://www.regionalstewardship.org

Alliance for Regional Stewardship (ARS), created in 2000, is a national, peer-to-peer network of regional leaders working across boundaries to solve tough community problems. They come from business, government, education and the civic sectors, but they share a common commitment to collaborative action and achieving results. ARS is committed to the idea that strong and vibrant regional communities are built on an innovative economy, liveable communities, social inclusion, and collaborative style of governance. The mission of ARS is to develop regional leaders and support regional initiatives that advance economic, social and environmental progress in America's metropolitan regions. It is through the following services that ARS helps community leaders to work together in a disciplined, structured way to achieve break-through results and build vibrant, competitive regions:

• learning network — the recognition that the combination of disseminating leading practices on regional initiatives and peer-to-peer exchange and learning is an incredibly powerful way to build the practice of regional stewardship;

• advisory services — deploying a network of consultants as strategic advisors to regional organizations and regional initiatives around the country, with a focus on practical, problem-solving approaches, has benefited 16 regions since 2003 and provided customized consulting and training to an estimated 500 leaders in regions around the country;

• action research — through its work, ARS is continually learning about diverse contexts for regional problem-solving, the changing nature of regional leadership and regional structure, and the lessons learned from both success and failure in regions around the country; the key steps identified to successful regional stewardship are: get together and get going; what's the big idea; dig in to the hard work of change; and, do it all over again, repeat, rebuild, renew.

The Greater Golden Horseshoe is one of the fastest-growing regions in North America. It is the economic engine of Ontario and Canada ... People from other parts of Canada and the world are drawn here because of the enviable quality of life and the economic opportunities that are available ... We must continue to ensure a high quality of life, economic prosperity, and the creation of quality jobs throughout the Greater Golden Horseshoe ... Clearly we can and must do a better job of planning for the future instead of responding to problems caused by growth as they arise ... We recognize the importance of accommodating growth in ways that maintain a high quality of life for our people and present stable and attractive conditions for businesses deciding where to locate jobs and investments. We must recognize that urban regions are becoming hubs of commercialization and competition as well as magnets for the highly skilled workers so necessary for innovation and productivity. As urban regions compete for these resources we can no longer afford to think short-term or municipality-by-municipality.

Government of Ontario (2004)

- *The setting of regional boundaries is as much a matter of value as of fact;*

- *The effectiveness of regional planning initiatives depends on the bundle of governmental resources they receive from the province;*

- *Regional plans concerned with land use seldom can be fully implemented by the regional planning agency;*

- *Metropolitan growth very soon spils over the political boundaries created to contain it;*

- *There is a need for an organ of governance at the urban region level to ensure that planning is holistic, integrated and considers the entire region;*

- *Successful metropolitan regional planning must be linked to a process of governing that is both more inclusive and possesses the requisite power to act in meeting regional needs and goals.*

Ira Robinson and Gerald Hodge
(1998)

qualified and creative people in cities and their regions would be a clear positive outcome of such agreements.

The approach to this closer collaboration between cities and regions should be premised on flexibility — new forums and networks — and not a ponderous governance structure. The key is not to replace existing governmental arrangements but to consolidate and strengthen them, often in an informal rather than a formal manner. The fundamental aim is to move cities and regions from relations of indifference or conflict at the best of times to a new state and culture of synergy. The results from this collaboration would far exceed those currently yielded by limited and conflicting relations.

A new dictum to describe local/regional interface and to capture this emphasis on collaboration could perhaps read as follows: *Citizens of central cities and their broader regions contribute to the funding for public services and other benefits based on when and where they enjoy those services and benefits, subject to fair and equitable taxation, and other governance arrangements.*

PLACE FOR DIALOGUE, EXPERIENCE AND LEARNING

Improving intergovernmental dialogue and workings amongst levels of government is crucial for the future of Canadian cities and regions. The following notes explore further the contours of these relationships, initially, at the operational level, in the context of Canada's Capital Region intergovernmental milieu, and later, through the scrutiny of tripartite agreements between the federal, provincial and municipal levels of government in western Canada.

Viewpoint:

Leading Intergovernmental Dialogue

It goes without saying that effective intergovernmental collaboration is at the heart of successful federalism as well as regional governance. But from my personal experience, while effective collaboration between levels of government does constitute a critical aim that needs to be realized by all, many factors and circumstances — both at the organizational and personal levels — can contribute to making it very difficult to achieve. Such organizational differences as culture, stages in development, agendas and priorities, and leadership and degree of commitment, can significantly constrain intergovernmental collaboration. Similarly, poor personal chemistry, language barriers, conflicting schedules, absence of support from senior management and lack of dedication, can seriously inhibit the development of effective collaboration between levels of government. However, the pay back of truly successful intergovernmental collaboration justifies doing everything possible to overcome such limitations.

Of particular importance should be the recognition that intergovernmental collaboration does not require an absolute top-down approach — all levels of organizations must be involved in making it happen and in sustaining it. As well, work behind the scenes — informal in nature — is as valuable under certain circumstances as more upfront efforts for the establishment of a productive framework of collaboration between levels of government. The existence of forums and networks of varying scope and reach that can help withstand changes in personnel and elected officials are also essential to the creation of intergovernmental momentum

and achieving consistency and results through work relationships. Operational and strategic considerations obviously influence the advancement of intergovernmental files, some requiring political directions and decisions while others are not as demanding. Through the following examples, I will illustrate the application of some of these aspects in the pursuit and conduct of intergovernmental collaboration.

The initial focus of my efforts at intergovernmental dialogue and cooperation was program and legislative implementation, this with representatives of the provincial administration. Although relatively modest in scope and scale — the work involved the establishment and operation of provincial-municipal steering committees. This collaborative effort resulted in important financial investments in and physical improvement to older neighbourhoods of the City of Saint-Jérôme. Later, in the course of my work with the regional county municipality, intergovernmental collaboration proved to be central to the completion of the first generation of planning documents under the Quebec planning legislation, including a first regional plan. In time, through the maintenance of this collaborative effort, it was possible to strengthen the dialogue and exchange of information on planning and development matters in the Saint-Jérôme region, especially with respect to how to harmonize first generation urban plans and by-laws with the regional plan. In all this, I learned a great deal about the management of intergovernmental work teams and the importance of forums of dialogue for nurturing and fostering local and regional collaboration.

By definition, Canada's Capital Region (CCR), with the presence of four levels of government, should be where intergovernmental collaboration is a dominant characteristic of its governance and the origin of many leading practices in how intergovernmental relations and affairs should be conducted and managed. CCR is indeed the scene of highly politicized relations between the different levels of government; however, the extent to which its intergovernmental relations can be described as collaborative is generally acknowledged as somewhat limited. In the course of work with the City of Ottawa and the National Capital Commission (NCC), I have been involved in both successful and less successful intergovernmental initiatives and undertakings.

Before the amalgamation processes that saw the creation of the new City of Ottawa in 2001 and the new City of Gatineau in 2002, several committees, mainly related to urban and regional planning in CCR, demonstrated some of the benefits of sustained intergovernmental dialogue and collaboration. The Regional Municipality of Ottawa-Carleton Planning Commissioners/Directors Committee, the Hull-NCC Coordination Committee, the PLANS Committee (bringing together planning personnel from the Regional Municipality of Ottawa-Carleton (RMOC), the Outaouais Urban Community and the NCC), and the Administrative Committee on Planning and Transportation (bringing together representatives from municipalities, provincial departments and the NCC) enabled the ongoing exchange of information, the resolution of problems and conflicts, the realization of joint initiatives, and the harmonization and integration of policies and regulatory frameworks. Following the municipal amalgamation on both sides of the Ottawa River, CCR has not seen the emergence of similar coordination structures that are clearly needed to steer to a new level of engagement and results between the cities, the provinces and the federal government via the NCC. The NCC Tripartite Planning

Committee — made up of the mayors of Ottawa and Gatineau and the chief executive officer of the NCC — offers the possibility of closing the gap in intergovernmental and, especially, interprovincial collaboration.

When we consider area-specific undertakings such as the Confederation Boulevard, the By-Ward Market, the Sparks Street Mall and Le Breton Flats, while some positive results have been achieved, comprehensive and sustained intergovernmental collaboration remains very much a work in progress. The completion of the Confederation Boulevard over the last twenty years did involve close collaboration between the NCC, the RMOC, the City of Ottawa and the City of Hull (now the City of Gatineau), but longer term arrangements for maintenance and life-cycle management of the different segments remain to be negotiated. The By-Ward Market has been relatively successful at redefining its core mission — from mainly commercial to mixed-uses — through the collaboration of all stakeholders with a leadership role played by the City of Ottawa and the NCC. However, the capacity and the ability of the By-Ward Market to renew itself and to maintain its vibrancy over the long-term will require improved stakeholder involvement, including intergovernmental dialogue and collaboration.

The Sparks Street Mall remains very much an area in search of a true vocation, this in spite of some recent efforts by the Sparks Street Mall Authority, the City of Ottawa, Public Works and Government Services Canada and the NCC to address and resolve longstanding concerns and problems, to highlight its heritage character and to reposition the mall with a mixed use profile, including the introduction of residential facilities. Lack of a common vision, conflicting mandates and failure to achieve a coordinated and sustained effort in the promotion, interpretation and development of the mall, account for its continuous difficulty to perform to its full potential. The Le Breton Flats area in the western part of downtown Ottawa has also witnessed long and protracted efforts by the RMOC, the City of Ottawa and the NCC to come to an integrated agreement in regard to the redevelopment of the site. Several decades went by before the conditions were right for initial development, including a major national institution, a large capital park and the first residential subdivision. Because of conflicting perspectives and expectations, the exact nature and character of the future evolution of Le Breton Flats remains to be fully determined.

The opportunity that was provided to me to participate in such high profile, complex and crucial initiatives for CCR, in some cases in a leadership position, has given me a more measured appreciation of what is needed to help bring intergovernmental collaboration greater recognition in the governance of CCR. It has also informed my approach to the management of intergovernmental relations, in particular, the requirement for constant adjustment and course correction if the relations are to be effective and to sustain adherence of all those involved.

Looking to the future, in order for Canada and its cities to be entirely and successfully responsive to the challenges and the opportunities that will confront them — demographic, cultural, environmental, economic — "raising the bar" in the management of intergovernmental relations will be an essential requirement. Boosting the "intergovernmental game" will not happen by virtue

of a magic wand or a special recipe. Rather, vision, leadership, commitment, dedication, flexibility and authenticity will constitute key ingredients in evolving new and much improved intergovernmental relations. Intergovernmental collaboration is very much context sensitive. Subject to local and regional realities and circumstances, the right forums, the right tools and the right institutions have to be established in close consultation with all levels of government and other stakeholders. To achieve consistency and sustainability in managing intergovernmental affairs, all must come to the recognition and acceptance that the whole is greater and more important than the sum of the individual parts. In a totally interdependent world, synergy must be substituted for autonomy as the new driving force in how governments relate to each other and to their constituencies. Furthermore, in addressing such issues as climate change, cultural diversity, aging population and improved productivity, Canada and its cities will not have the luxury of time. Time will be of the essence in bringing intergovernmental collaboration to the level that Canadians will expect from their leaders. The new intergovernmental *modus operandi* advocated must become fully ingrained in the life and organization of all governments and institutions. Ultimately, intergovernmental collaboration in the future will correspond to new decision-making chains, will reflect greater ongoing learning and the adoption of leading practices, while leveraging the legacy of previous generations of intergovernmental actors and players.

Leading Practices:

Intergovernmental Collaboration — Western Canada Tripartite Agreements

Envisioning, and ultimately realizing an increase in the breadth and the scope of intergovernmental collaboration and coordination is not only promoting good governance amongst the Canadian federation's partners. It is also, and perhaps more importantly, representing an essential ingredient for the success of Canada's urban agenda, and the achievement of sustainable, healthy and resilient cities and regions. Furthermore, in the absence of any foreseeable change to the Constitution, in particular of the roles and responsibilities of the different levels of government, it constitutes necessary "real politics", providing for pragmatism and flexibility in the delivery of governmental services and programs, as well as putting the needs and aspirations of Canadians above those of the government providers, making them, in the process, more "in tune" and more responsive.

For almost three decades, urban development agreements have been an important and successful platform for intergovernmental collaboration and coordination in western Canada. Starting with the 1981 Winnipeg Tripartite Agreement, and expanding with the 2000 Vancouver Tripartite Agreement and the 2005 Regina and Saskatoon Tripartite agreements, they have not only enabled cities and senior levels of government to harmonize and integrate their approaches to services delivery to citizens. They also represent a laboratory for innovation in urban governance and a wealth of experiences and experiments that other cities and regions in Canada can tap into and learn from. The Tripartite Urban Development agreements, as developed and managed by Western Economic Diversification

Canada (WD), have been praised and recognized nationally and internationally as an important advance in how governmental collaboration and coordination can be organized and be made to deliver expected outcomes and results. The following case study will highlight the factors that make tripartite agreements an important source of "lessons learned" in the context of Canada's urban agenda and for the practice of urbanism.

Achievements

The tradition of tri-level governmental collaboration in western Canada is premised on the following principles:

- the capacity of any one level of government to address and resolve major urban issues on its own is limited, and horizontal collaboration (working across jurisdictions) can yield powerful and more lasting results;

- the federal, provincial and municipal levels of government have different but, in some areas, complementary mandates directed at the same people, thus the importance to enhance their cooperation and coordination in responding to the needs and aspirations of Canadians;

- governmental action must be flexible in order to help find local solutions to local challenges and problems;

- a value-based approach to the planning, development and governance of cities and regions is central to the achievement of a new level of consciousness and confidence on the part of citizens, especially in the management of urban environments increasingly characterized by their socio-cultural and socio-economic diversity;

• the seamless provision of public programs and services is an important criterion to avoid duplication, align common priorities and foster innovative approaches to public engagement and delivery mechanisms; and

• western Canadian cities are growing centres of economic activity and as such, it is important for the three levels of government to coordinate their response to development and redevelopment opportunities and challenges as well to cooperate and share resources in matters of economic development and redevelopment.

Urban development agreements constitute one of the key means serving to frame and articulate the collaboration between the two senior levels of government and municipalities. Key characteristics of urban development agreements include: support activities that build on existing policies and programs; involve equal participation and decision making from the three partners; elicit results from joint planning for their overall development as well as development of sub-program components; include opportunities for complementary programming and funding through collaboration with external groups; provide for a community-driven approach to urban development, with ongoing public engagement; prioritize transparency of expenditures and accountability for the use of public funds; foster linkages to municipal strategic planning; and, promote the use of urban leading practices and continuous learning.

The policy underpinning of urban development agreements is generally vision driven, focusing on outcomes that will materially improve the lives of targeted residents by addressing gaps in the provision and delivery of services and leveraging the optimal use of different funding sources. The vision statement of the Vancouver Agreement illustrates the overall policy thrust of urban development agreements: the governments of Canada and British Columbia and the City of Vancouver share the vision of creating healthy, safe and sustainable communities. In such communities, all organizations work effectively together to improve the quality of everyone's life.

The geographical scope of urban development agreements varies according to the specific needs of participating cities:

• Winnipeg: city-wide, with a focus on neighbourhoods where the needs are greatest;

• Vancouver: downtown Eastside, with a gradual expansion to other neighbourhoods;

• Regina: downtown and inner-city neighbourhoods; and

• Saskatoon: older neighbourhoods.

The implementation and outcomes of the four tripartite agreements can be summarized as follows.

Since its inception in 1981, the Winnipeg Urban Development Agreement was renewed three times. It has resulted in significant physical improvements to the city's downtown. Two sub-areas have been the particular focus of attention: The Forks and the North Portage area. Key outcomes include: over $270 million invested by the different levels of government, which helped leverage over $675 million from private sector sources; and, enhancements to inner-city neighbourhoods and business street community facilities, new and renovated inner-city housing, and delivery of innovative education and training directed to immigrants, Aboriginal persons, youth and women.

The Vancouver Urban Development Agreement was renewed in 2005, with a continued focus on Downtown Eastside. Key outcomes have included and/or will include: revitalization of the Hastings Street corridor, the heart of Downtown Eastside; dismantling of the open drug scene, through the operation of North America's first supervised injection site; turning problem hotels into safe and clean places to live; making the community safer for the most vulnerable, particularly women, youth and children; developing the Carrall Street Greenway, a pedestrian and cyclist route linking False Creek to Chinatown and Gastown; establishing the inter-urban art gallery; introducing lighting projects in Victoria Square and Chinatown; developing the Chinatown Millennium Gate; supporting employment and business development organizations; and, integrating Downtown Eastside to the 2010 Olympic and Para-Olympic Winter Games through the Inner City Inclusiveness Commitment.

Urban development agreements were expanded to Regina and Saskatoon in 2005. Key priority interventions include: community-based approaches to affordable housing and homelessness in inner-city and older neighbourhoods; developing cultural and recreational opportunities to enhance quality of life; supporting environmental protection and climate change solutions; enhancing Aboriginal participation in the economy; promoting a positive business climate and enhancing the competitiveness of both cities; and, addressing the strategic infrastructure necessary for the continued physical, social and economic development of Regina and Saskatoon.

Limitations

On the basis of the 25-plus years experience of the City of Winnipeg, the following limitations of urban development agreements have been identified: the lack of attention to constituency building and succession management can make sustaining the intergovernmental collaborative effort very difficult, especially when initial leaders leave without having prioritized "agreement memory"; the diffusion over time of financial and program participation among a wider range of stakeholders can make the governance of agreements more unwieldy and less responsive; the combination of the constituency and succession issues with the broader participation issue can result in a loss of focus in the implementation of agreements, a greater difficulty to achieve consensus and the emergence of a greater level of conflict; the agreement as an intergovernmental collaborative model has not been able to generate clear strategic tripartite policy, producing instead narrower policy guidance in response to project specific contexts; the agreement has not shown, as a community development instrument, the capacity to evolve as might have been expected when considering the changes in the context and the environment of cities, a tendency for entrenchment and rigidity in both processes and content having been observed instead; the approach to communication in the management of agreements has not been as effective as intended, resulting in either unrealistic expectations or lack of awareness on the part of the public; and, in the absence of clear performance targets and measurements, the precise outcomes of agreements can be difficult to identify.

What Was Learned

Urban development agreements, despite their inherent limitations, represent an efficient and effective vehicle for the purpose of bringing the three levels of government to work together in the planning, development and governance of urban areas. They provide, at the same time, flexibility and comprehensiveness in addressing and managing urban issues and opportunities. They can foster intergovernmental coordination and collaboration by: helping to understand particular and common interests of the three levels of government; clarify problems and issues; emphasize project management capabilities; and, increase intergovernmental dialogue and communication. In order to optimize the value-added of urban development agreements in intergovernmental relations and affairs, a number of requirements appear warranted: equality among partners, especially for decision-making purposes; strong and accessible political support; the availability of consistent governance, capacity for program renewal and a focus on time-limited action agendas; the ability to re-enforce goals of other programs through a horizontal management approach; the flexibility to allow trial and error in the definition of roles and responsibilities to foster, over time, respect and adherence to these roles and responsibilities; the provision of a process of constant discussions and negotiations to adapt to changing political contexts and circumstances; promotion of community capacity building through skills and competency development to enable, in time, transition from program dependency to self-sustaining action; the capacity to balance partners' interests to create a sense of joint ownership; the possibility to combine risk taking and strict program accountability to ensure long-term successful engagement of partners; the opportunity to leverage funding from other sources through partnering and networking with governmental and non-governmental parties; and, the provision of stable sources of funding to make the management of change easier and more predictable.

Sources: Clatworthy, Lesliw and Associates (1990), Proactive Information Services, Inc. (2000), Western Economic Diversification Canada (2004, 2008).

Hamilton

Democracies grow from inside out and from bottom up rather than from outside in and top down. This is one of the reasons why democratization takes so long.

Benjamin Barber (2003)

CHAPTER 12

URBAN AGENDA: INSTITUTIONS

Institutions — Range of legal, political or social structures established by law, custom or practice to satisfy the public interest or respond to community needs.

Adapted from J.B. Sykes (1980) and Larousse (2000)

New social institutions are as vital to renewal as new products, services or technology.

Charles Landry (2000)

Our political institutions have not kept pace. They were designed for a different era. They are hierarchical and treat issues as discrete rather than connected.

Donald G. Lenihan (2006b)

[C]anadians really do want to be engaged, but ... they do not trust traditional forms of engagement, including political parties. They want our leaders to think creatively about new mechanisms for engagement — ones that would be more effective and responsive to their aspirations.

Donald G. Lenihan and Graham Fox (2005a)

C anadian institutions are doing well from a worldwide perspective and have already made progress at an institutional level in coming to grips with many of the complexities of urban areas. Nevertheless, more can be done.

The following question can help guide the discussion of institutional evolution in the context of the broader urban agenda: *how can Canada's institutions better embody the needs of cities and integrate planning, development and governance leading practices observed at the national and international levels?*

In more specific terms, how can such emerging challenges — achieving a more integrated approach to the resolution of problems and the response to opportunities, increasing resource constraints and competition, the transition of generations and greater cultural diversity, and the push to closer collaboration between levels of government — be addressed in governance terms, and be gradually undertaken through changes to existing institutions or the creation of new ones?

One of the main criticisms leveled at current institutions in Canada has to do with their relative inertia in the face of social, economic, cultural, technological and urban change occurring all around them. How can institutions better respond to society's trends, some of which involve being in conflict?

While this diagnosis is shared by many, a prognosis as to where institutions are headed and what can be done to solve some of their most urgent problems is much less clear.

Because of the many forces influencing the evolution of society and the difficulty experienced in harnessing those forces toward a definition of the common interests of Canadians, the institutional landscape has seen very little consolidation and, instead, has witnessed an increased amount of fragmentation in recent years. In the federal context of Canada, this fragmentation is not necessarily a problem and, in fact, could actually be construed as a positive turn of events. It can foster institutional flexibility, responsiveness, adaptability to diverse situations and environments, and the capacity to evolve more in tune with specific circumstances.

The response of federal, provincial and municipal levels of government to Canadians' needs and aspirations should not focus on their structures but instead relate to the many perspectives and processes that are needed to guide their future operations.

A key consideration should be to reduce the distance between the citizens and the institutions. Greater inclusion needs to be built around the improvements proposed to institutional make-up. Institutions have organized their work in the past on the premise that citizens would automatically go to them rather than the opposite — that the institutions go to the citizens. The new governance advocated by these reflections calls for a better balance between this "pull and push" in how institutions include citizens in their work and activities.

Increasingly, the expectations will be for greater push — on the strength, in particular, of improved technologies and other means — whereby citizens would be more involved in the determination of their needs, aspirations and expectations as well as how institutions respond, this under conditions that make it far easier to provide ideas and insights. To illustrate, employers and providers of services could be called upon to support more closely the work of institutions in the context of decision-making processes, e.g., through integrated consultative and participatory processes via access to the Internet and social media.

Institutions will be faced with challenging times and choices in the coming years as argued many times before. And their decisions will become more difficult to make. This more challenging environment will demand new abilities from decision makers:

• broadening the number of participants;

• reaching out to the "silent majority";

• creating better awareness of the root causes of problems and involving citizens in the development of solutions;

• developing greater capacity to build consensus;

• learning to say no more often;

• not trying to please everyone at the same time; and,

• bringing people to understand the importance of trade offs and compromises in determining the broader public interest.

As we move toward this new institutional context, the emergence of new community icons or symbols could influence how citizens come to understand and manage their changing reality.

Through a greater sense of identification with their institutions, citizens will be able to better appreciate what they have in common, what binds them together, and integrate the new outlook into their day-to-day lives, as well as into their expectations for the future of their communities and Canada.

The above themes — as well as others — underpin three proposals put forward for institutional change as part of the broader urban agenda: citizen houses; citizen forums; and ceremonies and celebrations.

CITIZEN HOUSES

The ability of the different participants in city planning, development and governance to interact and communicate has always been and will continue to be an essential dimension of cities' evolution, and of the work of their institutions.

A fundamental premise of New Urbanism is that if streets, sidewalks, and other public and semi-public spaces are laid out properly, community life will tend to flourish. But a growing number of new urbanists argue that it's not enough to get the physical design right. What's also needed is community institutions — particularly nonprofit organizations that will sponsor activities and enrich local life.

Philip Langdon (2006)

To maximize the number of citizens answering the questions, the overall strategy has been to go where people are.

Dick Ebersohn et al. (2005)

[A] solution to social problems like [poverty, health services, economic development, security, immigration] must involve the community directly. Parents, students, community groups and organizations, schools and governments must work together to help people change basic habits, attitudes and expectations that stand in the way of real change.

Donald G. Lenihan (2006b)

At first glance, this observation seems very much a matter of fact and of common sense. However, the capacity of cities to deal with the opportunities and challenges of the 21st century will hinge to a large extent on reframing and rethinking how interaction and communication take place between individuals, groups and organizations.

The greater role and participation of the public in the affairs of urban institutions — both as currently sought after and also as projected for the future — is perhaps suggestive that citizens should be given a more pre-eminent place in the structure and organization of cities.

In iconic and symbolic terms, the civic role of citizens in the life of Canadian cities, as regards their presence and representation, is clearly undervalued when compared to some of their other roles or domains of presence and representation, such as members of religious denominations through churches, as blue collar workers through factories, as white collar workers through office buildings, as consumers through retail streets and shopping areas, and as elected officials through Parliament and city halls, among others.

It was previously argued that better balance needs to be sought in the approach to and process of interaction and communication between citizens and institutions — citizens going to institutions to obtain services, and institutions reaching out to citizens to ease their participation in decision-making processes. This combination of centralized and decentralized interaction and communication — face-to-face or mediated — addresses in a direct way the proposed expanded relationships between citizens and institutions.

To capture the central role of citizens and civil society in the continued evolution of cities, new institutions should be established to ensure a transition from the simply functional and operational to a higher level of meaning — the creation of new icons and symbols representing the new balance sought between citizens and institutions in Canada.

"Citizen houses" could constitute an appropriate and timely proposal in the context of Canada's urban agenda. Variations already exist in Canada and other countries — advice bureaus in England, community exchanges in Scotland, business houses in Berlin, architecture/urban centres in Paris, Amsterdam, Montreal, New York, Chicago and San Francisco. Bringing public, private and volunteer sectors such as community associations, environmental groups, boards of trade, political constituency offices, social advocacy groups and others, under one roof, would provide a new space of dialogue in cities, acting to bring together the different forces and interests that will play a role in influencing and shaping cities' futures.

Beyond a key role in the evolving institutional make-up of cities, citizen houses could also play the following roles:

- as a nexus for information collection, sharing and dissemination among various interests;

- as a base for coordination between public, private and volunteer sectors, including joint planning, consultations and conferences;

- as a location for temporary exhibits and other displays of civic or community life, achievements and resources;

- as a place for welcoming new residents and visitors through the provision of orientation information;

- as a forum where specific issues, problems and/or opportunities can be discussed and addressed;

- as a resource for research and learning about the community, its activities, its organization and its citizens; and,

- as a meeting place for citizens where they can gather informally and engage in impromptu conversations and exchanges.

The proposed citizen houses could take as many forms as required by the specific context and needs of cities, including building on existing facilities. If it is indeed shown that citizen houses do respond to community needs, and that their feasibility is established, including sources of funding for their creation and operation, their development could be the subject of joint agreements between participants, with perhaps a leadership role played by municipalities and the private sector.

If conceived as gathering places, at a human scale, providing room for interaction, discussion and collaboration, and consisting of shared facilities between public, private and volunteer sectors, citizen houses could become, at one level, symbols of the new urban reality and agenda in Canada. At another level, they would also constitute a tangible and significant asset for cities that could influence the evolution of the urban form and fabric and the emergence of more integrated land uses, through strategic locations in central as well as in suburban areas.

In reference to some of the possibilities for action in Canadian cities previously presented in chapters 8-11, under the headings of connections, resources, generations and collaboration, citizen houses could play an important role in facilitating the following actions:

- new perspectives of citizenship in cities;

- alternative approaches to the delivery of goods and services;

- arrangements to enhance creativity and ingenuity;

- relations between generations and cultures; and

- the establishment of communities of practice.

Finally, they can complement "citizen forums" and "ceremonies and celebrations" as discussed below.

There is a need for new independent urbanism centres to actively help make urban strategy ... The ... centres, funded from a variety of sources, would be formed as a partnership representing a diversity of urban stakeholders and their role would be to provide a research and development function to the city.

Charles Landry (2000)

As the world evolves into one of ten-second TV sound bites, as local newspapers lose readership, and as the population becomes increasingly mobile, demand grows for new and better ways to keep citizens informed about development so that they can participate in the public process with knowledge, not just with emotion. The urban center can create a destination where the interested public can become informed players in shaping the future of its communities.

Diane Filipi and Jim Chappell (2008)

CANADIAN CENTRE FOR ARCHITECTURE, MONTREAL

http://www.cca.qc.ca

The Canadian Centre for Architecture was founded in 1979 as a new form of cultural institution, to build public awareness of the role of architecture in society, promote scholarly research in the field, and stimulate innovation in design practice.

The location of the new Multicultural Center in the North Building will significantly add to the cultural life of the area of our city which already includes the Canberra Museum and Gallery, the Playhouse and the Canberra Theatre. The co-location of many multicultural community organizations in the North Building will bring more vibrancy to that part of our city. The new Multicultural Center will provide a focal point for the administration, performance, displays, exhibition, radio broadcasting and social interaction for many members of Canberra's cultural community organizations, international students and members of diplomatic missions. The Center will provide an opportunity for the Canberra community to broaden its cultural experience and understanding ...

Australia Capital Territory Government
Building Our Community (2004)

[T]he Planning Exchange is being established in west central Scotland ... to improve communication and understanding between all those involved in planning — members of local authorities, research workers, professional planners, developers, property owners, the operators of public services, social workers, amenity societies, citizen groups ...

J.B. Cullingworth (1972)

LE PAVILLON DE L'ARSENAL, PARIS

http://www.pavillon-arsenal.com

Created in 1988, the Pavillon de l'Arsenal is the centre for information, documentation and exhibition for urban planning and architecture in Paris. It is a unique place, where information concerning urban development and architectural developments in Paris is available to everyone.

AMSTERDAM ARCHITECTURE CENTER

http://www.arcam.nl

The Amsterdam Center for Architecture (ARCAM) was set up as a foundation in 1986. ARCAM aims to reach the largest possible public in order to broaden architecture's appeal. It zeros in on topical issues and development in Amsterdam, so that the discussion on the future is constantly fuelled.

NEW YORK CENTER FOR ARCHITECTURE

http://cfa.aiany.org

The New York Center for Architecture, opened in 2003, is a hub for all interested in the built environment. It is a place to gather, share, learn, honour and advocate. Key aspects of its mission include: providing a centre of learning for the public and building industry professionals in order to improve the quality of the built environment; exploring cutting-edge topics, technological innovations and other issues concerning the built environment; and fostering an exchange and collaboration among members of the design, construction and real estate communities.

CHICAGO ARCHITECTURE FOUNDATION

http://caf.architecture.org

The Chicago Architecture Foundation (CAF), established in 1966, is dedicated to advancing public interest and education in architecture and design. CAF presents a comprehensive program of tours, exhibitions, lectures, special events, and adult and youth activities, all designed to enhance the public's awareness and appreciation of Chicago's outstanding architecture legacy.

SAN FRANCISCO URBAN CENTER

http://www.spur.org

San Francisco Urban Center, formed in 1959, promotes good planning and good government in the San Francisco Bay Area, through research, education and advocacy. The opening in May 2009 of the San Francisco Urban Center focussed on educational programs, public policy, urban planning and design with the ultimate goal of engaging citizens in SPUR's work and the issues that affect the entire region.

CITIZEN FORUMS

Canadians often are critical of their communications with different levels of government and institutions. While it certainly cannot be said that these communications are uniformly viewed as poor, they are nevertheless often perceived as confusing.

Some of the problems that afflict both the content and processes of these communications include, among others:

• information overload;

• what is said and what is left unsaid;

• biases in the presentation of information;

• varying levels of quality in the analyses and syntheses of information;

• lack of thoroughness in the treatment of information;

• failure to provide timely information; and,

• general impressions that final decisions have already been made.

When this complexity, confusion, and/or inconsistency in approach to communications by governments and institutions is combined with all the other claims on people's time and attention, it is not at all difficult to appreciate the reduction in the level of public understanding and participation, and that involvement in decision-making processes is seen as less and less relevant and appealing.

More and more citizens are seeking greater clarity in the information and communications emanating from governments and institutions, and are expressing clearly and sometimes loudly that they wish to be heard. In response to these demands for more participation and influence by citizens, governments and institutions have initiated some reforms in how they involve Canadians in decision making.[24] They have also established greater accountability through improved performance management and measurement.

If citizens are to assume a greater role, even taking centre-stage, in the evolution of Canada's urban governance and institutions, values such as accessibility, intelligibility, and reciprocity must guide information sharing and communications as well as the behaviours of politicians and administrators in their relations with citizens. In moving towards these new relations, conditions should be established to not only ease participation by citizens but also, and more importantly, to make the absence of mechanisms of public participation on the part of public authorities less and less acceptable. Attention to and focus on a more integrated approach to decision making and the delivery of goods and services would provide for and support those necessary conditions of participation by citizens.

[T]he urban centers are as different as the communities that spawned them; they represent the particularities of place ... This divergence of organizational structures and approach is appropriate for the continuing experimentation that is the heart of the urban experience. What is important is that so many communities have found that the urban center provides a significant way to encourage an ongoing dialogue about the future of the urban world.

Diane Filipi and Jim Chappell (2008)

Les mécanismes de délibération qui manquent ... sont les mécanismes permettant de réconcilier les valeurs, de dépasser les conflits de perspectives, d'engendrer un dialogue qui permette de déborder les conflits d'opinions et d'en arriver à une « réconciliation efficace des perspectives », fondée sur une information accrue et un apprentissage collectif plutôt que sur de simples convictions morales.

Gilles Paquet (2004)

---

[24] See "Planning First Nation Communities" at the end of the chapter.

The concept of civic citizenship means recognizing all adult residents of the municipal community as active participants in local governance, with contributions to make and responsibilities to assume as full members.

Peter Clutterbuck, Christa Freiles and Marvyn Novick (2005)

[A]ménager la ville des villes … [est] … un défi intellecuel et culturel, mais aussi … une exigence politique. « Faire de la ville » dans les grandes agglomérations demande de fortes politiques d'intérêt général. Pour lutter contre les dynamiques excluantes, l'hyperspécialisation territoriale, les inégalités entre les lieux. Pour satisfaire les exigences complémentaires de la compétitivité, de la durabilité et de la cohésion sociale. La gouvernabilité démocratique passe par l'innovation politique: non pas l'inflation institutionnelle, mais l'invention de nouvelles synergies entre villes et régions, ainsi que la mise en œuvre de formes de participation citoyenne qui ne se limitent pas à un quartier, mais qui vont au-delà … [L]a citoyenneté se conquiert et ce droit à la ville légitime le processus plus ou moins légal qui conduit à la conquête. Définir ce droit est une condition d'innovation politique et de progrès démocratique dans l'ère nouvelle qui s'ouvre.

Jordi Borja (2004)

A greater emphasis and priority accorded to the participation of citizens in civic affairs would contribute to altering the nature of the communications by governments and institutions. So would an "ethic of communications", whereby public participation in the work and decision-making processes of governments and institutions is guided by a broader view of leadership representing the community's priorities and reflecting common and shared interests of citizens, groups and organizations.

Obviously, such a new approach to communications calls for a different political culture. Again, overcoming the problems, challenges and opportunities to be faced by all levels of government and institutions in the context of the urban agenda and beyond will require political processes based on more — rather than less — collaboration and cooperation, and people able to deliver consensus and compromise.[25]

In order to respond to this changing communications context, a renewed perspective and approach to citizen committees or forums should be given consideration. As participatory mechanisms, these committees or forums are assuredly "old hat", having been, in many respects, one of the preferred approaches to involving citizens in decision-making processes, for quite a long time.

Notwithstanding this long history and legacy of citizen committees or forums in the governance of Canada and its cities, with their many advantages and also with their drawbacks, if reframed to integrate the new political culture that should underpin the urban agenda, they could provide a significant strategic and operational edge to communications with citizens.

The proposed citizen forums, while not fundamentally different from past citizen assemblies in terms of their structure, would find differentiation in their inclusiveness, activities and processes, by linking them more closely to the actual decision making by politicians and other decision makers on behalf of Canadians and by helping to improve the quality and pertinence of decisions made.

Citizen forums could deliver as well important benefits in the context of the urban agenda, including fostering a more engaged and responsible approach by citizens to civic life, tapping the creativity of people in the course of the work of their institutions, helping to bridge the different interests in communities, and leading the way to more participative decision-making processes.

The creation of citizen forums could also make an important contribution to the evolution of an ethic of communications previously mentioned. The key characteristics and roles of these citizen forums as envisioned here would be as follows:

• based on a citizen-centred and not a jurisdiction-centred model of governance;

---

[25] See "Working Collaboratively with Politicians" at the end of the chapter.

- comprised of citizens representing the range of interests in the communities;

- members of the forums would be appointed on a voluntary basis to permit an adaptable and flexible membership;

- mandated for targeted contributions in decision-making processes and complementary to other participation procedures involving the public and interest groups;

- based either on geographic areas or on common interests;

- focused on promoting and achieving consensus or resolving conflicts in the development of visions, policies, programs and services;

- used by federal, provincial and municipal elected officials as 'sounding boards' in decision-making processes;

- contributing to the integration of activities and decisions between governments and institutions;

- contributing to a renewed sense of citizenship in cities and regions as well improved relations between generations and cultures; and,

- supporting and participating in "communities of practice".

The risk exists that citizen forums could be perceived as an added layer of complexity in the work of governments and institutions and as slowing down decision making. They and their activities could also be viewed as threats to the power of politicians.

Based on the above description of their characteristics and roles, citizen forums must be imagined in the context of very specific mandates, involving very important or difficult community decisions. They would not be a substitute for political decision-making processes nor would they be involved in all aspects of civic governance.

More importantly, they should be looked at in terms of the enlightenment that they could bring to decision making by fostering greater participation, helping to identify needs and aspirations of citizens, and contributing to better and broadly accepted decisions. They could play a key role in the development of a new political culture in cities and regions by promoting shared values rather than self-interest.

CEREMONIES AND CELEBRATIONS

Ceremonies and celebrations reflect prevailing socio-economic, cultural, political trends and values. Their importance, meaning, scale and scope also vary in time and between groups and communities. As manifestations of both secular and religious traditions, they embody what Canadians have in common as well as their distinctiveness, their successes, their struggles, their different rituals and customs, from the local, to the national and even the global.

Over their short history, the people of Canada have created and nurtured a diverse and rich ensemble of ceremonies and celebrations at local, provincial and national levels. In the past, ceremonies were somewhat more dominant through the staging of regular and structured rituals,

Civic panels: This is the model for a civic-grounded federalism in which people and communities increasingly inform federal and provincial priorities.

Peter Clutterbuck, Christa Freiles and Marvyn Novick (2005)

Ceremony — Outward rite or observance.

Celebration — Engage in festivities after success.

J.B. Sykes (1980)

[F]estivals, held in various cities throughout Canada, mirror the kind of changes we can observe in the Canadian tapestry, and influence our society as well.

Paul A. Bramodat (2004)

Organized and impromptu events and activities in the public realm are extremely important, as they bring people together, help create social life and community, and make it easier for community members of all ages to collaborate, help each other, and celebrate together.

Suzanne H. Crowhurst (2006)

Community festivals generate a sense of joy and well-being ... and promote a shared sense of identity. They are the expression of community and a mechanism for developing community. They bring together people of different ages and different social, economic and ethnic backgrounds, and enable them to work together to achieve a common goal — the celebration of the community as a whole.

Suzanne H. Crowhurst (2006)

especially before the 1970s, associated with the image of a simpler life, focused more on the community and characterized by greater formality in relationships.

In recent times, with the greater complexity of the life of people — more fragmented, less polarized, involving local and global influences — in which communities of interest compete with physical communities for citizens' attention and time, celebrations have taken a higher profile, with particular emphasis on the profane and entertainment events and happenings.

Whether recurrent or ephemeral, ceremonies and celebrations can constitute powerful means for the creation of institutional meaning, and foster community cohesion and identity.

In the context of a rapidly changing and evolving Canada, different and creative ways will be needed to bring people closer together, formally and informally. This would ease and facilitate their coexistence within a more diverse and complex society and world.

Ceremonies and celebrations could provide new perspectives in matters of citizenship, relations between generations, and coordination between cities and their regions.

A higher priority accorded to ceremonies and celebrations in the day-to-day life and affairs of people could also help bridge Canada's diverse cultures and nurture common cultural bonds, with the creation of shared values and traditions, as longer term benefits.

Through new civic holidays and thematic days, special gatherings, impromptu or planned festivities, greater recognition of individual or group contributions and achievements, it would become possible to bring a higher level of appreciation on the part of Canadians as to what it means to share a unique, much admired and forward looking country.

Besides their physical manifestation in the lives of people and communities, ceremonies and celebrations can provide a sense of the passage of time, facilitating greater awareness of the need to integrate short- and long-term considerations in the life of people, organizations and institutions, and in the evolution of cities and regions. A key outcome of an improved sense of time could be the emergence of more balance within the lives of people at a personal, work and community level.

Other benefits to Canadians that could accrue from a fresh outlook at ceremonies and celebrations include:

- as counterpoint to societal forces pulling communities apart, helping to reconnect people, renew their commitment to each other, encouraging new perceptions, behaviours, and expectations of a different reality and a different world;

- as a way to help create a shared vision and a new ethic of communications, to promote better understanding of Canadians' common interests, and to encourage the building of consensus and the resolution of conflict; and,

- as key to achieving ultimately more sustainable, healthy and resilient communities and cities.

Integrating this new perspective and approach to ceremonies and celebrations in community life will obviously demand some investment — more specifically the necessary leadership to convince Canadians of its importance and value. This commitment could also strengthen the ability of Canadians to work together as well as further the role and recognition of Canada in matters of institution and governance.

PLACE FOR DIALOGUE, EXPERIENCE AND LEARNING

Two notes consider more closely the working of institutions in their evolving context as set by the urban agenda. They relate to the recent institutional change in the planning, development and governance of First Nation communities and the importance for politicians and professionals of working collaboratively.

NATIONAL CAPITAL COMMISSION — DISCOVER THE CAPITAL

http://www.canadascapital.gc.ca

All year long, Canada's Capital Region is alive with a range of interesting activities. The National Capital Commission provides public programming and events that promote national pride and unity, make the Capital Region Canada's meeting place, and communicate Canada to Canadians as well as to visitors from outside Canada. Programs and activities are hosted in every season in the heart of the capital, in the region's parks and green spaces, on Parliament Hill, along Confederation Boulevard and the Rideau Canal Skateway. Canada Day celebrations on July 1st provide an opportunity to take pride in our country and its customs, symbols and traditions. It has also an amazing assortment of activities for the whole family to enjoy together, a day of discovery, adventure, entertainment and fun. Every February, Canada's Capital Region is host to Winterlude, Canada's winter celebration. From spectacular ice carvings, to skating on the world's largest skating rink to an amazing playground made of snow, Winterlude is a great way to take in the best of our Canadian winter. Christmas Lights Across Canada is another celebratory event created to liven up winter months. Originally, only Parliament Hill was illuminated, but the celebration of light in the capital has grown to include over 60 sites along Confederation Boulevard. A significant achievement of Christmas Lights Across Canada is the way it brings Canadians together and links the Capital Region with Canada's 13 provinces and territories. Sound and Light Show is a way to experience the story of our country through original music, giant images and spectacular lighting effects on Parliament Hill. Every fall, the NCC, through Fall Rhapsody, invites residents of and visitors to Canada's Capital Region to experience the magical fall colors of Gatineau Park.

J'aime beaucoup les cérémonies d'investiture des présidents aux Etats-Unis ... Il y a quelque chose de rassembleur dans ces célébrations dont le Canada devrait s'inspirer ... Comparons avec ce qui se fait au Canada. Le lendemain de sa victoire, le nouveau premier ministre rentre dans sa capitale et disparaît pour former son gouvernement ... Des célébrations? Il y en a guère au Canada sinon quelques réceptions réservées aux diplomates, aux hauts fonctionnaires et à quelques bailleurs de fonds du parti. Pas de feux d'artifices ... ni de bals populaires. Au Canada l'avènement d'un nouveau chef de gouvernement est une affaire de protocole ...Le peuple est en quelque sorte dépouillé de son vote. Le premier ministre et son Conseil devraient être assermentés au Parlement et la journée pourrait donner lieu à des célébrations populaires.

Michel Vastel (2005)

Leading Practices:

Planning First Nation Communities

First Nations are one of the founding peoples of Canada. For demographic, cultural, political, judicial and environmental reasons, they have gained greater standing and influence in the recent evolution of the country, and will play an even more important role in the future. This larger profile is of particular relevance and significance to Canada's urban agenda, in consideration of First Nations increased presence in Canadian cities, e.g., 50 percent of their people now live in urban areas.

Planning in and for First Nation communities is a relatively recent undertaking in the context of their broader governance. Because this planning work is still very much in its infancy, characterized by a great deal of trial and error, and often lacking appropriate institutional underpinnings, it is early to talk of and identify First Nation communities "urbanism leading practices". On the other hand, if we want to "grow" the practice of urbanism in their communities, set the stage for an expanded and more mature "urbanistic culture", it is of great value to review and take stock of what has been achieved so far. The following case study will document this planning experience in First Nation communities, with the hope that it can provide urbanists and other stakeholders useful insights, and help them to develop a world-view on how to approach this new area of practice of urbanism.

Achievements

In establishing positive and fruitful collaborative relationships with First Nations, the following institutional and cultural aspects help clarify their world-view and inform their life-histories and their lifestyles: the enshrinement in the 1982 constitutional amendments of First Nation

treaty rights has legitimized their quest for control over ancestral lands all across Canada (the "land claims process") and for full control over their destiny through self-government; some of the distinctive cultural traits of First Nation communities include a multi-generational world-view, the key role of elders and of the extended family, the priority accorded to traditional knowledge and the land as the source of their most fundamental values; because they are dispersed throughout Canada, on reserves and in urban areas, First Nation communities find it difficult to speak with one voice, which makes the recognition and affirmation of their interests very complex and challenging; First Nation communities have the highest population growth rate in Canada, the outcome of a birthrate that approaches the population replacement threshold of 2.1; First Nation communities are confronted with many deep-seated socio-cultural and socio-economic problems that have significant effects on their cohesiveness and identity, e.g., high suicide rate, unemployment, drug abuse, school drop-out, inadequate housing; and, the coexistence of members and non-members of First Nation communities in urban areas requires an appropriate perspective, one involving more nuance, based on the respect of specific cultural differences.

Before the late 1990s, planning in and for First Nation communities was characterized by: a lack of framework; a focus on compliance to external administrative requirements; an expert-driven approach; limited, if not non-existent community engagement; and, an absence of link to the implementation phase of the process. With the turn of the century, First Nation communities were introduced to comprehensive community planning (through Indian and Northern Affairs Canada, in partnership with the Canadian Institute of Planners (CPP)), which made possible: a focus on the needs of communities as defined by them; a broad world-view, where all aspects of a community are considered; a community-based process, where the residents play a central role in the development of plans; and, a better understanding by external stakeholders of the community interests, both immediate and longer term.

The CCP has enabled First Nation communities to bridge their past traditions, anchored in distinct environmental values as well as sound land stewardship practices, and their contemporary aspirations and search for self-sufficiency, improved governance, and a road-map to sustainability, evolved by and for First Nation's people. As a planning tool designed for First Nation communities, the CCP exhibits the following key traits: it is proactive, allowing the emergence of forward-looking leadership groups as well as an active citizenry; it can help address and resolve long-standing conflicts in communities; it can help channel and manage the pace of change in communities; it is integrated, capturing all the internal and external relationships of communities; it is an evaluation tool, enabling communities to ascertain the effects and impacts of proposals; and, it is an information and communications tool, contributing to the understanding of the vision and facilitating the participation of citizens.

The process of elaboration of the CCP serves as a means to building capacity within First Nation communities, ensuring that planning constitutes an ongoing requirement to decision making, that is based on their own exigencies, that it is conducted in a culturally appropriate manner, and that it is managed on the basis of local expertise and knowledge. Through the process of engagement of external stakeholders, the development of the CCP can also contribute to an improved understanding between cultures, while allowing for the sharing of experience, the introduction of planning partnerships, and the creation of reciprocal learning opportunities.

In response to the challenges faced by First Nation communities in Atlantic Canada — socio-economic disparities, land use conflicts, inferior housing stock — a Joint Community Planning Committee (JCPC) was established to help put in place comprehensive community planning. The committee was composed of representatives of First Nation communities and federal departments, along with planning professionals from Dalhousie University. The principal aim of the JCPC was to develop a planning capacity in First Nation communities, initially through three pilot projects (Red Bank, New Brunswick; Abeqweit, Prince Edward Island; and Pictou Landing, Nova Scotia), in order to demonstrate how community planning can make a difference, develop the necessary professional and technological expertise, and support and create among First Nation's people an awareness of the value added that planning can bring to community life, governance and decision-making processes.

The First Nation's Community Planning Model represented a key outcome of the work of the joint committee. Some of the key drivers in developing the model were to:

• find more effective and efficient methods of dealing with development issues in First Nation communities;

• play a pedagogical role for First Nation's people by fostering a journey of discovery, capturing their imagination, and promoting a new community spirit;

• think over the long-term in order to move away from short-term reactive approaches;

• establish a vision based on a better identification of needs and an open, inclusive process that can engage all members of First Nation communities and involve them in decisions about their future; and,

- support negotiations related to funding agreements and the attainment of tangible results through planning and implementation processes.

A number of ideals helped to further anchor in and make relevant the First Nation Community Planning Model to the reality of First Nation communities: strategically consider how limited resources are to be used; protect natural resources and processes; protect traditions while embracing positive change; and, work toward self-sufficiency. The First Nation's Community Planning Model has been used by 22 First Nation communities in Atlantic Canada and its application has expanded to communities in western Canada.

In assuming its fiduciary responsibilities and obligations, the federal government has put in place over time (through Indian and Northern Affairs Canada) a structured process of engagement and collaboration with First Nations in order to address and redress all outstanding issues, e.g., how treaties are honoured and new ones negotiated, settlement of land claims, their evolution towards self-sufficiency and self-government. The commitment made to comprehensive community planning reflects an evolving and consolidating set of relationships between the federal government and First Nation communities, in particular: respecting their traditions and values; ensuring an appropriate two-way flow of information and communication; championing their interests inside the government and the administration; adhering to international agreements as related to their rights and the stewardship of ancestral lands; and, aligning funding with planning and implementation processes. In promoting a new world-view in the rapport between First Nations and the rest of Canada, the federal government is intent on bringing their communities to a level of well-being, prosperity and quality of life comparable to other Canadian communities. The transition of First Nation's people from a way of life based mainly on reserves to one split between reserves and urban areas, reinforces the need for new models of relationships, with their challenges but also their possibilities.

Limitations

For many reasons — some under, others outside the control of First Nation communities — comprehensive community planning has not, so far, lived up to the benefits promoted by officials and to the level of people's expectations. The most important limitation has been the difficult transposition of "plans on paper" to their implementation in the "day-to-day reality of people". An important test of CCP — the delivery of tangible results to First Nation communities — has not been met, mainly because the necessary resources have not been provided. Other limitations associated with the application of comprehensive community planning in First Nation communities include:

- the absence of consistent funding to sustain the planning effort;

- the challenges involved in building a constituency for community planning — with a limited planning culture, turnover in leadership often entails starting all over;

- the failure to establish long-lasting planning institutions that could help embed planning rules and protocols in the governance of communities;

- the lack of attention dedicated to training — the development of necessary skills is a key requirement to help people sustain the demand placed on them by planning processes;

- the inconsistent engagement of people in planning processes, resulting for the most part in failure of communications, of not reaching out to people consistently and sufficiently;

- the absence of planning champions, of change agents, of a distributed leadership that could bring about bottom-up approaches as countervailing measures to the dominant top-down governance and decision-making structures;

- the lack of alignment between the content of community plans and the political and fiscal realities underpinning their realization; and,

- the pursuit by the federal government of "silo" responses to the comprehensive community planning processes and outcomes.

What Was Learned

The use of comprehensive community planning is a relatively recent addition to the governance and decision-making processes of First Nation communities. The fact that CCP has encountered difficulties and roadblocks when considering the results obtained from its application is a normal occurrence whenever attempts are made to integrate planning systems in local cultures. Achieving planning in local communities — in terms of process, content and outcomes — can never be perfect, nor totally successful. It requires time, patience, a long-standing commitment, acceptance of errors and risks, the need to empower people and the presence of leaders at all levels of communities. In making a contribution to comprehensive community planning, giving it its rightful place in the governance and decision making apparatus of First Nation communities, planners must espouse a broader perspective, one that bridges the local focus of plan making with an ensemble of global links and connections. Through such a more encompassing world-view, they can help First Nation communities identify and appreciate their distinct qualities, consider problems and opportunities from different lenses, and ascertain positively and creatively possible alternatives to the realization of their vision.

Successive federal governments have made firm commitments in renewing and even transforming their collaboration with First Nation communities. The application of comprehensive community planning as a means to aligning federal program administration with the governance of First Nation communities is a good illustration of this new approach to relations. In the process of further strengthening First Nation communities, federal authorities should take a more horizontal view of responding to their needs and aspirations. A broader support system is needed to dovetail and complement planning systems in ensuring the sustainable and consistent application of CCP and in obtaining more tangible results. Key system elements — both tangible and intangible — include: nurturing relations, developing networks and technological capacity, providing appropriate levels of resources, respecting commitments made, evolving context specific governance, enabling different human resource solutions such as coaching and mentoring, and ensuring necessary flexibility and adaptability.

Grounding the planning, development and governance capacities of First Nation communities through adherence to and respect of their particular culture and local history constitutes a key requirement for their successful transition to sustainability, health and resiliency. In broadening the application of comprehensive community planning, First Nation communities should nurture sharing practices among themselves, building on their strong traditions of information exchange, knowledge and experience. Strengthening and sustaining the development of a planning culture will clearly benefit from such enlightened collaboration.

Sources: Jeffrey Cook (2008), Colin Harivel and Colette Anderson (2008), Indian and Northern Affairs Canada (2003), Laura Mannell and Heather Ternoway (2008), Frank Palermo (2003), Kasio Tota (2003), Tracey L. Wade (2008) and Ryan Walker (2005).

Viewpoint:

Working Collaboratively with Politicians

Throughout my professional career, I have always welcomed the opportunities offered by my work to establish positive and fruitful working relationships with politicians. In the planning and development process, politicians do indeed play a very important, if not a crucial role. Conversely, in recognition of the important role played by the professionals of urbanism in contributing to the achievement of the goals and aspirations of politicians in the governance of cities, it is critical to also examine how they view, value and approach their relations with professionals. In fact, this relationship is often complex and multi-faceted, taking place simultaneously at different levels — obviously politicians as decision makers but also as interested parties in the planning and development of the area they represent, as hierarchically superior to the professional cadres and also, at times, as individuals sharing similar interests and participating in the same professional networks. As the following examples will show, I have tried in my collaboration with politicians to achieve a reciprocity in roles, with the recognition that in getting to outcomes and results, politicians and professionals have to complement each other and have to work hand in hand to ultimately make possible sustainable, healthy and resilient cities and regions.

Politicians, like other stakeholders in the planning and development of cities, are confronted with policy issues and decisions in and for which they have varying levels of knowledge, experience and expertise. As they address the different problems and proposals that come their way at council tables and in other decision-making instances, they have to find and evolve their own comfort zone. In my work, initially for the City of Saint-Jérôme and later for the RCM of La-Rivière-du-Nord, I was placed in situations where I had to lead the delivery of planning programs and regulatory processes and instruments that were often "first generation". They required, on my part and also on the part of the politicians I was working with, steep learning curves. The lack of familiarity of politicians with these specialized council agenda topics and the centralization of political power in the mayor's and reeve's offices created additional challenges in advancing this work. Through the establishment of good communication channels and protocols with the director general/secretary treasurer as well as the mayor's/reeve's offices, combined with open lines of communication with key community stakeholders and leaders, I was able to gradually create the necessary political and operational comfort zones. Through a value-based approach in creating and nurturing working relationships with politicians, it was possible for me to implement projects that had a positive influence on four neighbourhoods in Saint-Jérôme and set the stage for the establishment of the necessary conditions for longer term land use and environmental change in the broader Saint-Jérôme region.

When I joined the Planning Department at the City of Ottawa, a whole new political environment opened up to me. While noting an absence of polarization in how city council conducted its affairs, the divisiveness often exhibited in addressing and deciding on issues and proposals struck me as peculiar and difficult to relate to in comparison to my prior experience in working with politicians. Very early on, I discovered a political class highly experienced and knowledgeable in and appreciative of urban planning and development matters, which created some interest in my work but also, at times, made it very challenging. To the tense and distant working relationships with politicians forecasted for me by colleagues in the department, I found instead a deep passion and commitment to their work and a willingness to collaborate with me if I was ready to engage them and their constituents in open, transparent and timely ways. Some politicians were very demanding but through dedication and hard work, I was able to determine their interests and priorities which made possible close collaboration and led to several successful streetscape improvement projects in and around downtown Ottawa. When failure in communication happened, related in most cases to conflicts between some of my staff and politicians, I did manage to rectify the situation by clarifying the lines of communication, this through the use of diplomatic and respectful approaches.

Of the many relationships that the urbanist must engage in and nurture in her/his work, collaboration with politicians is one of the most important and requires careful attention and management. Collaboration with politicians is a demanding endeavour; the ability and the capacity of the urbanist to sustain and make the collaborative effort fruitful over the long haul depends on a sustained investment of time, effort, quality of work and goodwill. In order to strike a positive collaborative relationship with politicians, I have found that two key considerations must inform the efforts of the urbanist.

First, getting to know the politicians is key to ascertaining what makes them who they are as people, which can then help shed light on their interests, goals and aspirations. By definition, politicians are people with a distinct world-view, capable of articulating it in different public forums and animated by a wide range of motives in serving the public interest. In some cases, it is for the personal standing and the other advantages that come with the position. But in the majority of instances, they are driven by a sincere and vibrant commitment to the well-being, prosperity and order of their community and its citizens. Through an understanding of the "character" of an individual politician, it becomes possible for the urbanist to open up appropriate lines of communication and to determine the requirements for positive engagement and collaboration with them.

The second consideration relates to the ability and capacity of urbanists to evolve working relationships with politicians based on trust, mutual respect, reciprocity and predictability. At one level, working with politicians is obviously influenced by the relation of hierarchical authority that defines their interaction with urbanists. But at another level, their collaboration needs to be set by the responsibility they share in determining the policy agenda of their community and in making sustainable, healthy and resilient development happen. The "ideal" of shared responsibility is often trumped by the "reality" of hierarchical authority. However, in charting the future requirements for the relationships between urbanists and politicians, the ideal will need to be given more attention if the reality of communities is to be responsive to the planning and development challenges of the 21st century.

Saskatoon

I know of no safe repository of the ultimate powers of the society but the people themselves; and if we think them not enlightened enough to exercise their control with a wholesome discretion, the remedy is not to take it from them but to inform their discretion.

Thomas Jefferson quoted in John Punter (2003)

CHAPTER 13

GETTING ON CANADIANS' RADAR SCREEN

RE-IMAGING CANADIAN CITIES

It is now opportune to consider again an important fact that best captures the essence of contemporary Canada: more than 80 percent of Canadians — and now 50 percent of the people on Earth — are living in urban areas.

This may very well be at the root cause of many of our society's ills and dilemmas, however it is also the launching pad for many creative ideas and innovations absolutely fundamental to our survival in the long-term.

But a particularly thorny difficulty exists for the urbanists and others who plan, manage and govern in cities. The roles of urban areas — in terms of their challenges but also their possibilities — surprisingly, and also worryingly, often do not register in citizens' world-view. They live, work, travel, recreate and consume in cities, but they seem oblivious to the meaning and significance of these places for their future and the future of Canada.[26]

When looking at the urban agenda under the prism of the perceptual challenge posed by Canadians' world-view of their cities, or lack thereof, it becomes imperative to distinguish between a second level and a first level of change.

The second level corresponds to the support and commitment by Canadians to the vision and policies that underlie the urban agenda, this based on the reconciliation between perceptions of urban reality and what is needed to achieve a sustainable, healthy, and resilient urban transformation.

At the first level, the focus must be on capturing the cities and their regions in the imagination of Canadians, creating an "urban presence" in their lives, and fostering a shared perspective and appreciation of the meaning of city living. This chapter will further explore and underscore the importance of the first level of change for the successful determination and realization of Canada's urban agenda.

Citizens must be equipped to look at their cities and regions with new eyes, as a source of shared perceptions that can be the basis for shared meanings that can then be translated into shared visions and shared actions. In other words, the future of cities and regions should be seen and approached as being largely in the hands of their citizens. In setting that future in motion, obviously taking into account extraneous factors, they must come to the realization that they are really in it "all together".

---

[26] Key sources of inspiration for this chapter include David Gordon (2001), Kevin Lynch (1969), Henry Mintzberg (2004), and Gareth Morgan (1988, 1998).

This chapter will deal with the necessary ingredients for a renewed appreciation of what city living should entail, in three parts: how the transition to a shared perspective of the city could be achieved; the strength of this shared perspective or shared image as an underlying base for greater civic engagement; and, the role of the urbanist as a key actor in making the case for and advancing a proper framing of the urban agenda as a "place for dialogue, experience and learning".

A SHARED IMAGE OF THE CITY

Citizens share many things in their day-to-day experience of the city, including the physical space on which it is built and of which it is made up. In evolving a more wholesome perception of the city, this sharing of the "physical reality" by citizens is of particular significance in that it is, in many instances, an important source for the shaping of images that they then use to describe and remember their places of origin and/or living.

Acknowledging this symbolic value of the physical reality of the cities, confirmation of a deeper meaning could, potentially, contribute to the sought after change in perceptions on the part of citizens. Initially, the simple association to the physical reality of the city would likely continue to prevail and dominate; however, over time, it could take a whole new symbolic dimension, as a distinct source of identity, pride and even broader meaning. This is "my city"!

A shared image of the city, if appropriately communicated and nurtured, could lead to the expression of greater equanimity and respect for the "shared commons" that

the city represents, and be capable of positively influencing the decisions and behaviours of citizens, in the context of achieving sustainability, and healthy and resiliency objectives and outcomes.

Of course, a shared image of the city and its attendant perceptual change will not happen spontaneously nor will it materialize from nowhere. Furthermore, it is unlikely that such a shared image would ever touch a large majority of the citizens of any city.

The aim should be, instead, to reach-out initially to a minority of citizens — perhaps up to 10 percent — that would include, in as much as possible, representatives from the different "walks-of-life" and from the various constituency groups. Based on this initial contingent of champions, more citizens could be enlisted as the urban agenda progressively takes shape, and its broad influences on the lives of people and their experiences of the city become increasingly evident and manifest.

But before even contemplating the possible outcomes of a shared image, it is necessary to address and answer a more basic question: how can a city go about establishing such a shared image in the first place?

Articulating and conceiving of a shared image of the city, in all its essential content and process details, should be as unique as the place and the people it will be striving to represent, symbolize and embody as a source of identity, pride and meaning.

However, it is possible to identify a set of common characteristics that can guide the articulation and conception of a shared image of the city:

Tout citadin a longtemps fréquenté certaines parties de sa ville et l'image qu'il en a baigne dans les souvenirs et les significations ... Le besoin de reconnaître et de rattacher à un modèle ce qui nous entoure est si crucial, et plonge si profondément ses racines dans le passé, que l'importance pratique et émotive de cette image pour l'individu est immense ... Un cadre physique vivant et intégré, capable de « produire » une image ... bien typée, joue aussi un rôle social. Il peut fournir aux communications de groupe la matière première des symboles et des souvenirs collectifs.

Kevin Lynch (1969)

... [M]any people have ... lost the ability to form and express opinions about the look and feel of their surroundings ... [V]isual literacy seems to have slipped down the agenda.

The Economist Intelligence Unit (2010)

- The "physical reality" of the city as a starting point, acting like a "shared domain of reference" for all participants.

- The "shared leadership" perspective and approach, bringing together municipal, business and community leaders, and involving as many citizens as possible and the different constituencies.

- The different professional, technical and artistic disciplines as providers of the creativity and ingenuity required by the process, including artists, designers, marketers, urbanists, among others.

- The process as a source for the identification of a "deeper order" that underlies the civic reality and the civic culture, helping to connect the different aspects and realms of the city in the imagination and consciousness of its citizens.

- The shared image as a "container" sufficiently powerful to convey meaning and foster awareness by way of:

  ▸ abstraction — reflecting different ideas about the city in very simple terms, easy to grasp and to understand;

  ▸ evocation — linking and bridging the past, present, and possible futures of the city;

  ▸ representation — depicting concretely and vividly the aspirations that citizens have and share for their city; and,

  ▸ association — describing the bonds that bring citizens together in the planning, management and governance of their city.

- Ultimately, the shared image becomes a source of "resonance" for all citizens and constituencies, providing a "unifying force" in moving toward a more sustainable, healthy and resilient future for the city.

To achieve this and be successful, the shared image of the city should integrate both didactic and practical strands in the process of its development. To promote and encourage the participation of citizens in its inception, it is important that the tools and approaches used be a source of reflection, but also be friendly in nature and a pleasure to work with.

Metaphors could be such tools, constituting an original and interesting way of looking, apprehending, understanding and creating insights in the structure and working of cities.

For the purpose of articulating and conceiving of a shared image of the city, the adoption of a metaphorical approach could help stretch the community's thinking, allowing citizens and other participants in the process to consider their city in a new light and from a diversity of points of view.

Although each metaphor, in and of itself, offers only a partial and limited view of the city, it is in combination that metaphors find their true value, because in approaching the same subject or idea through various means, they can suggest perspectives and actions that may not have been possible and achievable before.

For the purpose of illustrating the image-making power of the metaphor-as-the-city, we will briefly consider three examples below: a tapestry-as-the city, a chessboard-as-the-city, and a hologram-as-the-city.

Initially, the strengths and limitations of each as an image for the city will be reviewed. The identification of some of the insights the three metaphors can provide will follow with a discussion of the structuring and working of the city when the insights are collapsed in one analytical tool.

Tapestry-as-the-city

Strengths:

- The framing, anchoring, and tight weaving characteristic of the tapestry reveals an inner structure that is comparable to the layout of the city and its different networks.

- The tight weaving is also suggestive of deep inter-connectedness and inter-dependency, where one "loose thread" can signal the unravelling of some city constructs.

- The variety of threads, colors and patterns reminds us of the diversity typical of the city, including its people and land uses.

- The texture and variable thickness of the tapestry is illustrative of the range in intensity of activities found in the city.

- The tapestry as a piece of art strongly engages the visual sense, similarly to what we experience when looking at a city.

- The combination of the particular elements of a tapestry makes it a unique art piece in the same way that the distinctive constitutive elements and characteristics of a city are sources of identity for its citizens.

- The tapestry as a simple, organized and creative art form is not dissimilar to the city as a unique and structured socio-political entity.

Limitations:

- The tapestry is static while the city is dynamic.

- It is bi-dimensional while the city is multi-dimensional.

- It engages the senses in a limited way while the city is multi-sensory in its make-up.

- It is not changing while the city is in a constant state of flux.

- It has firm boundaries while the footprint of the city can expand over time.

- When observing a tapestry, we are focusing in on the object, while when looking at a city we can simultaneously focus in and scan out.

Chessboard-as-the-city

Strengths:

- Its chequered appearance and the figurines confer to the chessboard an inner structure that can be related to the layout of the city and its demographic profile.

- The squares of the chessboard make it grid-like corresponding to a typical city street layout.

- The chessboard when in play is interactive which is also a key attribute of the city.

Metaphor — an expression to achieve meaning by using one aspect of a life perspective or experience to understand and describe another.

Adapted from Gareth Morgan (1998)

- The chessboard and its rules of play refer to two distinct levels of reality which is comparable to the city as a physical entity and as a living and governing body.

- The unique design of the chessboard and of its figurines make reference to the diversity and source of identity that a city represents.

- The game of chess, with its two opponents and its win-lose strategies, reminds us of the often adversarial relations in the city and the role of political/public institutions in managing those relations.

- The chessboard as both simple and complex in its make-up and rules of play is an apt description of the inherent nature of the city and of its rich environment.

Limitations:

- The chessboard is three-dimensional (when considering the movement of figurines) while the city is multi-dimensional.

- It is generally "black-and-white" while cities are much more nuanced, with shades of grey and colors.

- It is a closed system, rule-based while the city is an open system, with a propensity for self-organization.

- It engages the senses in a limited way while the city is multi-sensory in its make-up.

- It is not changing while the city is in a constant state of flux.

- It has firm boundaries while the footprint of the city can expand over time.

- It reflects a constant level of activity while the city displays a range in the intensity of its activities.

- When observing the chessboard and the people playing on it, we are focusing in on the object, while when looking at the city, we can simultaneously focus in and scan out.

Hologram-as-the-city

Strengths:

- The morphological versatility that characterizes the hologram, from a scale and dimension standpoint, mimics the variety and complexity of the different components of the city, such as shape, layout, patterns.

- The variety of angles of view made possible by the hologram, especially the shifts in the visual field that it allows, is reminiscent of the richness and diversity of the city's viewscape.

- The hologram, similarly to the city, is inherently multi-dimensional, by virtue of its tangible and intangible aspects, the latter found in a digital form of organization and expression.

- The capacity for the hologram to embed the whole in each of its constitutive parts suggests the symmetry, flexibility and connectedness characteristics of the city associated to the relations between the community as a whole and its different districts and neighbourhoods, its sectors of activity and their sub-sectors, and its systems of networks and their sub-systems.

- The capacity of the hologram to organize, store, retrieve and mine information exemplifies key characteristics of the city, including growth, evolution, learning, dynamism, responsiveness.

- The digital character and possibilities displayed by the hologram enables the broadening of the visual field, encompassing inward and outward scanning motions, much like the visual experience afforded by the city.

- The hologram as a distinctive, sophisticated and broadly used technological marvel is a reflection of the city as a source of identity that can be branded and reaches out locally and globally.

Limitations:

- The hologram is a perceptual sleight of hand while the city is real and authentic.

- It has a distance to it while the city is close-by and proximate.

- It is a cold medium while the city can be both cold and hot.

- It engages the senses in a limited way while the city is multi-sensory in its make-up.

- It has firm boundaries while the footprint of the city can expand over time.

- It is a closed system while the city is an open system.

These three metaphors provide a number of valuable insights in the structuring and working of cities including the following:

- They help to illustrate the multi-faceted character of the city:

  ▸ its diversity,

  ▸ its dynamism,

  ▸ its multi-dimensional nature,

  ▸ its intensities of use and activity,

  ▸ its inner structure and infrastructures,

  ▸ its identity,

  ▸ its socio-political characteristics,

  ▸ its expanding footprint,

  ▸ its evolving nature,

  ▸ its openness,

  ▸ its learning capacity,

  ▸ its responsiveness to internal and external factors, and

  ▸ its interactivity.

- They help also to demonstrate some of the contrasting aspects of the city:

  ▸ its tangible and intangible aspects,

The metaphor of the hologram invites us to think of systems where qualities of the whole are enfolded in all the parts so that the system has an ability to self-organize and regenerate itself on a continuous basis.

Gareth Morgan (1998)

Virtuellement la ville est en soi le puissant symbole d'une société complexe. Bien exprimée visuellement, elle peut aussi avoir une forte signification.

Kevin Lynch (1969)

Those societies most able to engage their citizens have tended to generate greatest economic wealth.

Henry Mintzberg (2004)

▸ its simplicity and complexity,

▸ its hot and cold characteristics,

▸ its local and global reach,

▸ its wholeness and separateness,

▸ its physical reality and living properties, and

▸ its inward and outward visual field.

• Finally, they help to identify aspects of the city that were ignored or left unsaid:

▸ the importance of values and ethics in planning, managing and governing the city,

▸ the role of the senses in how the city is experienced,

▸ the economic reality of the city, and

▸ the time dimension of the city.

The metaphor-as-the-city is one of several approaches that can be used to create a shared image of the city — others include visioning and "listening to the city" processes, search conferences, charrettes, public forums, and web-based interactive initiatives.

Whatever the means retained, the end result should remain the same: achieving a city-wide consensus on how to comprehend, describe and communicate the city.

Having articulated and conceived of a shared image of the city constitutes an important first step toward the first level change of the citizens' world-view of their city, within the broader context of the determination and realization of the urban agenda. Citizens should also be able to consider the city in a broader context, how its physical reality and their living environment connect to a larger whole, and what their role should be in helping to move toward a more sustainable, healthy and resilient future. They should feel an engagement to the city and the urbanist can and should help.

AN ENGAGEMENT TO THE CITY

While the shared image of the city can be powerful in altering the world-view of citizens, it should also be the point of origin for a more fundamental enactment: the emergence of new relationships between citizens and their city. In order to make possible and feasible a more sustainable, healthy and resilient city future, citizens need to reclaim a greater role and place in how this future is charted.

For citizens, the sources of distraction or diversion from a commitment to the city and involvement in shaping the response to their needs and aspirations are many. For some, a daily preoccupation with basic survival makes it definitely not top-of-mind, unfortunately. For others, the usual distance or neglect is only superseded when their particular interests are perceived to be or are put at risk, whether as a result of a change in alignment between their interests and the broader community interests, or through the imposition of others' interests on top of theirs.

For others still, the lack or absence of any motivation to participate or get involved is ascribable purely and simply to a failure to grasp the connection between their appreciation of city living — such as the implications of individual decisions and/or actions on the environment of the city — and such broader issues as what healthy living entails, the consequences of energy over-consumption and scarcity, the ramifications of the home/work location choices, the long-term impact of short-term consumption patterns, and the meaning of climate change for the future of cities.

How to bridge this gap between the actions of living in the city and the appreciation of the implications of such actions for the ever changing and evolving reality of the city, constitutes a key policy dilemma and also a crucial aspiration for Canada's urban agenda. Similarly to this sense of empowerment that citizens of developing countries feel and get as a result of their involvement, initially, in capacity building initiatives — such as learning to secure and protect a source of water or how to build a house — and later in the ongoing development of their communities, Canadians must take the necessary steps to define and decide for themselves the roles and responsibilities they wish to assume in the determination and realization of their cities' future orientations and destinies.

Under Canada's circumstances, such a decision can be reached with the knowledge that "peace, order, and good government" is not at risk or on the verge of being irretrievably lost. Furthermore, the place of cities in the life of citizens should be well positioned, put in its right balance, not overbearing nor overwhelming, but a seamless engagement as much as possible in consideration of all the other preoccupations and priorities that Canadians have.

The power of engagement and the promotion of all that can be achieved through the complementary or joint actions of the individuals and of the broader community, need to become a key mantra and a key strategy, respectively, for Canada's urban agenda.

The whole is much more than the sum of the individual parts …

In breaking new boundaries of commitment and engagement, Canadians must obviously, on the one hand, leverage what they are currently doing right in what they contribute to their cities, and on the other, focus the bulk of their efforts on addressing areas that require changes in approaches or behaviours. An ideal step-wise change management approach would include:

- building on the current areas of strength;

- adapting to new realities and circumstances;

- modifying what is no longer tenable; and,

- adopting new practices when a transformation agenda is necessary.

In order to sustain the commitment and engagement of Canadians toward their cities and regions, the contribution of some key constituencies will be of paramount importance. Politicians, print and electronic media, and

To make the [State of the Union Message] memorable, the president and his speechwriters have to dig deeper … Obama needs one or two brief images or metaphors that linger in the mind … But if it's lacking a line that can be chiseled in marble … he won't set the tone he needs for the remainder of his term … President Obama's task in 2011 is to frame our choice … then offer instructional tips on inventing the future.

Jonathan Alter (2011)

The media is key to urban reinvention. Most city media disappoint. They are geared to complaining rather than helping to create. Cities are often projected as clichés, with little sense of their depth or richness. There is much about problems, but little about achievement and aspiration.

Charles Landry (2006)

Never tell people how to do things. Tell them what to do and they will surprise you with their ingenuity.

General Georges Patton quoted in Andrew Heintzman and Evan Solomon (2003)

Sustaining a network over time and improving its capabilities requires cultivating deep ties. Creating the infrastructures and conditions that support long-term relationships building is tricky work.

Stephen Goldsmith and William D. Eggers (2004)

community leaders will need, in particular, to be at the forefront of the change agenda, more specifically by:

- listening to the preoccupations and insights of Canadians;

- keeping a steady and relevant flow of information;

- engaging Canadians in a variety of creative ways; and,

- ensuring that they are provided with the appropriate and necessary skills and competencies to enable the transformation of their world-view and of their behaviours.

Imperative also to the success of Canada's urban agenda should be the substitution of a concentration on "control" of all kinds with a "continuum" of measures that, while including controls, would as well favour incentives, facilitation, collaboration and self-organization.

As part of the first level change advocated to appropriately set the path for Canada's urban agenda and help create a new civic spirit and culture in cities, an important consideration will be how to evolve the city "in the round" and thus move away from the current "silo mentality". This change demands an investment in trust building, the development of "deep ties" between Canadians themselves and with their cities.

In the end, an engagement to the city will be about establishing key building blocks that will include transformative change but, as crucially, tapping into civic memories as well as enabling individuals and communities to "learn how to learn" their way toward a sustainable, healthy and resilient urban future.

THE ROLE OF THE URBANIST

Urbanists provide, through their professional practice, a great deal of knowledge of and experience in the planning, designing, developing, managing and governing of the city. The soft and hard skills and competencies of the urbanist — corresponding to the substantive and procedural dimensions of urbanism — make possible their contribution to the first and second level changes underpinning Canada's urban agenda.

Through the work of urbanists in the public, private and volunteer sectors, the multi-faceted interfaces and interactions between the different constituencies involved in giving form, appeal and value to cities, can be structured, facilitated and coordinated. The major aim, and also the key outcome pursued, is a generally more predictable, enlightened and distributed decision-making context and process.

Because of this unique place that the professional practice of the urbanist occupies in charting the future course of urban evolution and transformation in Canada — with the acknowledgement that not all is satisfactory and that improvements are definitely in order — expanding the contribution of urbanism in Canadian cities should constitute a key priority for the profession.

Helping to broaden the perspective that Canadians have and share of their cities, fostering a greater commitment and engagement by the different constituencies to cities and their future, and introducing new approaches, strategies and tools in the planning, designing, developing, managing and governing of cities, correspond to some possible actions that hold promise but that reflect also a sense of urgency.

The question that can be posed is the following: how ready are the professionals of urbanism to rise to the challenge? Are they willing to play the role as "agent of change" in the context of Canada's urban agenda?

An initial answer could be that institutional, corporate and political barriers are inhibiting a broader role for urbanists. However, from a value- and ethics-based perspective, the practitioners of urbanism in Canada, at the beginning of the 21st century, are really called upon to re-assess and re-examine, as professionals, their own perspectives of and approaches to change. Only by renewing their world-view, e.g., moving away from a strict definition of roles, strict specialization, a focus on the spatial aspects, are they going to continue to exert a positive influence on the future direction of urbanism in Canada and, ultimately, contribute to the change in world-view and behaviour by Canadians called for by the urban agenda.

In setting out an updated vision for their professional practice, urbanists must look beyond their current "horizon of concern" and instead, picture themselves as leading the wave that will transform in time Canada's cities. On the strength of their past accomplishments and legacies, and especially leveraging their many partnerships and networks of support, they can help put in place the building blocks and create the conditions of success for an urban agenda "tipping point".

By re-positioning their actions and influence, urbanists would move their practice forward, giving it a greater socio-economic, socio-political, and socio-technical reach and depth. At the same time, they would be helping in the process to mobilize a broader and more distributed civic leadership for the purpose of planning, designing, developing, managing and governing Canadian cities.[27]

In the process of advancing their professional practice, the professionals of urbanism could consider the following areas of inquiry as worthy of closer examination and integration.

Re-framing **their perspective of urbanism**:

▸ As a professional undertaking, urbanism is considered a privileged domain of practice, but as a subject of reflection and intervention, it is not.

▸ Urbanism, through this more encompassing perspective, is indeed everywhere one looks, and is part and parcel of every city's inhabitant life domain; it can be compared to a kind of "glue" that helps hold the different aspects and dimensions of the city together.[28]

▸ In arriving at a new perspective of urbanism, urbanists must be encouraged to break stifling boundaries, move away from professional silos, and instead, adopt an interdisciplinary perspective and approach in all professional work.

[P]rofessional qualities now being highlighted for city-making …

- *An ability to cross boundaries and think laterally.*
- *The ability to pick out the essence of a professional position and to see how it relates to other aspects.*
- *Practical and open to new ideas.*
- *An openness of thinking and willingness to hear other things.*
- *To be able to listen and to hear.*
- *To be able to bring out the best in others, to facilitate, to draw together arguments and attitudes.*
- *People who know their place, have walked its streets, can feel what it is like.*
- *A sense of vision combined with realism, a patience garnered from having experience, a mix of drive and focus on the nitty-gritty, a tenacity to see things through.*

Charles Landry (2006)

[27] See "Steering Controversial Initiatives and Advocating For A Planning Constituency" at the end of the chapter.
[28] From Daniel Solomon (2003).

Creative learning environments have characteristics including exuding trust; freedom of action; variety — where you can transfer knowledge across contexts and disciplines; a balance between the skills people have; challenge — a context where ideas are bounced back and forth with continued feedback and evaluation; direct relevance to the outside world; and an organizational leadership culture that is open-minded and boundary-crossing.

Charles Landry (2006)

▶ Urbanism is part of a larger whole of socio-economic, socio-political, and socio-technical endeavours, that should be shared, but with a clear and concise delineation of roles and responsibilities, through which urbanists can define and exercise their professional prerogatives.

Taking a more **reflective perspective** and approach to the professional practice of urbanism:

▶ Urbanists, through the advancement of their professional practice, should take the opportunity to step back somewhat from their profession to better step forward.

▶ Although they advocate a context sensitive practice of urbanism, often urbanists do not deliver, as attested by the poor results in the planning, designing and developing of many parts of cities.

▶ What is required is a more thoughtful approach to the future of cities, where urbanists can be seen taking a professional stand for quality outcomes, and help to put in place practices and processes that can bring more context sensitive, more appealing, and more value-based interventions.

▶ The broader use of design reviews, improvements to how projects are planned and managed as well as the budgeting process of projects, are some of the means that can help push the envelope of quality results in the planning, designing and developing of cities.

Fostering and promoting a more **creative and innovative** practice of urbanism:

▶ The tools, methods and processes of the professional practice of urbanism often come under criticism and attack.

▶ It is often argued that these tools, methods and processes have not always followed the evolution of society (zoning is often cited in this regard) and do not meet the requirements for the sophisticated, complex contemporary planning, designing and development of cities.

▶ Obviously, such criticisms and attacks do not reflect some of the advances in the practice of urbanism, consisting more often than not in manœuvres to side-step the rigorous requirements for the planning, designing and development of cities.

▶ Nevertheless, the professionals of urbanism would do well to invest more energy and effort in the ongoing search for more creative and innovative tools, methods and processes, including their roles as advocates for legislative change provincially.

▶ As for tools and methods, the broader use of "gradients" (such as the "transect" in new urbanism), "thresholds" (range in densities and carrying capacities), "linkages" (such as the transportation/ land use, health/urban development, fiscal framework/planning, development and governance policies, and energy/urban development nexuses), "overlays" (such as heritage, environmental, mixed-uses ones) and "forms-based codes" (as an alternative to traditional zoning), constitute some examples that warrant more reflection and inquiry.

▸On the procedural front, the recognition of the importance of linking awareness, appreciation and engagement in the design of participatory processes is one insight that could be further examined by urbanists; the recourse to greater experimentation, and trial and error (such as the use of metaphors in visioning processes) should also be more widely promoted in the practice of urbanism.

Prioritizing more **accountability** in the practice of urbanism:

▸While practitioners of urbanism have individual accountability regimes, in consideration of the special importance of the practice of urbanism for the future of Canada and its cities, the establishment of a professional system of accountability, echoing and complementing the values and ethics code of practice, should be investigated.

▸As noted above, the results of the practice of urbanism are not always aligned with society's best interests and with professional leading practices.

▸While urbanists can certainly not be entirely faulted for such poor outcomes, they do share some of the responsibility, and perhaps by strengthening and clarifying the definition of this responsibility and reporting more consistently on its exercise, the profile and value of the work of urbanists and,

of urbanism more generally, could be enhanced and their credibility increased.

▸The importance of such a performance-based approach to the practice of urbanism takes on an added meaning and dimension when considered in light of the key role of the urbanist in achieving a critical mass for the change of the awareness, appreciation and engagement of Canadians toward their cities, and crafting win-win-win approaches and solutions in charting the future course of urbanism in Canada.

▸The possible performance indicators that could ensure the grounding and the conditions to make operational the proposed accountability regime could include: to what extent the citizens of Canadian cities are positioned at the centre of their planning, designing and developing; also, the level of advocacy and direct contribution of the professionals of urbanism in achieving more context sensitive development, in line with professional leading practices; and finally, the degree of openness and transparency of urbanists in reporting on their professional practice, e.g., such as web-based registries that could outline annual professional activity highlights.

The linkages between the advancement of the practice of urbanism and the determination and realization of Canada's urban agenda require special attention, for obvious reasons. The urbanists, both as key contributor and key stakeholder of the urban agenda, can be looked

The key is to transform regulations, especially zoning, from an exercise in separating land uses and constraining development to a culture of managing complex mixes of intensive development that will facilitate results consistent with good urban design principles and plans.

Larry Beasley (2003)

Those urban regions where ... experimentation is given the most latitude, where the profound challenges of urban sustainability are seen as opportunities rather than crises, will emerge as the economic winners of the 21st century.

John Lorinc (2006)

upon to play an important leadership role. They would be expected to act as a model for other constituencies, and also model and evolve their practice upon the orientation, policies and consensus arrived at during the urban agenda process.

Accordingly, in the context of the practice of urbanism, the urban agenda can be conceived as a "place for dialogue, experience, and learning" about cities. This reflects the dynamic nature of the inter-relationships between urbanism and charting a course for the future of cities in Canada, and at the same time, signalling the pedagogical requirements inherent in moving a professional practice into a new and often uncharted terrain. This suggests a fifth and final area of inquiry in the context of the re-definition of the urbanist's practice.

Reviewing how **knowledge management, succession planning, and learning strategies** are approached and handled in the practice of urbanism:

> ▸Urbanists have developed, over time, a rich body of knowledge that includes, among other elements, values, principles, theories, guidelines, and leading practices as well as strong and influential professional institutions such as the Canadian Institute of Planners (CIP).

> ▸While this body of knowledge is not necessarily the subject of a broad consensus among practitioners of urbanism, it should, nevertheless, command a certain level of support and respect for the purpose of guiding and steering the evolution and improvement of the profession, and ensuring that

its transmission from generation to generation of urbanists is organized and delivered as effectively and efficiently as possible.

▸As such, the profession must, as a matter of priority, determine the best approaches to maintain and nurture the urbanist's body of knowledge; consideration could focus on the role of annual professional gatherings, the establishment of professional *observatoires*, e.g., associated with universities, they could conduct on an ongoing basis "environmental scans" of the profession and its practice, and the formalization of an "urbanism body of knowledge" (UBOK — similar to the Project Management Institute PMBOK).

▸The appropriate management of succession in the practice of urbanism — throughout the career paths of urbanists — is another important underpinning to the positive and enlightened evolution of the profession.

▸Toward managing career paths more formally and proactively, coaching and mentoring activities and programs constitute appropriate succession initiatives.

▸The youth in the practice of urbanism — either as apprentices or as beginners — should represent a segment of the profession of urbanism that is provided with special attention; the close links between the Canadian Association of Planning Schools and CIP is a positive contribution to this goal.

▶Nurturing the development of young urbanists, through professional probationary programs or professional skills and competency-enhancing activities, is not only key to the successful succession planning strategy, but also fundamental to the long-term health and sustainability of the profession.

▶As part of the evolving culture of Canada, and as a means to diversify and enrich the profession, the appropriate and timely integration of newly immigrated foreign professionals must be another priority segment, for the development of the body of knowledge as well as a cornerstone to a successful succession strategy.

▶Despite being part of the management of knowledge and the planning and management of succession, learning management requires obviously some consideration on its own.

▶While traditional approaches include formal educational and training programs as well as professional development programs, the evolution of the profession, in the context of the requirements of Canada's urban agenda, will call for innovative learning approaches — not separate or distinct from the practice — but subsumed in the day-to-day work of the urbanist.

▶In this particular learning context and environment, the role of outreach activities, collaboration with colleges and universities, the priority given to experimentation, the use of technologies and new media, and the focus on greater accountability in the work of the urbanist will become key components of an expanded learning strategy.

In reference to the "public place for dialogue, experience and learning" previously proposed as a useful interface between the profession of urbanism and the determination and realization of Canada's urban agenda, each urbanist, through his/her professional practice, will be making a distinct contribution toward its meaning, its ongoing actualization, and its transformation over time.

The writing of these reflections represents one contribution on my part toward the enactment of this "public place for dialogue, experience, and learning". Hopefully, the ideas, insights and proposals contained herein will help the advancement of the profession of urbanism and support positively and proactively Canada's urban agenda

PLACE FOR DIALOGUE, EXPERIENCE AND LEARNING

Two final notes address specific engagement processes: the steering of controversial initiatives and advocating for a planning constituency. These reflect the role of the urbanists in helping to resolve conflicts in communities and in nurturing the support of key stakeholders to successfully bridge the short-term and long-term planning, development and governance of cities and regions. They are based on my professional practice.

A true learning city develops by learning from its experiences and those of others. It is a place that understands itself and reflects upon that understanding — it is a reflexive city. Thus the key characteristics of the learning city is its ability to develop successfully in a rapidly changing socio-economic environment.

Charles Landry (2006)

Viewpoint:

Steering Controversial Initiatives

As generally accounted for and described in the planning/ urbanism literature, controversial situations should definitely be exceptional in nature rather than frequent in occurrence. While in my professional experience controversies have indeed been few and far apart, they have nevertheless taken unexpected dimensions in relation to what the conventional wisdom would appear to suggest. More importantly, they have opened up my eyes to aspects of the practice of urbanism that are clearly instructive and of significance for the lives of communities as well as the evolution of the profession.

In the early 1980s, the Quebec government began the implementation of a new planning legislation requiring all municipal governments to put in place a comprehensive planning framework for the territory under their jurisdiction. This legislation also created a new governance level in municipal affairs, the regional county municipality (RCM). In light of the environmental issues and risks prevalent at the time in less urbanized areas — especially in non-municipally serviced areas and along shorelines — the first order of business for RCM was the adoption and application of an interim control by-law that set strict guidelines over municipal development activities, including minimum lot size, standard distances between water wells and septic systems, and minimum separation between buildings and rivers and lakes shorelines.

Working for one of the 95 RCMs established by the planning legislation, I was mandated to write and oversee the implementation of such an interim by-law. The public and the political reaction to these new rules was very intense, as was to be expected, and altered in

important ways the atmosphere and relationships in the course of planning decisions. Through a collaborative effort with the mayors of the nine municipalities making up the Council of the RCM of La-Rivière-du-Nord and their planning staff, as well as through extensive public consultation sessions, I helped to generate greater awareness of the problems underlying the need for such strict measures and to start the difficult transition to a whole new governance context. While change did not occur overnight and resistance proved very difficult to overcome in certain municipalities, my work showed me the merit of concise and well articulated communication strategies and tools in reaching out to the different stakeholders and, perhaps more importantly, the virtue of flexible and progressive approaches in addressing the root causes of such resistance.

In 1983, almost a decade in the making, a revitalized and transformed western end of Rideau Street, immediately east of the Rideau Canal, began a new stage in its eventful evolution in downtown Ottawa. Combining a major internalized shopping concourse (Rideau Centre), a hotel belonging to an international chain (Westin) and a level-3 convention facility (Ottawa Congress Centre), the Rideau Street revitalization project clearly aimed at repositioning this area as one of the main commercial magnets in Canada's Capital Region (CCR). Designed as a bus mall, the "new Rideau Street" had its sidewalks enclosed in glass, as a way to create a more comfortable environment for the bus riders and at the same time, ease the transition of the shoppers into the internalized retail environment of Rideau Centre. Unfortunately, the enclosed Rideau Street failed to deliver the benefits intended and instead gradually became a negative force for the commercial vocation of downtown Ottawa. The combination of a poor image — the result mainly of safety and security concerns of the users — and a rapidly deteriorating physical environment, led to early calls for the removal of the glass enclosures.

When I joined the City of Ottawa, Planning Department in 1990, the Rideau Street Enclosures Removal Project had already been initiated. I undertook to coordinate all the planning activities needed to provide the necessary conditions that could help return Rideau Street to its original vocation and physical conditions. While the different stakeholders generally agreed on the overall objective for the Rideau Street Project, the approach to implementation became a source of significant conflict between the City of Ottawa and the building/property owners and members of the Rideau Street Business Improvement Area (BIA) — the cost sharing formula being at the centre of the conflict. My involvement toward the resolution of this controversial situation demonstrated, more particularly, the benefit of using a third party expert in conflict resolution in order to better understand the interests of the other party in the dispute, develop alternative communication channels that can ease the identification of possible avenues of solution, and maintain throughout the negotiation process a positive and proactive perspective and engagement approach that can facilitate the eventual determination of a negotiated solution. The conflict resolution process did deliver a "made in Ottawa" solution, allowing the demolition work to proceed and avoiding the costly intercession of the Ontario Municipal Board.

In the late 1990s and early 2000s, the National Capital Commission (NCC) advanced several projects that were met with a great deal of opposition. Throughout its storied history, spanning over a hundred years, the commission has acted as an important "change agent" in CCR, principally through its visions for the capital and the implementation of its plans. As a result, it is definitely no stranger to

controversy and in some instances, such as with the establishment of the National Capital Greenbelt, its decisions and actions have been challenged in front of judicial tribunals, including all the way to the Supreme Court. However, some of the more recent controversial undertakings differed in that they never went beyond the conceptual stage, having been stopped not by judicial decisions but instead in the court of public opinion. As NCC Planning Director, I was called upon to manage these initiatives/projects under very demanding and challenging professional circumstances. That these controversies would have a negative effect on the reputation of the NCC was a likely outcome. The way they were managed allowed the application of conflict resolution methods and other public participation approaches that helped bring them to appropriate closure or lead to the exploration of other proposals that allowed the NCC to reach out in a positive way to the different stakeholders and start the process of regaining the public trust.

Planning and development processes, by their very attempt at striking acceptable balances and trade-offs between a variety of community interests, are, as a result, inherently susceptible to spikes of public and stakeholder anger, triggering the emergence of passionate debate and controversial situations. The urbanists and other professionals, whether they professionally agree or disagree with any undertaking, are called upon to help resolve these difficult times in the life of communities. It is tempting to consider controversies with some contempt because of the high emotions and conflict they create and generate. But, assuming the necessary communication strategies and conflict resolution mechanisms are in place, they do constitute an essential dimension to urbanism, allowing communities to debate what fundamental values and principles they wish to espouse and adhere to, enabling creativity and ingenuity to flow, and informing the boundaries and limits of what development is acceptable and what is not acceptable.

Viewpoint:

Advocating for a Planning Constituency

In carrying out their work, the professionals of urbanism are confronted with a double dilemma. The majority of citizens are generally focused on the immediate aspects and dimensions of their life, and as a result, find it very difficult, if not impossible, to contemplate what the long-term future has in store for them and their communities. Related to this short-term perspective and focus of the citizenry is the political process at all levels of government which emphasizes short cycle agendas and priorities spanning only a few years with only cursory reference and consideration paid to the longer term.

Although certainly not ideal, I have personally accepted that this is the reality with which professional practices have to work. Rather than looking at the future of cities as a "long distance race", it is more productive to approach it as a "relay race" whereby a given generation of the public and their politicians build on the accomplishments of prior generations and "pass on" its legacies as building blocks for the next generations' achievements. Bridging these several generations successfully requires the development and nurturing of a "planning constituency" that enables reaching out to key individuals that will harness the energy and resources to realize the vision and plans of a community over the short-, medium- and even long-term. Some examples of my efforts to build planning constituencies follow.

In Saint-Jérôme region in the 1980s, I was dealing with an area and a city characterized by a very limited planning tradition and community leadership that was operating very much in isolation. Despite the interesting attributes of its location — in the lower Laurentian, to the north of Montreal — and the role of tourism as the main economic engine, there was limited collaboration and cohesion exhibited by regional stakeholders. In consideration of the little synergy to be found among actors in the area for which I had planning responsibilities, it became evident that building some *esprit regional* (regional spirit — I was not familiar with the concept of planning constituency at the time) as a way to underpin urban and regional planning should be a key dimension of my work.

Gradually, in a step-wise fashion, I initiated a number of activities that were intended to put in place the conditions for the emergence of better regional cohesion: close collaboration with municipal officials, constant liaising with regional media, the writing of different popularizing documents dedicated to fostering a better understanding and appreciation of planning, presentations to interest groups and municipal councils, priority given to the revitalization of downtown Saint-Jérôme, and a leadership role in provincial and national planning organizations. The subsequent, post 1980s, evolution of the Saint-Jérôme area, has confirmed the importance for the professionals of urbanism of advocating for a planning constituency in and for their work.

In 1999, the National Capital Commission (NCC) celebrated one hundred years of planning Canada's Capital Region (CCR). Conscious of the symbolic importance of having CCR enter the 21st century in a meaningful and memorable way, the NCC launched an important visioning initiative, with a particular focus on the core area of the capital. Despite the innovative character of the planning proposals and the outreach efforts to include and involve all the key stakeholders, the NCC was confronted with a poor public image, stemming from all those years of cutbacks, some controversial proposals and the public perception of an organization primarily focused on itself, and not very open and transparent in its governance.

With the view to helping overcome this conundrum, I initiated a reflection in the NCC about the lessons to be learned from the successful implementation of the 1950 Gréber Plan (based on the work of David Gordon from Queen's University). Key success factors identified included vision, leadership and the adequate endowment of resources. However, in order for those success factors to imprint any depth and momentum to the planning and development process, a key requirement was also noted: the building over time of a broad-based constituency. The work of the NCC between the late 1950s and the early 1980s in realizing the major proposals contained in the 1950 plan indeed involved nurturing the participation and commitment of several generations of federal elected officials from different political affiliations.

Initially, my efforts at constituency advocacy received positive support and struck a chord. But as the strategy to reach out for the 21st century vision and the implementation of its more specific elements evolved, the focus was placed on the development of a more limited constituency. It proved to be very ephemeral and, as a result, could not provide the necessary "push" to extend our "relay race" in the planning of the capital and its core. With the recent (2006) review of the mandate of the NCC, the need for a sustained, broad-based constituency for the organization and, in particular, for its planning role was reconfirmed.

In furthering our understanding of what constituency building entails, it is useful to use another metaphor: constituency building as "shifting gears", realizing the vision of a community is the result of the cumulative work of many generations of leaders and decision makers. Over the short-, medium- and long-term, progress on implementing the vision will also depend on the interplay of several factors, including evolving political ideologies, shifting power coalitions, the ups and downs accompanying economic cycles with their influence on the investment of public and private resources, and how continuity and change in the development of communities is brought into some kind of balance. The forward, fast-forward or backward thrusts of the action of leaders and decision makers as influenced by the above factors illustrates the dynamic and often unpredictable nature of constituency building. Planning constituencies are absolutely crucial for the long-term sustainability, health and resiliency of communities. In the current governance of cities, sustained planning constituencies are more of an exception than the rule. But in light of the dividends and pay-offs they can contribute to the successful evolution of cities, they clearly need to be pursued diligently and given higher priority.

Saint John

[L]a planification efficace des agglomérations humaines dans les démocraties occidentales va dépendre davantage des contacts humains à l'intérieur du processus décisionnaire que de la compétence des urbanistes et de leur savoir-faire dans la préparation des plans … C'est la qualité des rapports entre les acteurs qui peut faire la différence entre l'échec et la réussite.

Harry Lash (1976)

CHAPTER 14
PULLING IT ALL TOGETHER

A CALL FOR TRANSFORMATION

This last chapter brings our journey along the path to the "projet de société" to a close. The implications of the five priorities and the fourteen action items — the proposed action plan — for charting and implementing an urban agenda will be identified. More specifically, I suggest that the action plan, in fact, fundamentally challenges the *status quo*, calling for a transformation in how cities are perceived and approached in Canada. Four types of transformation are critical:

• transformation of perspective;

• transformation of roles;

• transformation of processes; and,

• transformation of policies.

The consideration of these transformations, each in turn, will allow us to connect the priorities and action items to specific aspects of the urban agenda, discussed in previous chapters, i.e., the notion of synergies (chapter 6), the definition of key collective abilities and the identification of the roles and responsibilities of key stakeholders (chapter 13), the linkages between the action plan and key urban outcomes (chapters 4 and 13), and the determination of policy implications (chapters 8-12).

Transformation of Perspective

Adopting the right perspective or outlook when dealing with complex and distinctive places like urban areas must constitute a *sine qua none* condition for, ultimately, achieving a successful urban transformation. As a starting point, the way we consider and approach the urban phenomenon needs to be holistic, in recognition of the interdependent nature and character of all that is urban. The discovery of a deeper order and meaning — beyond the strict visual and physical — and the determination of a unified field of inquiry — corresponding to a convergent rather than divergent/fragmented approach to urban diagnoses, prognoses and syntheses — is crucial to the establishment of a shared understanding of the urban reality by all participants and stakeholders of the urban agenda. Fostering top-down/bottom-up and lateral/horizontal perspectives and approaches to the planning, development and governance of urban areas — instead of a hierarchical world-view — must play a big part in substituting an ecological/empowerment paradigm for a control/bureaucratic paradigm.

How the different dimensions or aspects of the urban reality interrelate and work together — the notion of synergy — is a good example of the application of perspective to the urban agenda. The identification of such synergies must constitute an important determinant of Canada's urban future. **Table 1** identifies the strength of relationships — high, medium and low — between the fourteen action items. Through the determination of such synergies between the components of the proposed action plan, it becomes possible to define and refine how the different components of the urban agenda are combined and brought together.

Table 1
Synergies Between the Proposed Actions

Legend: ◎ High ● Medium · Low

	1. Land Use and Transportation	2. Urban Development and the Environment	3. Citizenship in Cities	4. Professional Work in Cities	5. Life-Cycle Perspective and Approach	6. Alternative Management Strategies	7. Ubiquitous Creativity and Ingenuity	8. Relations between Generations and Cultures	9. Intergovernmental Relations	10. Communities of Practice	11. Cities and their Surrounding Regions	12. Citizen Houses	13. Citizen Forums	14. Ceremonies and Celebrations
1. Land Use and Transportation	—	◎	●	◎	◎	●	●	●	◎	◎	◎	●	●	·
2. Urban Development and the Environment	◎	—	●	◎	◎	◎	◎	◎	◎	◎	◎	◎	●	◎
3. Citizenship in Cities	●	●	—	●	·	●	◎	◎	●	●	●	◎	◎	◎
4. Professional Work in Cities	◎	◎	●	—	●	●	◎	●	●	◎	●	·	●	◎
5. Lyfe-Cycle Perspective and Approach	◎	◎	·	●	—	●	◎	·	◎	◎	◎	●	·	●
6. Alternative Management Strategies	●	◎	●	●	●	—	◎	◎	◎	◎	◎	◎	●	◎
7. Ubiquitous Creativity and Ingenuity	●	◎	◎	◎	◎	—		◎	◎	◎	◎	◎	◎	◎
8. Relations between Generations and Cultures	●	●	◎	◎	·	●	◎	—	●	●	●	◎	◎	◎
9. Intergovernmental Relations	◎	◎	●	●	◎	◎	◎	●	—	◎	◎	·	●	◎
10. Communities of Practice	◎	◎	●	◎	◎	◎	◎	●	◎	—	◎	●	●	·
11. Cities and their Surrounding Regions	◎	◎	●	◎	◎	◎	◎	●	◎	◎	—	·	●	◎
12. Citizen Houses	●	◎	◎	·	●	●	◎	◎	·	●	·	—	◎	◎
13. Citizen Forums	●	●	◎	●	·	●	◎	◎	●	◎	●	◎	—	◎
14. Ceremonies and Celebrations	·	●	●	◎	·	●	◎	◎	●	·	●	◎	◎	—

Transformation of Roles

Throughout Part III of the book, I have advocated a dialogue over the roles of the different participants involved in the planning, development and governance of Canadian cities. From this dialogue should emerge not only a clearer identification of these roles but also and, importantly, the recognition that distinct prerogatives correspond to sets of distinct responsibilities. It is through this duality of roles and responsibilities that the conversation over Canada's urban future can advance, from more entrenched positions, to a situation more propitious to the recognition of shared interests.

In light of the interdependent and complex character of urban areas, as noted above, ensuring a shared appreciation of roles and responsibilities can, in addition, contribute to the establishment of a collaborative frame of mind that helps recognize that nothing in cities is achieved by "going it alone" but, instead, that anything of any consequence is the result of a spirit of cooperation and coordination, with appropriate dispute resolution mechanisms in the case of differences or conflicts. From such a collaborative frame of mind and spirit can evolve a comfort level in facing and addressing nuances, "shades of grey" characteristic of urban areas — those tangible and intangible, formal and informal elements and processes that need to really drive the charting and enacting of an urban agenda.

Ultimately, what must result from a mastery of roles and responsibilities in an urban context is the emergence of constituencies that can advocate for the urban agenda and the creation of a new culture of decision making and

leadership, one that moves away from hierarchy to espouse a shared and distributed approach to leading in cities.

An essential ingredient to the dialogue on roles and responsibilities and, eventually, to the success of the urban agenda, is the definition and honing of selected collective abilities and competencies. The significance of these abilities and competencies can be found in enabling individuals and groups to evolve over time the necessary dispositions for fruitful and results-based collaboration in an urban context.

Tables 2 and 3 represent an attempt on my part to define key collective abilities and identify roles and responsibilities of key stakeholders.

Table 2 identifies five key collective abilities that can help frame the determination and realization of Canada's urban agenda. These abilities are:

- bridging or spanning different realities and interests;

- aligning with or to place in relation of agreement;

- capacity building or to help achieve a pre-determined proficiency;

- managing change or to enable an appropriate and acceptable transition between two or more states of being;

- and learning or to acquire additional knowledge and experience in fields of endeavour.

They should be considered together and not separately, in a dynamic perspective, and within cycles of evolution.

Table 2
Five Key Collective Abilities

Bridging

▶ local and global

▶ cities and regions

▶ long- and short-term

▶ levels of government

▶ citizens and governments/institutions

▶ generations

▶ ethnic groups/cultures

▶ schools of thought

▶ professions

▶ urban development and
the environment

▶ land uses and transportation, etc.

Aligning

▶ visions

▶ public, private, and volunteer sectors

▶ interests

▶ languages

▶ reality and perceptions,
expectations and behaviours

▶ market and regulatory responses

▶ good design and security, etc.

Capacity Building

▶ leadership

▶ collaboration

▶ dialogue

▶ synergy

▶ consensus building

▶ conflict resolution

▶ mediation

▶ participation in decision making

▶ scenario development

▶ risk management

▶ creativity, innovation and ingenuity

▶ partnerships

▶ integration

▶ long-term support networks

▶ accountability

▶ performance measurement, etc.

Managing Change

▶ demographic

▶ level of indebtedness

▶ resource allocation

▶ priority setting

▶ role of citizens

▶ accessible governments/institutions

▶ power and influence

▶ life-cycle management

▶ succession in organizations

▶ service delivery

▶ diversity

▶ resistance to change

▶ governance, etc.

Learning

▶ sharing best practices

▶ new citizenship

▶ coaching and mentoring

▶ ethics in communication

▶ learning to learn/continuous
learning

▶ communities of practice

▶ citizen forums

▶ new ceremonies and celebrations

▶ use of pilot projects

▶ flexibility

▶ adaptability

▶ active versus reactive approaches
to problems

▶ symbolism

▶ community memory as
living memory

▶ approach across organizations
rather than isolated silos

▶ co-evolution

▶ auto-organization

▶ emergence

▶ resilient communities

▶ healthy communities

▶ sustainable communities, etc.

[Ils] scellent chaque année un peu plus les liens entre le Québec et la Région française Rhône-Alpes en abordant des problématiques communes … En une vingtaine d'années, la Région Rhône-Alpes, la deuxième en importance de France, sera devenue un partenaire privilégiée de la Belle Province … À l'origine de cette multiplication des échanges, on trouve la céation du Centre Jacques-Cartier [à Lyon] … pour dynamiser les liens entre les différents milieux — culturel, scientifique, politique … Le Canada et le Québec surtout furent choisis pour assurer une ouverture sur le plan international en raison des liens très forts qui unissaient déjà les villes de Lyon et de Montréal … [D]epuis 1991, la synergie entre les deux rives de l'Atlantique repose aussi sur la participation croisés d'acteurs économiques majeurs … Résultat, en 17 ans d'existence, les Entretiens Jacques-Cartier auront permis à pas moins de 12000 conférenciers … de se succéder au fil des 350 colloques organisés devant quelque 40000 auditeurs au total … Les Entretiens Jacques-Cartier … sont des ponts entre des disciplines qui ne se fréquentent pas.

Martin Kouchner (2004)

Building local capacities is as important for the long-term as tailoring funding programs to fit local circumstances.

External Advisory Committee on Cities and Communities (2006)

Resistance must be understood to be a natural and inevitable response to virtually anything that is new or different. It cannot be ignored or avoided without risking disaster. In a diverse, democratic society, resistance cannot be overcome either by rational logic or by force. Neither does resistance have to be merely endured until, somehow, it goes away. It can be dealt with … Members of rapidly and constantly changing organizations can enhance their adaptiveness if they develop their previously unrecognized potentialities. Examples include personal qualities such as tolerance for ambiguity and uncertainty, talent for managing and making use of conflicts, willingness to take risks … empathy, intuition, … and a visionary, future-oriented perspective. If they are to participate in creating — or adapting to — organizational changes, people must master a great many new, unprecedented competencies …

Arthur M. Freedman (1997)

Table 3 identifies the roles and responsibilities of four key stakeholder groups: the public; the politicians; the media; and the community leaders. Their roles (what is expected) and responsibilities (what to account for) should be well defined, be monitored, and be the subject of constant and critical review and communication, in consideration of the importance of these four groups in achieving sustainable, healthy and resilient cities and regions in the medium- to the long-term.

Table 3
Identifying Roles and Responsibilities of Key Stakeholders

PUBLIC

Roles

• Key beneficiary of the work and decisions of governments and institutions;

• As citizens: elected members of Parliament, legislative assemblies, municipal councils, and other elected bodies; participate in varying degrees in the work of democratic institutions (as individuals or through community groups), and pay for public goods and services through taxes and other charges; and,

• As consumers: wish to optimize and maximize their access to public goods and services in response to their needs and aspirations, while seeking to minimize the taxes and other charges they must pay for them.

Responsibilities

For those who already participate in governmental and institutional decision making, and are seeking additional opportunities for involvement:

▸ to broaden their awareness of the public interest, including participation in community-based groups;

▸ to avoid undue polarization and "not-in-my-backyard" reaction; and,

▸ to help reconcile public and private interests through improved decision-making processes, such as consensus building and alternative dispute resolution.

For those who do not currently or usually participate in governmental and institutional decision making:

▸ to reduce the ranks of the silent majority;

▸ to help diminish the gap between opportunities provided for democratic participation and actual involvement; and,

▸ to improve the nature of public debate while increasing the quality of decisions, through their participation in consultations with governments and institutions, in combination with improved public participation processes.

For both participants and non-participants in the work and decisions of governments and institutions:

▸ to commit to the collective resolution of problems and response to opportunities, this consistent with Canadian traditions and values; and,

▸ to seek more information and educational venues — through individual efforts and participation in community groups — about public affairs, adjust expectations, and modify lifestyles consistent with the reality of cities and regions in the 21st century.

Link to the Urban Agenda

The dual roles of the public — as citizens and as consumers of public goods and services — should be brought into a better balance in order to contribute to the efficient use of limited public resources. The public goods and services consumed should also be valued according to their true cost to society. Conditions necessary to increase and enhance the engagement of citizens in the work of governments and institutions need to be put in place.

POLITICIANS

Roles

• Leadership of governments and institutions;

• Advocates: for certain approaches to public affairs and public interest questions, problems and issues, based on political ideology and/or personal priorities; and,

• Champions: of the public interest in Parliament, legislative assemblies, municipal councils, and other elected bodies, with the obligation to serve all constituents in responding to their needs, aspirations and concerns, this irrespective of ideology and political affiliation.

Responsibilities

• To provide vision and inspiration to constituents, other members of the public, and other stakeholders, in advancing, explaining, debating and/or deciding about general and specific public interest questions, problems, issues, and opportunities;

• To act with integrity in representing, communicating, and/or acting upon their beliefs, perspectives and approaches to public affairs and public interest questions, problems, issues and opportunities; and,

• To acquiesce to the monitoring, measurement and evaluation of their performance, not only in the context of electoral processes but also, through more thorough review processes, e.g. public debates on specific issues, report card on level of representation of constituents, etc.

Link to the Urban Agenda

The complexity and difficult choices that will underpin the determination of the urban agenda will require politicians to substitute for strict partisanship more collaborative approaches, ones spanning the political and ideological continuums. Politicians should act also as advocates and champions of the five collective abilities previously identified as key for the realization of the urban agenda: bridging, aligning, capacity building, managing change, and learning.

MEDIA

Roles

• Central conveyors and providers of information on public affairs and governance questions, problems, issues and opportunities, in print or electronic formats, through reporting, opinion pieces, research and analytical work, and other activities;

• Media outlets: mainly the private sector media, with activities commercially oriented and focused; and,

• Media industry: both public and private sector media, as provider of information whereby objectivity, diversity and equity in coverage and perspective are offered to play a critical role in open and accountable governments and institutions.

The Kispiox Music Project ... is only one of many NACO efforts to reach out to young audiences who would'nt ordinarily have access to an orchestra. Another is the Music Bridge ... broadband event ... linking ... students ... by videoconferencing technology. One of the very special things about Music Bridge, aside from the kids learning about music ..., is that they're learning about each other ...

Lara Mills (2004)

The professional journalist's covenant with those who read or hear him or her is central. But its terms have been left vague and undefined. Greater clarification and definition are needed if professional journalists are to discharge responsibility more fully. … [T]he press should take responsibility for performing four functions. The first is a political function. By informing the citizenry of what its government and other centers of power are doing, the press becomes itself an integral part of the political process. By monitoring the centers of power — political, economic, social — the press functions to keep them in check. The second role of the press involves an educational function. It includes reporting on and promoting discussion of ideas, opinions and truths … In this role the press follows the tradition of the town meeting. Third, the press functions as a utility, a conduit of information about what is happening. It operates as the society's "bulletin board". The fourth function is social and cultural. The press holds up a mirror to society and reflects the kind of people we are, shows us our heroes and villains, recalls our shared values.

Louis W. Hodges (1986)

Responsibilities

- For those media involved in public affairs, strive to provide:

  ▸ sound reporting: by communicating the facts, ensuring that different points of view are heard, and encouraging as objective and balanced a coverage as possible;

  ▸ balanced understanding: by communicating analyses of problems, questions, issues and opportunities, within their proper context, detailing their different aspects and helping readers, listeners and/or viewers form an opinion and a judgment; and,

  ▸ enlightened orienting: by communicating possible solutions, looking at alternatives, their advantages and disadvantages, and supporting public debate and public decision making.

- To promote and foster the emergence of a new "ethics in communications" that could allow for the debate of both individual and community-wide positions and interests, so that when decisions are made, they actually reflect the values of respect, fairness and order, and help meet the goals of efficiency, effectiveness, equity and sustainability.

- To help create greater public awareness, comfort and commitment in participating in public affairs.

Link to the Urban Agenda

The definition, determination and realization of Canada's urban agenda will call for the provision of information in a responsible manner by the media that voluntarily balances their private and public interest roles, so that public debates and public decisions support the long-term sustainability, health and resiliency of cities and regions.

COMMUNITY LEADERS

Roles

- From the business, volunteer/NGO, professional, academic and public sectors: speak to the diversity of circumstances, needs and aspirations in communities, and of alternative approaches;

- Represent, on their own or through their organizations, the social, economic, cultural and environmental interests, among others, of the communities; and,

- Participate, through different forums, in discussions and debates, and support decision making in public affairs.

Responsibilities

- To provide alternative sources of community leadership in the debates and decisions on public affairs;

- To forge new and innovative community partnerships with other stakeholders that can advance the definition and realization of the shared vision and common interests of cities and regions; and,

- To support politicians in promoting the five collective abilities identified as key for the definition and realization of the urban agenda.

Link to the Urban Agenda

The citizen-centred, decentralized, and network-based approaches to the definition and realization of the urban agenda will demand a distributed community leadership, evolving at all governance levels and in all societal sectors of cities and regions.

Transformation of Processes

Evolving Canada's urban agenda must first and foremost reflect an orientation and predisposition to the awareness, appreciation and engagement required of Canadians living in an urban world. Charting and eventually enacting our urban agenda will require a capacity and ability to step back when considering the needs, aspirations and requirements of Canadians and their communities, this in order to be able to move forward confidently and competently.

Changes in perceptions and behaviours will constitute key prerequisites to evolving the awareness, appreciation and engagement of citizens. As counterpoint to this important breakpoint in the reality of Canadians, incentives of different sorts — fiscal, financial, regulatory, legal, market-based, value-based — will have to be given careful consideration and be progressively put in place as the components of the urban agenda are gradually advanced.

Charting and implementing an urban agenda in Canada will also demand the "breaking of boundaries" — political, legal, social, fiscal and financial, environmental, professional, etc. — that will rely and depend on open, inclusive and transparent processes of dialogue and decision making. Acknowledging the many transitions that will represent the urban agenda in the life of citizens, institutions and organizations, the continuum of "dialogue, experience and learning" will constitute an important facet of "managing change" in urban Canada.

Other key characteristics of this transformation of processes in the context of Canada's urban agenda include:

- the cumulative effects of "small actions" and the importance of selected "big moves";

- the value accorded to discovery, trial and error, the acceptance of failure and the management of risk;

- the importance of integrated and harmonized approaches, leading away from "silos" and advancing a more consensual approach to priority decisions; and,

- more of a proactive rather than reactive outlook for the future of urban Canada.

A final important process requirement of the urban agenda will be a clear link between the proposed action plan and well-articulated urban outcomes and results (as proposed in chapter 4). This essential linkage will need to be underpinned by a performance-based approach to the planning, development and governance of cities that must include an accountability regime for all leaders and decision makers.

Figure 3 and tables 4-8, found at the end of the chapter, illustrate such a linkage framework. Integrating the end-state goals of sustainability, health and resiliency, the fourteen action items are related to five categories of urban outcomes and their associated result areas: natural environment, built environment, communities, institutions and economies. Through this linkage framework, the contribution of the proposed action plan to the urban agenda is clarified and brought to light and life!

Transformation of Policies

The transformation of policies in relation to Canada's urban agenda must underscore a basic notion about urban areas: not an individuals' life domain, rather as a "shared commons" for the benefit of all. The "shared commons" paradigm needs to be accented and supported by an

Leadership ... is direction ... It is direction in that it is ultimately geared towards action. But leadership will be effective and real only if the direction makes sense with respect to a given situation, to what the moment ... demands ... [L]eadership [can be analysed] in terms of three elements which ... are the "diagnosis" — the phase during which the leader grasps the situation intellectualy and assesses what has to be redressed; the "prescription" of the course of action — designed to meet [the] problems or ... [the] conclusion ... based on advice ... [of] what the better course of action should be; and the "mobilization" of those who will be involved in ensuring that the action does take place — ... subordinates ... the population as a whole or ... the fraction of the population that is relevant to the course of action ... [Political] leadership is always more than analyses and decision making: it consists also in affecting the minds and energies of those who have a part to play in the implementation.

Jean Blondel (1987)

evolving political culture, where "politic" is construed as "the art to determine the public interest amid the collision and collusion of individual/particular interests". Emerging policies for the planning, development and governance of cities must involve the consideration, in a rigorous and thoughtful manner, of all upstream and downstream aspects and facets as well as all cumulative effects and implications of proposals, projects and other initiatives.

The realization of an urban agenda must also invoke a shift from a basic management approach to cities to a higher-end notion of stewardship, that can better bridge the different realities of cities.

Additional policy considerations in charting and enacting an urban agenda include:

• the inclusion of leading practices premised not on a monolithic outlook at urban problems and opportunities, rather as an ensemble of building blocks that iteratively and cumulatively can inject new insights, a renewed foresight and serve as sources of new collective energies;

• the evolution of a "unifying force" that underlies the concepts of "shared understanding" and "shared commons" that were seen as central tenets of an urban agenda;

• the progressive development of an "ethics of communications" that can help highlight and focus the public interest in all decisions made in and for cities; and,

• the special attention that "urban diversity" and "urban creativity" must command toward charting and enacting Canada's urban agenda.

Table 9, found at the end of this chapter, addresses the policy implications of the fourteen action items taken

separately. When envisaged as a policy ensemble, the proposed action plan does advance a comprehensive program for charting and enacting Canada's urban agenda. Furthermore, combining perspective, roles, processes and policy transformation with the five categories of urban outcomes identified above, the contours of the central tenet advocated in this book emerges: a "projet de société" for the future of Canada and its cities.

CYCLE OF TRANSFORMATION

The implementation of the proposed action plan should not be envisaged in a strictly static manner. To the contrary, reflecting the inherent characteristics of urban areas that are in constant flux and evolving, it needs to be seen within dynamic interplay, over time, between perspective, roles, processes and policies with the achievement of sustainable, healthy and resilient natural and built environments, communities, institutions and economies. Our call for transformation is fundamentally a trigger point for launching, maintaining and nurturing a cycle of change along the path to the "projet de société".

Diagram 3 illustrates the complete journey towards the "projet de société". Anchored in the vision, the five priorities and fourteen action items — the action plan — constitute key proposals for charting and enacting Canada's urban agenda. At the apex of the path, the cycle of transformation — illustrated by the "infinity" notation — conveys the ongoing dynamic nature of the implementation of this action plan. Completing the diagram is the continuum of "awareness, appreciation and engagement" that reinforces the development on the part of Canadians of a world-view of their cities, through changes in their perceptions and behaviours.

Figure 3
Linkages Between the Suggested Action Plan and Key Urban Outcomes

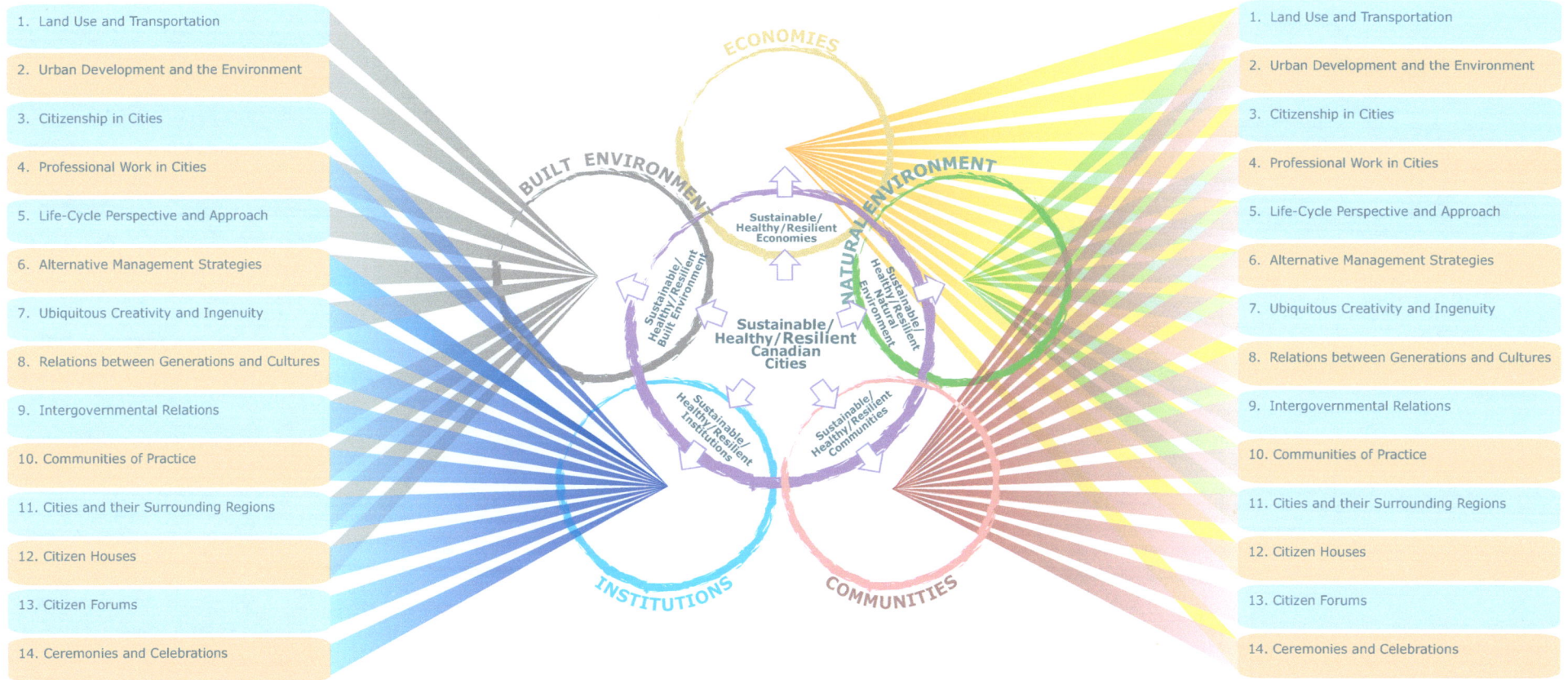

1. Land Use and Transportation
2. Urban Development and the Environment
3. Citizenship in Cities
4. Professional Work in Cities
5. Life-Cycle Perspective and Approach
6. Alternative Management Strategies
7. Ubiquitous Creativity and Ingenuity
8. Relations between Generations and Cultures
9. Intergovernmental Relations
10. Communities of Practice
11. Cities and their Surrounding Regions
12. Citizen Houses
13. Citizen Forums
14. Ceremonies and Celebrations

ECONOMIES

BUILT ENVIRONMENT

NATURAL ENVIRONMENT

Sustainable/Healthy/Resilient Economies

Sustainable/Healthy/Resilient Built Environment

Sustainable/Healthy/Resilient Natural Environment

Sustainable/Healthy/Resilient Canadian Cities

Sustainable/Healthy/Resilient Institutions

Sustainable/Healthy/Resilient Communities

INSTITUTIONS

COMMUNITIES

1. Land Use and Transportation
2. Urban Development and the Environment
3. Citizenship in Cities
4. Professional Work in Cities
5. Life-Cycle Perspective and Approach
6. Alternative Management Strategies
7. Ubiquitous Creativity and Ingenuity
8. Relations between Generations and Cultures
9. Intergovernmental Relations
10. Communities of Practice
11. Cities and their Surrounding Regions
12. Citizen Houses
13. Citizen Forums
14. Ceremonies and Celebrations

Table 4
Linkages Between the Suggested Action Plan and Key Urban Outcomes — Built Environment

Abbreviations

LU & T	Land Use and Transportation
UD & E	Urban Development and the Environment
C in C	Citizenship in Cities
PW in C	Professional Work in Cities
LCP & A	Lyfe-Cycle Perspective and Approach
AMS	Alternative Management Strategies
UC & I	Ubiquitous Creativity and Ingenuity
RbG & C	Relations between Generations and Cultures
IR	Intergovernmental Relations
C of P	Communities of Practice
C & SR	Cities and their Surrounding Regions
CH	Citizen Houses
CF	Citizen Forums
C & C	Ceremonies and Celebrations

Key Urban Outcomes	Suggested Action Plan													
	Connections				Resources			Genera-tions	Collaboration			Institutions		
	LU & T	UD & E	C in C	PW in C	LCP & A	AMS	UC & I	RbG & C	IR	C of P	C & SR	CH	CF	C & C
Built Environment														
The physical footprint of cities has been reduced through increased intensification of land uses	●	●		●	●	●	●		●	●	●	●		
Mixed uses account for an increased share of new development	●	●		●	●	●	●		●	●	●			
Densities reflect sensitivity, not only to the economic value of lands, but also to human scale and their local impacts	●	●		●			●		●	●	●	●		
Quality of design is not only inspired but also inspires a sense of identity, helps contrast the public from the private realms, and contributes to a positive civic image	●	●		●	●	●	●		●	●	●			
Land uses are integrated with accessible, affordable and energy efficient transportation	●	●		●	●	●	●		●	●	●			
Public transit is accessible at less than 10 minutes on average from all residential and employment areas	●	●		●		●			●		●			
Modal share of public transit has increased over recent years relative to private vehicles	●	●		●		●			●		●			
Transport demand management measures constitute a key stewardship strategy at the majority of major employment centers	●	●		●		●	●		●	●	●			
Cultural, heritage and/or archeological resources are preserved and/or rehabilitated	●	●		●	●	●	●		●	●	●	●		
Universal accessibility is a standard feature of all development projects	●	●		●	●	●	●		●	●	●	●		
Use of green construction and green technologies is a standard feature of all development projects	●	●		●	●	●	●		●	●	●	●		

Table 5
Linkages Between the Suggested Action Plan and Key Urban Outcomes — Natural Environment

Key Urban Outcomes	Suggested Action Plan													
	Connections				Resources			Generations	Collaboration			Institutions		
	LU & T	UD & E	C in C	PW in C	LCP & A	AMS	UC & I	RbG & C	IR	C of P	C & SR	CH	CF	C & C
Natural Environment														
Watersheds constitute a key territorial reference unit in the planning, development and governance of cities and regions	●	●		●	●	●	●		●	●	●			
The ecological integrity of natural ecosystems is protected	●	●		●	●	●	●		●	●	●			
Natural areas are protected from encroachment and development	●	●		●		●	●		●	●	●			
Prime agricultural lands are protected and their re-designation for urban uses strictly limited or prohibited	●	●		●	●	●			●	●	●			
Local food is provided and supplied to markets	●	●		●	●	●			●	●	●			
Surface and ground water supplies are legally protected	●	●		●	●	●	●		●	●	●			
Public access to shorelines is allowed with an on-going monitoring of negative impacts	●	●		●			●		●	●	●			
Urban development uses context-sensitive, storm-water management methods	●	●		●	●	●	●		●	●	●			
Urban development is respectful of the sounds of nature and minimizes the level of ambient noise	●	●		●			●		●	●	●			
Urban development minimizes the production of CO$_2$ and other greenhouse gases while fostering the maintenance of an air of quality	●	●		●	●	●	●		●	●	●			
Urban development emphasizes renewable energy sources and minimizes the production of ambient light through the protection of the dark sky	●	●		●	●	●	●		●	●	●			
Urban development fosters a water consumption regime maximizing recycling and re-use measures	●	●		●	●	●	●		●	●	●			
Urban development enables the recycling and re-use of urbanized lands, including soil decontamination through brownfield sites decontamination	●	●		●	●	●	●		●	●	●			

Table 6
Linkages Between the Suggested Action Plan and Key Urban Outcomes — Communities

Key Urban Outcomes	Suggested Action Plan													
	Connections				Resources			Genera-tions	Collaboration			Institutions		
	LU & T	UD & E	C in C	PW in C	LCP & A	AMS	UC & I	RbG & C	IR	C of P	C & SR	CH	CF	C & C
Communities														
Supply of land provides for short and longer term housing needs	●	●		●	●	●	●		●	●	●			
Range of housing types and tenures made affordable to people at different income levels	●		●	●	●	●	●	●	●	●	●			
Development of housing reflects proximity between employment and residential areas, also supports public transportation and other non-automobile transportation	●	●		●		●	●		●	●	●			
Efforts are coordinated among concerned stakeholders to address and reduce homelessness	●		●	●	●	●	●	●	●	●			●	
Discussions between generations and cultures occur on an on-going basis at work and in communities			●	●		●	●	●	●	●		●	●	●
Immigrants receive their work permit and/or professional accreditation in a timely manner			●	●				●	●	●				
Children have their basic needs and aspirations looked after			●	●		●	●		●	●			●	
Minorities, including aboriginal people, are full members of communities and an integral part of the working of governments and institution			●	●			●	●				●		●
Range of community facilities responsive to both local and external needs and aspirations	●	●	●	●	●	●	●	●	●	●	●	●		
Community facilities help shape the urban form and contribute to the quality of life, of the environment, healthy living and lifestyles	●	●		●	●	●		●	●	●	●	●		●
Community facilities contribute to community economic development, as key component of their tourism infrastructure	●	●		●	●	●		●	●	●	●			
Community facilities as contributor to the safety and security of communities	●	●	●		●	●	●	●	●			●		●
Community facilities express and reflect community values	●	●	●			●	●	●		●		●		●
Planning and development of community facilities based on public discussions while shaping local identity and mirroring the local diversity	●	●	●	●		●	●	●	●			●		●

Table 7
Linkages Between the Suggested Action Plan and Key Urban Outcomes — Institutions

Key Urban Outcomes	Suggested Action Plan													
	Connections				Resources			Generations	Collaboration			Institutions		
	LU & T	UD & E	C in C	PW in C	LCP & A	AMS	UC & I	RbG & C	IR	C of P	C & SR	CH	CF	C & C
Institutions														
Succession management is integral to the operations of all governments and institutions			●	●			●	●	●	●	●	●	●	●
Citizens are involved and engaged in governments' decisionmaking			●	●			●	●	●	●	●	●	●	●
Intergovernmental collaboration is embodied in major decisions and actions in the governance of cities and regions				●			●	●	●	●	●	●	●	●
Dispute resolution is a common method to resolve conflicts			●	●			●	●	●	●	●	●	●	●
Professionals of urbanism collaborate through inter-disciplinary teams and work groups			●	●			●	●	●	●	●			●
Regional planning is a compulsory requirement under provincial planning legislations			●	●			●	●	●	●	●	●	●	●
Content of land-use plans is coordinated between levels of government			●	●			●	●	●	●	●	●	●	●
Integrated intergovernmental online delivery of services is accessible to citizens			●	●			●	●	●	●	●	●		●
An integrated, preventive and holistic perspective structures the delivery of health services			●	●			●	●	●	●	●		●	●
Life-long learning is integrated in all aspects of the operations of governments and institutions			●	●			●	●	●	●	●	●	●	●
Creativity and ingenuity are integrated in all aspects of the operations of governments and institutions			●	●		●	●	●	●	●	●	●	●	●

Table 8
Linkages Between the Suggested Action Plan and Key Urban Outcomes — Economies

Key Urban Outcomes	Suggested Action Plan													
	Connections				Resources			Genera-tions	Collaboration			Institutions		
	LU & T	UD & E	C in C	PW in C	LCP & A	AMS	UC & I	RbG & C	IR	C of P	C & SR	CH	CF	C & C
Economies														
Diversity of employment locations are supported by an adequate supply of lands for a range and mix of office, retail, and industrial uses	●	●		●	●	●	●		●	●	●			
Locations for employment growth are identified and prioritized	●	●		●		●	●		●	●	●			
Vitality of central areas and main streets is maintained and enhanced	●	●	●	●	●	●	●	●	●	●	●	●		●
Planning and maintenance of infrastructure is based on the long view through a life-cycle perspective and approach	●	●		●	●	●	●		●	●	●			
Public investments are increasingly prioritized along or adjacent to public transportation corridors	●	●		●	●	●	●		●	●	●			
Funding and financial incentives are available for the redevelopment of brownfields	●	●		●	●	●	●		●	●	●			
Public incentives combined with market mechanisms support the integration of environmental preservation to urban development	●	●		●		●	●		●	●	●			
Fiscal, financial and regulatory aspects of environmental planning, management and stewardship are fine tuned and the source of incentives	●	●		●	●	●	●		●	●	●			

Table 9
Contours of a "projet de société"

Suggested Action Plan	Key Policy Implications

CONNECTIONS

1.Giving priority to the integration of land uses and transportation infrastructure in the planning, development and governance of Canadian cities –

Making seamless cities, whole cities ...

To create different policy choices in regard to the spatial configuration of cities, the diversity and intensity of urban activities, the scale and scope of infrastructure networks, the modal share of alternative modes of travel, the housing – employment nexus, the use of alternative energy sources, the production of GHG, among others.

2.Linking urban development and the environment through a symbiotic perspective and approach –

Making the integration of the environment to urban development top of mind ...

To put in place the fiscal, financial, regulatory and market conditions and incentives necessary to achieve innovations and trigger new behaviours.

3.Broadening the definition of citizenship to ensure a more meaningful involvement of Canadians in the life of their cities –

Making cities more inclusive and propitious to citizen engagement ...

To foster a more horizontal and proactive governance of cities with priority attention given to the alignment and steering of policy areas that matter in the life of citizens in cities.

4.Fostering an inter-disciplinary perspective and approach by the professionals of urbanism in the planning, development and governance of Canadian cities –

Focusing professionals' work at the interface of their practices ...

To enable greater professional leadership and collaboration through more integrated and unified project and portfolio management.

Table 9 *(continued)*

RESOURCES

5.Espousing a life-cycle perspective and approach in facilities and infrastructure development, stewardship and management –

Building cities with the long view in mind ...

To provide greater predictability in decisions related to resource expenditures over the short, medium and longer term.

6.Using alternative delivery mechanisms in the provision of public goods, services and programs –

Making integration and seamlessness the standard rather than the exception ...

To achieve more effective and efficient use of public resources through the inclusion of a variety and diversity of functions and uses in allocation and program decisions.

7.Envisaging creativity and ingenuity as integral to all operations of the different levels of government –

Making the cities of ideas and imagination ...

To make better use of the creative abilities and skills in public organizations to attract and retain talented people.

GENERATIONS

8.Enhancing the quality of life in the work environment, in communities and for immigrants through inter-generational and inter-cultural dialogue, practice and learning –

Realizing the cities of many transitions and distinctive voices ...

To expand wealth generation in organizations, institutions and communities through the systematic transfer of knowledge, the sharing of memories and the enrichment of people's life achieved by more encompassing and valued relations between generations and cultures.

COLLABORATION

9.Renewing inter-governmental relations through new governance structures and processes that recognize Canadian cities as full partners –

Empowering cities in an increasingly urban world ...

To bring inter-governmental relations to a new level of understanding and practice through the creation of an urban federalism reflecting closer collaboration and coordination between senior levels of government and municipalities.

10.Expanding the scope and range of inter-governmental collaboration through the use of communities of practice for the planning, development and governance of Canadian cities –

Experimenting our ways to urban solutions ...

To foster innovation from the different levels of government in how they collaborate and jointly plan and deliver goods, services and programs to Canadians.

11.Focusing the collaboration between Canadian cities and their surrounding regions on the governance of the environmental commons that they jointly share –

Viewing whole what is often considered apart ...

To consolidate and broaden regional planning practices in support of the establishment of a stewardship perspective and approach to resources management.

Table 9 *(continued)*

INSTITUTIONS

12. Creating citizen houses as new symbols of the civic role of citizens and their renewed engagement in the life of their communities and cities – *Putting citizens at the core of cities ...*	To strengthen the sentiment of civic belonging of Canadians through the establishment of destinations and meeting places that can foster the emergence of an urban citizenship.
13. Bringing citizens closer to institutions and other decision-making structures and processes through redefined and expanded citizen forums – *Improving democracy by empowering citizens as change agents ...*	To support a broader and a more direct exposure and involvement of Canadians in the workings of their governments and institutions.
14. Bridging cultural diversity and nurturing common cultural bonds by adding new ceremonies and celebrations to the institutional make-up and fabric of Canadian cities – *Creating stories and myths in the midst of cities ...*	To create new informal and formal places and spaces where Canadians can experience what defines their identity and the cultural richness of their communities and cities.

Diagram 3
Schematic of the Development of the Urban Agenda, Part III

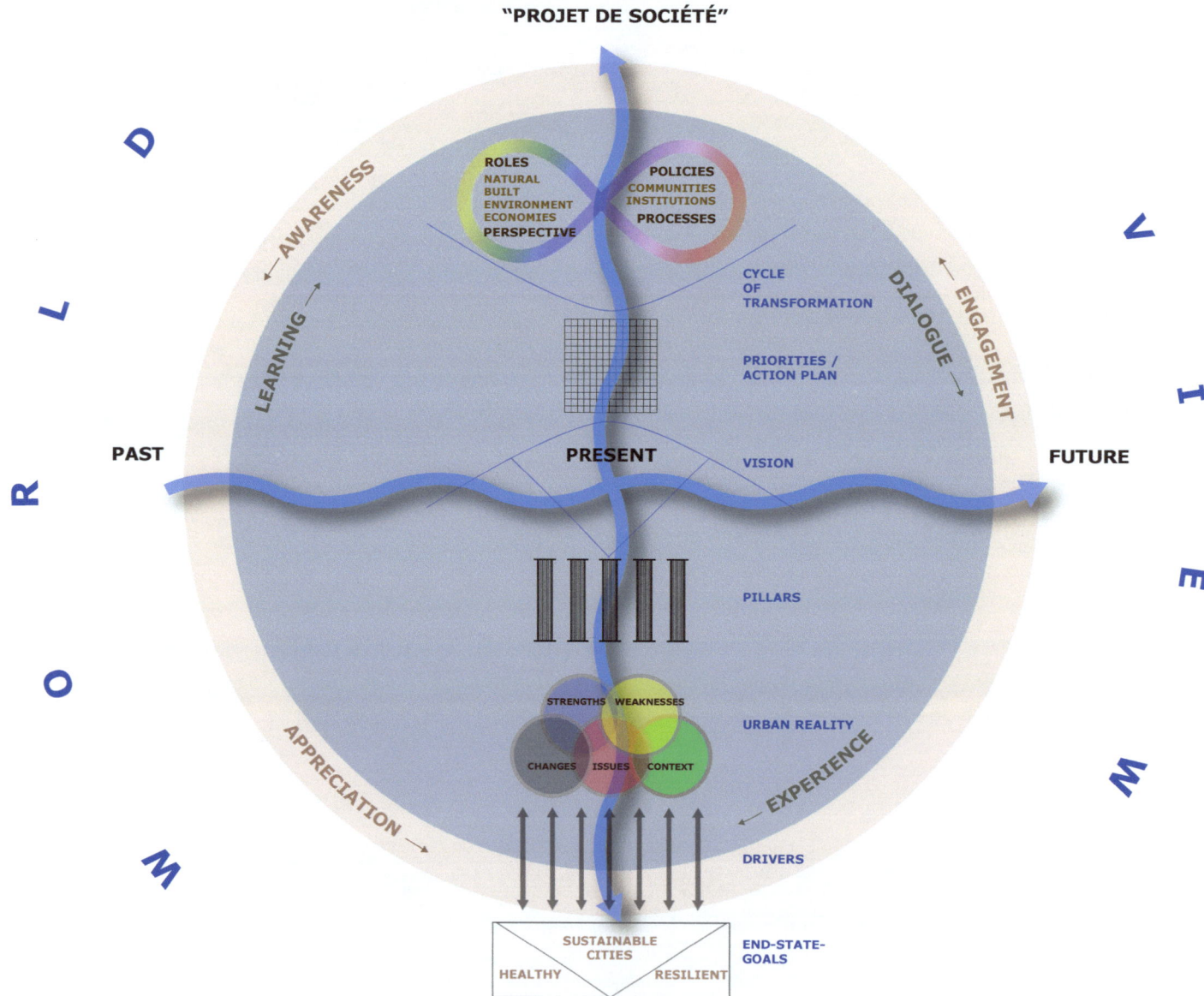

WORLDVIEW

"PROJET DE SOCIÉTÉ"

AWARENESS

DIALOGUE

ENGAGEMENT

LEARNING

ROLES
NATURAL
BUILT
ENVIRONMENT
ECONOMIES
PERSPECTIVE

POLICIES
COMMUNITIES
INSTITUTIONS
PROCESSES

CYCLE
OF
TRANSFORMATION

PRIORITIES /
ACTION PLAN

PAST

PRESENT

VISION

FUTURE

PILLARS

APPRECIATION

STRENGTHS WEAKNESSES

CHANGES ISSUES CONTEXT

URBAN REALITY

EXPERIENCE

DRIVERS

SUSTAINABLE
CITIES

END-STATE-
GOALS

HEALTHY RESILIENT

Yellowknife

[Y]es, the force of technological change sets the challenge which society has to face; but no, there is nothing inevitable about the way society then orders itself. By the same process, technology in its headlong march also creates choices and opportunities; and, faced with those, urban societies can and must decide for themselves the way they want to go.

Peter Hall (1998)

To make ... urbanism work, people must identify with it. It must be vested with meaning and cohere with local culture and values.

Jeb Brugman (2009)

CONCLUSION

WHY AM I CAUTIOUSLY OPTIMISTIC?

I would like to close my reflections, initially, by summarizing the main points developed in the book. Next, key inferences that can be drawn from the reflections will be outlined. Some additional considerations will follow that provide the reader with the elements that I see as essential conditions for the successful transition to sustainable, healthy and resilient cities and regions. In the postface, I offer a poem conveying and describing my aspirations for an ideal Canadian city.

SUMMARY

Canada's urban agenda must address the many changes confronting Canadian cities and regions — demographic, economic, environmental, institutional, etc., as well as their many challenges — urbanization, globalization, aging and health, level of debt, absence of long-term outlook, fiscal and financial situation, democratic participation, climate change, security, etc. But it must also be able to respond to several opportunities, existing and emerging — a diverse population, the mixing of generations, the prospects for life-long learning, Canadians' creativity and ingenuity, promising scientific discoveries, etc.

Canadians, individually and collectively, have risen and responded to the changes, challenges and opportunities that have confronted their society and country in the past. Canadian cities have a degree of comparative advantage in relation to cities in the United States in such areas as their urban form, the mobility of their residents, their community character and cohesion, the quality of their environment, their safety and security, and their governance. If conceived as the "projet de société" for Canada in the early decades of the 21st century,

the urban agenda could be looked upon as a unique and critical means to help define the future of Canada. The pessimism, cynicism and scepticism often expressed and heard when debating and envisioning this future does not reflect and is not informed by the legacies and successes of earlier generations of Canadians.

There appears to be an emerging societal and political consensus concerning the urgency of an urban agenda for the future of Canada. However, when moving from a more conceptual level of consideration to the actual governance of Canadian cities and regions, there is less unanimity, more division, and even conflict. The lack of recognition of cities as a force to be reckoned with in the Canadian intergovernmental, environmental, macroeconomic and socio-economic context and dynamic is a good illustration of a missed opportunity in the recent evolution of Canada's governance. The hesitant approach in embracing key urban outcomes and results in such dimensions as urban form, environmental aspects, physical infrastructure and natural resources areas, etc., also exemplifies the difficulties in charting a proactive urban future. The development of a unifying vision for the future of Canada, as well as its cities and regions, could help overcome these differences, and contribute to the creation of a synergistic force that could bring Canadians closer together in regard to the medium- to long-term outlook of their country.

The future planning, development and governance of Canadian cities and regions can be approached with some cautious optimism. The foundations, on which the urban agenda is to be defined and ultimately realized, are generally sound, e.g., positive urban legacies, good reputation and credibility of Canada, Canadian culture and values. Five pillars have been proposed for the purpose of further anchoring this definition and realization of Canada's urban agenda:

• making Canadians the fundamental reference point in Canada's governance;

• strengthening the role of cities in Canada's federalism;

• providing an appropriate weight to major cities in the governance of the country;

• valuing experimental and unusual processes and solutions; and,

• balancing regulatory, fiscal, market and value-based mechanisms.

In order to achieve consensus, resolve conflicts and counter divisiveness, I believe that the definition, determination and actual implementation of an urban agenda should be based on "key priorities" that can guide/steer the evolution of Canadian cities and do so in an efficient, effective, equitable, orderly and sustainable manner. To each of these priorities can be associated possible action items making up a plan of action in the context of the urban agenda. Five priorities and fourteen action items — bases for the development of urban policies — are put forward:

• **Connections**: looking at issues in terms of their relationships rather than in isolation, i.e., land use and transportation, urban development and the environment, citizenship in cities, professional work in cities;

• **Resources**: balancing the supply and the demand of limited public resources, i.e., life-cycle perspective and approach, alternative management strategies, ubiquitous creativity and ingenuity;

• **Generations**: considering the needs and aspirations of current and future generations and different cultures of decision making, i.e., relations between generations and cultures;

• **Collaboration**: building greater consensus or at a minimum, a climate and ideal conditions for the resolution of differences, i.e., intergovernmental relations, communities of practice, cities and their surrounding regions; and,

• **Institutions**: creating new institutions and symbols in response to the evolving fabric of Canada and its cities, i.e., citizen houses, citizen forums, ceremonies and celebrations.

While the urban agenda must heed the needs, aspirations and concerns of Canadians for the purpose of charting a new course for the country, it must also, and perhaps as importantly, address the performance of all the actors responsible for the response to these needs, aspirations and concerns, and for mapping out this new path for Canada. The ongoing monitoring and reporting on the performance of governments, institutions, managers, professionals and other stakeholders in moving toward and achieving sustainable, healthy and resilient urban development must constitute a key outcome of the urban agenda.

The greater engagement and even central role advocated for citizens in the development and realization of the urban agenda requires a transition from a bureaucratic "top-down" approach to one that is more ecological and "top-down and bottom-up", especially at senior government levels — something based on a network frame for the planning, development and governance of cities. The perspective of life in cities and regions as a constantly shifting "place for dialogue, experience and learning" will have to be communicated, valued and encouraged to take hold in the consciousness of Canadians.

The change and evolution in the perceptions, expectations, behaviours and lifestyles of Canadians that is needed in order for them to fully assume their roles and responsibilities in the emerging societal context will be an important consideration for the successful planning, development and governance of sustainable, healthy and resilient cities. And as a result, it will ensure that the country's international commitments in matters of urban development and the environment are met.

KEY INFERENCES FROM THE REFLECTIONS

Achieving sustainable, healthy and resilient cities and regions will require the provision of sound governance systems, practices and institutions.

Recognizing Canadian citizens as the *raison d'être* of our public governance institutions is very much akin to recognizing the very special place that shareholders occupy in the corporate governance sector: at the pinnacle of organizational interest and consideration.

Sustaining the health of our democracy will depend on the maintenance and nurturing of a lively, vigorous and engaging "political milieu", with the proviso that a qualitative shift takes place: leaving behind the ideological edge that too often characterizes our current political debates, i.e., polarization of issues, and evolving a new political culture and new decision-making forums that put Canadian citizens at the centre of their deliberations.

Governing our country as well as our cities and regions will equally demand a qualitative shift, from a command and control mindset to one of empowerment, based on incentive/disincentive systems, and the crucial notion that distinct domains of responsibility correspond to individual entitlements.

Stewarding Canada's shared commons will benefit from a clear sense of purpose on the part of our governing institutions and their leaders, emphasizing what unites Canadians instead of what divides them.

Evolving new governance systems, practices and institutions must be given a sense of urgency; time is really of the essence in striking the appropriate balance between interests in good governance of Canadian cities.

Describing and implementing Canada's urban agenda must not rest on happenstance and the vagaries of changing times; it must be propelled forward, informed by vision, intention and a unity of purpose around a shared "projet de société".

Conceiving Canada's urban agenda as a substitute to constitutional change, while possible, does not in and of itself constitute the probable path in charting Canada's future governance; the urban agenda as an experiment in governance, with its share of dialogue, experience and learning, more likely and appropriately could lead the way to future evolution and transformation of our constitutional regime.

Advancing Canada's urban agenda as an integrative mechanism across all sectors, levels and regions of Canadian society, must be given clear preference over a menu that is a hodge-podge of disparate and fragmented policies.

Evolving a "made in Canada" urban agenda must stimulate Canadians to stand tall, taking pride and celebrating their achievements, while acknowledging that some areas make them role models; at the same time, they must be ready to look for lessons and leading practices from other people and other places around the world.

Creating not "a one size fits all" but rather "to each community its own" urban action plan must constitute the guiding *leitmotiv* of Canada's urban agenda; in parallel, each community's policy menu should include, in whole or in part, for the short-term or the longer term, five distinct but interrelated priorities: connections, resources, generations, collaboration and institutions.

Playing a leadership role in the enactment of Canada's urban agenda must become each urbanist's first priority; it can be achieved through the development of a "unified field" of professional practices, i.e., by integrating core societal values, values associated with the experience of place, and finally, urban form values, with the needs and aspirations of Canadians throughout the planning and design process as the primary reference point, and by working across political and professional interfaces and/or boundaries.

CONDITIONS FOR SUCCESS

Let me introduce these conditions for success by first noting that discussions on sustainable, healthy and resilient cities and regions are often carried out in technical, scientific, bureaucratic or political terms. Less often are they approached from a human point of view.

As I have observed either explicitly or implicitly throughout the book, urban areas are complex by their nature, and as a result, achieving sustainability, health and resiliency goals involves addressing this complexity. One significant contributor to the complexity is the myriad of human aspects and relationships inherent to the life and reality of urban areas, that dictates to a large extent their development. It is crucial to consider these human factors if we want to be successful in matters of sustainable, healthy and resilient urban areas.

My point is not that these factors are totally ignored now, but that perhaps they are not given sufficient attention. As is often the case

with any complex phenomenon, not giving enough attention or overlooking a single element can have a profound effect on how the whole works, holds together, and is transformed.

Some examples of the human dimension of life in urban areas include:

• how citizens view their day-to-day reality according to different and often conflicting lenses — social focus versus economic focus, individual perspective versus community outlook;

• the existence of forces of change that coexist or conflict with forces of continuity and inertia — globalization versus relative stability of institutions and their processes;

• the different degrees of consciousness that citizens bring to their experience of urban areas — knowledge of how decisions are made, level of participation in public processes;

• the different perspectives of time that exist between citizens and throughout society — time at a personal level versus time from the perspective of institutions.

When I look at the future of Canadian cities and regions, and the requirements that the human dimensions of sustainable, healthy and resilient urban development make on Canada's society and its governance, three distinct but related sets of considerations best capture my outlook and my hopes for urban Canada: areas of evolution, characteristics of a sound governance framework, and management of certain risks.

The first set of considerations relates to **areas of evolution** that can ease significantly the transition to sustainable, healthy and resilient urban development in Canada. Three areas are identified in order of precedence:

1. encouraging a greater awareness by Canadians of the changing reality of their country and especially of the role of cities and regions in this evolution — through education, media, public events;

2. ensuring that, over time, the different levels of appreciation that Canadians exhibit of the organization and working of civic and democratic institutions are narrowed to the greatest extent possible and that they be replaced by a more shared understanding — by illustrating the connections between the different dimensions of cities and regions and their governance, and making them perceptible in the daily life of citizens; and,

3. enabling a broader and more meaningful engagement of Canadians in their civic and democratic institutions — by facilitating how citizens access their institutions and how institutions reach out to citizens in the conduct of their day-to-day activity.

Building on the above areas of evolution, the second set of considerations consists of **key characteristics of a governance framework** that can best ensure the realization of sustainable, healthy and resilient urban development in Canada. Five characteristics are proposed:

1. The need for a defining **vision** for the evolution of cities and regions, one:

    That determines the kind of community we want in the future, including the nature of the relationships that should exist between citizens — values, ethics, culture;

    That helps citizens reconcile the day-to-day and the long view of their community — through consideration of life-cycles as an example;

That reflects the importance of looking at the community in terms of what links their different elements and citizens rather than in isolation — land use and transportation, health and urban development, energy and urban development, education and citizenship; and,

That is clearly articulated and communicated in order that it be shared by citizens — facilitating their understanding, leading them to assume their roles and responsibilities.

2. The need for a shared and distributed community **leadership**, one:

    That articulates, communicates, commits to, and realizes the vision — leaders as "champion" of the vision;

    That can bridge the long view and short-term decisions — translation of the vision into achievable actions;

    That establishes a multi-generation constituency for the realization of the vision over the medium- and long-term — linking community elected officials over many election cycles to ensure some continuity of purpose among the many short-term demands and decisions as well as overcoming forces of inertia; and,

    That transcends the different levels of consciousness that citizens bring to their experience of cities and regions — through top down/ bottom up approaches to decisions, reaching out to the silent majority, ensuring the participation of all interests, and building commitment through partnerships and networks.

3. The need for a **flexible** perspective and approach to the governance of cities and regions, one:

    That envisages cities and regions in terms of nuances, shades of grey, in an open perspective and not in black and white terms, from an ideological perspective or in terms of strict polarities — while mixed uses and higher densities may be the broad objectives, segregated land uses and lower densities can also be considered acceptable in certain areas;

That recognizes that plans and by-laws developed and approved to translate the vision are, in reality, never an absolute true reflection of the evolving reality of cities and regions — a development proposal filed the following day of a plan's approval can be consistent with the vision but in contravention of the plan and existing by-laws;

That acknowledges that priorities will evolve according to the needs and aspirations of citizens and communities but will also depend on internal and external forces that have little to do with the prevailing governance framework — the nature of leadership, the existence of personal agendas, the community power structure, decisions made outside the community's governance structure;

That enables a community's governance structure to deal with a fluid decision-making environment and to balance over time conflicting perceptions, behaviours, and realities — the vision can call for improvements in both the socio-economic and environmental aspects of the community but the leadership at any given time may be pressed to address more important or even conflicting priorities; and,

That allows the evolution of cities and regions to be approached in the context of "continuums" that can enable the capture in space and time of different realities — to ensure appropriate transitions and the establishment of acceptable timeframes, the use of variable regulatory requirements and variable development frameworks depending on the situation of specific communities.

4. The related need for a **progressive** approach to decisions associated with the realization of sustainable, healthy and resilient urban development, one:

That facilitates the necessary adjustments of perceptions and behaviours that are key to the evolution toward the shared vision — starting with a broad awareness of the vision and its importance to the future of the community;

That fosters the emergence of a shared understanding of the vision, which can give rise to a leadership that can guide, eventually, cities and regions toward sustainable, healthy and resilient development;

That eases the efforts of "catalysts" in the community which can involve as early as possible all relevant stakeholders in the process of change and help focus on "small victories" that demonstrate the benefits of certain actions — whether emerging from the public, private or volunteer sectors, the actions and realizations of some individuals can play a determinant role in creating the "spark" toward a more sustainable, healthy and resilient approach to the governance of cities and regions; and,

That values the work of "change agents" to ensure that "learning by doing" is not lost nor forgotten and that whatever is achieved is captured through the building of the community's memories and legacies — monitoring and evaluation become key to community learning and the building of community memories that can contribute to ongoing adjustments in response to changing realities.

5. The need for **innovative governance arrangements** for the purpose of realizing sustainable, healthy and resilient cities and regions, ones:

That provide for the development of leading-edge urban policies that can help steer and push forward the shared community vision and ensure the integration and harmonization of plans, regulations, programs and projects between different levels of government and other stakeholders — coordination between planning priorities and infrastructure investment decisions, between physical and non-physical policy areas;

That allow the establishment of governance and institutional processes that can frame and nurture a distributed community leadership and help connect the different interests and agendas — transition to new collaborative relationships between federal, provincial and municipal levels of government, reflecting the need for 21st century governance decision-making processes; and,

That foster and facilitate the creation of new governance and institutional structures and mechanisms to provide for appropriate decision-making frameworks, help achieve shared understanding, resolve conflict, and contribute to consensus building — the Council of the Federation and the structuring of federal-provincial-municipal collaboration through intergovernmental agreements, such as the Vancouver Agreement, are examples of the capacity of Canadians to create innovative governance or institutional arrangements.

The third and final set of considerations addresses some **risks** that could limit or inhibit the capacity of Canada to successfully make the complete the transition to a sustainable, healthy and resilient urban future. Three risk areas that must be managed and mitigated are noted.

1. Canadians neglect to recognize and accept that the world in which they will live in the next decades will be very different from the one they have grown accustomed to and have experienced in the late 20th and early 21st centuries — transformational change in the areas of demography, economy, environment and technology will result in a much different appreciation and experience of day-to-day life;

2. Canadians, when looking at their futures, tend to focus their attention often exclusively on their situation and fail to appreciate and recognize that circumstances in other countries and continents can and will affect their reality and their capacity to plan for it — the projected high level of poverty in some countries and the reduced availability or even the disappearance in other countries of key resources that Canadians take for granted, such as water and sources of energy, will become key factors in how Canada interfaces with the rest of the world in the future; and,

3. Canadians are becoming too complacent in their appreciation of what they have achieved in the past and how these achievements can support or not their aspirations and shared view of the future — Canadians have always taken a lot of pride in their ability to resolve their conflicts in a relatively peaceful manner, this in comparison to the violence that exists in and afflicts other parts of the world; however, it can be argued that violence can take many forms and that consistent failure by a society to address over time some key issues or areas requiring adjustment or change is in and of itself a form of psychological/intellectual violence, that can undermine the foundations of any society, even one as solid as Canada.

I have tried in my reflections on the future of Canada and its urban areas to put forward many positive and constructive suggestions to further advance Canada's urban agenda. But I also think that not all is well in Canada and the three areas of risk noted above pose for me the greatest threat for the future of Canada and its cities and regions.

Earlier on, I have posited the notion of approaching the urban agenda as a "projet de société" for Canada in the 21st century.

Such an approach could indeed be the key to successfully bringing Canadians together in a shared vision of their country, but they must first find the will and the courage to resolve some of the long-standing difficulties they have had in governing themselves. Achieving a sustainable, healthy and resilient urban future is definitely in the realm of the possible but it will depend ultimately on the resolution of these governance challenges in the short-, medium- and long-term.

Ottawa-Gatineau

What is the city but the people?

Shakespeare, Coriolanus, quoted in Rachelle L. Levitt (2009)

Nothing can stop an idea whose time has come.

Victor Hugo quoted in John Micklethwait (2010)

POSTFACE
MY IDEAL CANADIAN CITY

Let's think about this!

Isn't a great city fundamentally about …
The well-being and prosperity of its people!
Openness to all kinds of influence!
Variety in all its aspects!
Quality of place!
Autonomy to set and realize its destiny!
Its deep-rooted meaning for its citizens!
Constant change!
Its day-to-day reality, with ups and downs! and,
The passage of time!

My Ideal Canadian City
Is indeed such a place
Where Canada loves to congregate
Driven by democratic values and an alliance of three equal
*   governing partners*
Which provides for living at its best and to its fullest
Both origin and destination where Canadians come first.

Let's think about this!

People do make a city
Its physical expression is often a mirror image of their culture,
    spirit, and well-being
Humanity in scale and scope begets friendliness, recognition,
    and also hope
Accessibility reflecting response to needs and fulfillment of dreams

Proximity being heralded and celebrated through memorable
    gestures of good will and warm expressions of welcome
Depth of economic opportunities conveying the breadth of reach
    by the city's prosperity.

My Ideal Canadian City
Is indeed such a place
Where Canada loves to congregate
Driven by democratic values and an alliance of three equal
*   governing partners*
Which provides for living at its best and to its fullest
Both origin and destination where Canadians come first.

Let's think about this!

An open city is like a breath of fresh air
It is similar to having the world at its doorsteps
Letting people move in from all over
Yet allowing them to leave to discover
New ideas and new ways of the world
From those influences they can return and create wonder up close
Or let the city take notice and make it proud from afar.

My Ideal Canadian City
Is indeed such a place
Where Canada loves to congregate
Driven by democratic values and an alliance of three equal
*   governing partners*

Which provides for living at its best and to the fullest
Both origin and destination where Canadians come first.

Let's think about this!

A diverse city is a generous and prosperous city
It is fulfilling for all generations of people, wherever they
    come from
Inclusiveness is a hallmark of its accomplishments
Various urban forms creating appeal and enjoyment
Senses in all those activities finding true wonderment
Choices of lifestyles a drawing card really it is
That provides to all those creative minds a lot of satisfaction
    and merriment.

My Ideal Canadian City
Is indeed such a place
Where Canada loves to congregate
Driven by democratic values and an alliance of three equal
    governing partners
Which provides for living at its best and to its fullest
Both origin and destination where Canadians come first.

Let's think about this!

Quality is the utmost that a city can aspire to
Starting with the life of its citizens at the fore
The design of buildings in harmony with their surroundings in
    and outside of the core
The high achievements of the city in many fields of endeavour,
recognized by peers and others
The transparency and openness of the relations between citizens
    and their institutions

The imperative put on sustaining the environment and
    infrastructures in evolving the city's plans for the future.

My Ideal Canadian City
Is indeed such a place
Where Canada loves to congregate
Driven by democratic values and an alliance of three equal
    governing partners
Which provides for living at its best and to the fullest
Both origin and destination where Canadians come first.

Let's think about this!

An autonomous city is truly a city for which time has come
No longer is inability to decide and realize one's destiny a
    viable regime
A new order is slowly but surely on the rise
Conjuring up a thoughtful and mature leadership style
That Canadians have longed for awhile
With choosing its fate comes to the city the credentials that the
    21st century world calls for
New prerogatives in financial decisions being the beachhead for
    this transformation of the city at its core.

My Ideal Canadian City
Is indeed such a place
Where Canada loves to congregate
Driven by democratic values and an alliance of three equal
    governing partners
Which provides for living at its best and to its fullest
Both origin and destination where Canadians come first.

Let's think about this!

The meaning that a city carries
Is really the soul of that city
Flowing from this are shared feelings of pride and identity
Often it is the credo of leaders in the branding of their city
    to the outside world
But a meaningful city is much more
It is one of an engaged citizenry
They come to appreciate what works for the city and what hurts
    the city
Created is an awareness that they are part of a larger collective
    and universe
Also provided are cues and signals on the battlefield for a
    sustainable, healthy, and resilient future
Really shedding light on what behaviours need alignment with
    what actions to ultimately realize the city's vision.

My Ideal Canadian City
Is indeed such a place
Where Canada loves to congregate
Driven by democratic values and an alliance of three equal
    governing partners
Which provides for living at its best and to its fullest
Both origin and destination where Canadians come first.

Let's think about this!

Change is inherently what the city is about
Whether low pace or high pace
It is the engine that sparks the city's dynamism
There is for sure the need to steer change to the benefit of all

Creativity finding nurturing in a state of constant change
Destabilizing yes change is, but from change often emerge enhanced
    and improved conditions
Through changing circumstances, the city can assess where it stands
    on its vision and aspirations
As well decide to be proactive instead of being reactive
And periodically, a stepping stone to a city reinvented and transformed
    change can be.

My Ideal Canadian City
Is indeed such a place
Where Canada loves to congregate
Driven by democratic values and an alliance of three equal
    governing partners
Which provides for living at its bvest and to its fullest
Both origin and destination where Canadians come first.

Let's think about this!

Ah! The daily existence of a city
There are definitely trade-offs and paradoxes to be had in seeking
    an ideal
The city has necessarily its rough edges, all too real and
    sometimes detrimental
It must dovetail down-to-earth practicalities with high minded visions
For it to be successful, it must balance perfection with imperfection
And the messy with the beautiful
Some civic actions and decisions are in the public interest
    and beneficial
Others are susceptible to darker schemes and influences, that
    can bring distraction and be harmful.

My Ideal Canadian City
Is indeed such a place
Where Canada loves to congregate
Driven by democratic values and an alliance of three equal
*   governing partners*
Which provides for living at its best and to it fullest
Both origin and destination where Canadians come first.

Let's think about this!

A city in time is a wealthy city
Rich with its memories and legacies of the past
Optimist in what the present can bring and fulfill
Hopeful in its future potential anchored in well crafted visions
    and exemplary succession practices
It is a place that naturally bridges the past and the future
Citizens acquainted and conversant as they are with the subtleties
    of the short and long view of their city
The dialogue between generations helping to unravel the meaning
    of the passage of time
For such an important and crucial aspiration of a sustainable,
    healthy, and resilient city in the future.

My Ideal Canadian City
Is indeed such a place
Where Canada loves to congregate
Driven by democratic values and an alliance of three equal
governing partners
Which provides for living at its best and to its fullest
Both origin and destination where Canadians come first.

Let's think about this!

REFERENCES

AirScapes. 2007. Photos of 18 Canadian Cities by Ron Garnett, www.AirScapes.ca [accessed on March 18, 2011].

Alcock, Reg and Donald G. Lenihan. 2001. *Opening the E-Government File: Governing in the 21st Century*, Results of the Crossing Boundaries Cross-Country Tour. Ottawa: Centre for Collaborative Government, Changing Government, volume 2.

Alexander, Christopher et al. 1977. *A Pattern Language: Towns, Buildings, Construction.* New York: Oxford University Press, pp. 140-144.

Alexander, Jim and Christopher Comeau. 2008. "Collaborative Transformation — The Key to High Performance Results in a Complex World," *Canadian Government Executive*, May, p. 19.

Alliance for Regional Stewardship, http://www.regionalstewardship.org [accessed on March 18, 2011].

Alter, Jonathan. 2011. "A Script for 'Sputnik' — Obama's State of the Union Challenge," *Newsweek*, January 10 & 17, p. 18.

Andrew, Caroline. 1994. "Federal Urban Activity: Intergovernmental Relations in an Age of Restraint." In *The Changing Canadian Metropolis: A Public Policy Perspective,* Volume 2, ed., Frances Frisken. Berkeley/Toronto: Institute of Governmental Studies, University of California, Canadian Urban Institute, pp. 427-454.

Andrew, Caroline. 1995. "Provincial-Municipal Relations; or Hyper-Fractionalized Quasi-Subordination Revisited." In *Canadian Metropolitics — Governing our Cities,* ed. James Lightbody. Toronto: Copp Clark Ltd., pp. 139-140.

Andrew, Caroline, ed. 2004. *Our Diverse Cities.* Ottawa: Metropolis Project, Number 1, spring.

Arbour, Louise. 2005. "Freedom From Want," Lafontaine-Baldwin Lecture, *Maclean's*, March 14, pp. 36-37.

Amsterdam Architecture Center (ARCAM), http://www.arcam.nl [accessed on March 18, 2011].

Arsenault, Michel. 2004. "Planète mafia —Entrevue avec Xavier Raufer," (Institut de criminologie de Paris; auteur de Le Grand Réveil des Mafias, J.C. Lattès), *L'Actualité*, October 15, pp. 20-22.

Australian Capital Territory Government. 2003. *The Economic White Paper for the Australian Capital Territory.* Canberra: Australian Capital Territory Government, pp. 20-22.

Australian Capital Territory Government. 2004. *Building Our Community — The Canberra Social Plan.* Canberra: Australian Capital Territory Government.

Australian Capital Territory Government. 2004. *The Canberra Plan.* Canberra: Australian Capital Territory Government, p. 10.

Australian Government. 2003. *Urban Design Guidelines for Perimeter Security in the National Capital.* Canberra: National Capital Authority.

Bakopanos, Eleni. 2005. "Can Distressed Urban Areas Become Poles of Growth?" OECD International Conference on Sustainable Cities: Linking Competitiveness with Social Cohesion, Montreal, p. 2.

Banting, Keith and Richard Simeon, eds. 1985. *Redesigning the State: The Politics of Constitutional Change in Industrial Nations.* Toronto: University of Toronto Press.

Barber, Benjamin. 2003. *Fear's Empire: War, Terrorism and Democracy.* New York: W.W. Norton, pp. 194, 223.

Barber, John. 1995. "Urban Canada Needs to Develop New Resources," *The Globe and Mail*, September 9, D1 and D5.

Beasley, Larry. 2003. "Laws and Processes Behind the Urban Designer's Pencil: Thoughts from the Vancouver Experience," *Plan Canada*, autumn, p. 41.

Beasley, Larry. 2004a. "Re-Inventing the City for People — A City by Design," *Ontario Planning Journal*, January-February, p. 15.

Beasley, Larry. 2004b. "Moving Forward in Canadian Communities: Soliloquy of an Urbanist," *Plan Canada*, winter, pp. 16-18.

Bedford, Paul. 1997. "When They Were Kings: Planning for Reinvestment," *Plan Canada*, July, pp. 18-23.

Bedford, Paul. 2005. "Looking Back, Looking Forward," *Ontario Planning Journal*, March-April, p. 19.

Bedford, Paul. 2006a. "Discovering Tokyo to Rediscover Toronto," *Ontario Planning Journal*, January-February, pp. 23-25.

Bedford, Paul. 2006b. "Positive Civic Engagement: Can Ontario Learn from Other Places," *Ontario Planning Journal*, April-May, p. 19.

Bedford, Paul. 2006c. "Chance of a Lifetime for Greater Toronto Region," *Ontario Planning Journal*, July-August, pp. 23-25.

Bergeron, Pierre. 2005. "Se réconcilier avec la planète," *Le Droit*, December 12, p. 16.

Blondel, Jean. 1987. *Political Leadership: Towards a General Analysis.* London: Sage, pp. 16-17.

Blumenfeld, Hans. 1983. "The Metropolis — Summing Up." In *The Metropolis: Proceedings of a Conference in Honour of Hans Blumenfeld*, eds. John Hitchcok and Ann McMaster. Toronto: Centre for Urban and Community Studies, University of Toronto, pp. 233-236.

Boarnet, Marlon G. 2006. "Planning's Role in Building Healthy Cities," *Journal of the American Planning Association*, winter, pp. 5-9.

Bolger, Len and Eddy Isaacs. 2003. "Shaping an Integrated Energy Future." In *Fueling the Future: How the Battle over Energy is Changing Everything,* eds. Andrew Heintzman and Evan Solomon. Toronto: Anansi, p. 58.

Borde, Valérie. 2004a. "L'ignorance nous coulera! — Entrevue avec Camille Limoges" (historien des sciences), *L'Actualité*, November 1, p. 22.

Borde, Valérie. 2004b. "Innovations — Les cartes du Québec," *L'Actualité*, November 1, p. 38.

Borja, Jordi. 2004. "Nous avons tous droit à la ville," *Courrier International — Hors-Série: Maison*, October-November-December, p. 81.

Boucher, Isabelle. 2006. "Can We Plan for a Feeling of Security?" *Plan Canada*, autumn, pp. 22-25.

Bourne, Larry S. and James Simons. 2003. "New Fault Lines? Recent Trends in the Canadian Urban System and their Implications for Planning and Public Policy." In *Perspectives on a Canadian Urban Strategy,* ed. Ian Skelton. Toronto: *Canadian Journal of Urban Research*/Canadian Institute of Planners, p. 24-25.

Bramodat, Paul A. 2004. "Mirror and Mortar: Ethno-Cultural Festivals and Urban Life in Canada." In *Our Diverse Cities*, ed. Caroline Andrew. Ottawa: Metropolis Project, Number 1, spring, p. 93.

Brender, Natalie, Marni Cappe and Anne Golden. 2007. *Mission Possible: Successful Canadian Cities*. The Canada Project Final Report, volume III. Ottawa: The Conference Board of Canada.

Broadbent, Alan. 2006. "Brighter Lights, Bigger Cities," *The Walrus*, June, pp. 56-61.

Broadbent, Alan. 2008. *Urban Nation: Why We Need to Give Power Back to the Cities to Make Canada Stronger*. Toronto: HarperCollins Publishers Ltd.

Brown, David D. 1999. "Learning from First Nations," *Plan Canada*, November, pp. 22-23.

Brown, John S. and Paul Duguid. 2000. *The Social Life of Information*. Boston: Harvard Business School Press.

Brugman, Jeb. 2009. *Welcome to the Urban Revolution — How Cities Are Changing the World*. Toronto: Viking Canada, p. 219.

Busby, Peter. 2007. *Learning Sustainable Design*. Gatineau: Janam.

Calthorpe, Peter. 1993. *The Next American Metropolis*. New York: Princeton Architectural Press.

Canada-British Columbia-Vancouver. 2000. *Urban Development Agreement Regarding Economic, Social and Community Development in the City of Vancouver*, p. 1.

Canada-Manitoba-Winnipeg. 1995. *The Winnipeg Development Agreement*.

Canadian Center for Architecture, http://www.cca.qc.ca [accessed on March 18, 2011].

Canadian Climate Impacts and Adaptation Research Network. 2006. *Adapting to Climate Change: An Introduction for Canadian Municipalities*. Ottawa: Canadian Climate Impacts and Adaptation Research Network.

Canadian Institute of Planners: Awards for Planning Excellence
• 1995 — City of Vancouver: CityPlan Public Process (*Plan Canada*, July, 1995)
• 1996 — Northern Cityscape: Linking Design to Climate, Norman Pressman (*Plan Canada*, September, 1996)
• 1997 — Greenbelt Master Plan, National Capital Commission (*Plan Canada*, November, 1997)

• 1999 — Master Plan, Schematic Plans and Landscape Patterns for the Lachine Canal National Historic Site, Malaka Ackaoui (*Plan Canada*, November, 1999)
• 2001 — First Nations Community Planning Model, Frank Palermo *et al.* (*Plan Canada*, July-August-September, 2001)
• 2006 — Canada's Capital Core Area Sector Plan, National Capital Commission (*Plan Canada*, winter, 2006)
http://www.cip-icu.ca/web/la/en/pa/a65a44dcd9ae42fe89f31c898e27ac33/template.asp [accessed on March 18, 2011].

Canadian Institute of Planners: Vision in Planning Award
• 2001 — National Capital Commission, 1950 Plan for the National Capital — Gréber Plan (*Plan Canada*, July-August-September, 2001)
• 2002 — Greater Vancouver Regional District, Liveable Region Strategic Plan (*Plan Canada*, July-August-September, 2002)
• 2006 — City of Vancouver, The Accessible/Inclusive Cities and Communities (*Plan Canada*, winter, 2006)
http://www.cip-icu.ca/web/la/en/pa/1918A9FCF65D40D495EC9B4798D56E60/template.asp [accessed on March 18, 2011].

Canadian International Development Agency. 1998. *An Urbanizing World: Statement on Sustainable Cities*. Ottawa: Canadian International Development Agency.

Canadian International Development Agency. 2001. *Sustainable Development Strategy 2001-2003 — An Agenda for Change*. Ottawa: Canadian International Development Agency, p. 1.

Canadian International Development Agency. 2002. *What We Are Learning About Sustainable Development*. Ottawa: Canadian International Development Agency.

Canadian Urban Institute. 2001. *Federal, Provincial and Municipal Governance in Canada,* Toronto: Canadian Urban Institute.

Capra, Fritjof. 2002. *The Hidden Connections: A Science for Sustainable Living*. New York: Anchor Books, p. 126.

Cervero, Robert and John Landis. 1990. "The Transportation — Land Use Connection Still Matters," *Access*, pp. 2-10.

Chambre de commerce du Montréal métropolitain. 2004. *Transport en commun: Un puissant moteur du développement économique de la région métropolitaine de Montréal*. Montreal: Chambre de commerce du Montréal métropolitain.

Chartier, Bob. 2007. "Generational Differences," *Canadian Government Executive*, November, p. 11.

Chicago Architectural Foundation, http://caf.architecture.org [accessed on March 18, 2011].

Chisholm, Stewart. 2002. "Protecting Urban Greenspace," *Plan Canada*, July-August-September, p. 19.

CIRAIG, Interuniversity Research Centre for the Life Cycle of Products, Processes and Services, Montréal, École polytechnique, http://www.ciraig.org/en/index_e.html [accessed on March 21, 2001].

City of Calgary. 2005. Photo of Calgary, Ken Richardson photographer. Calgary: Customer Services & Communications.

City of Hamilton. 2008. *Vision 2020 Hamilton*.
http://www.myhamilton.ca/myhamilton/CityandGovernment/ProjectsInitiatives/V2020 [accessed on March 21, 2011].

City of Ottawa. 2004. "Choosing Our Future: Planning for Long-Term Community Sustainability," Overview of the conference, November 1, p. 2.

City of Toronto. 2002. *Regeneration in the Kings: Directions and Emerging Trends.* Toronto: City Planning Division, Urban Development Services. http://www.toronto.ca/planning/kings_execsum.htm [accessed on March 21, 2001].

City of Toronto. 2002. *King-Spadina Secondary Plan Review.* Toronto: City Planning Division, The Planning Partnership. http://www.toronto.ca/planning/pdf/king_spadina_final_pt1.pdf [accessed on March 21, 2001].

City of Toronto. 2005. Photo of Toronto, Brad Ross, photographer. Toronto: Media Relations.

City of Vancouver. 1995. *City Plan.* Vancouver: Planning Department. http://www.city.vancouver.bc.ca/commsvcs/planning/cityplan/cityplan.htm [accessed on March 21, 2011].

City of Vancouver. 2005. Photo of Vancouver, Larry Beasley, co-director. Vancouver: Planning Department.

City of Vancouver. 2008. *EcoDensity Planning Initiative.* Vancouver: Planning Department. http://www.vancouver-ecodensity.ca/ [accessed on March 21, 2011].

City of Vancouver. 2008. *Community Services.* Vancouver: Development Permit Board. http://www.city.vancouver.bc.ca/commsvcs/planning/dpboard/DPBOARD.HTM [accessed on March 21, 2011].

City of Vancouver. 2008. *Community Services.* Vancouver: Urban Design Panel. http://www.city.vancouver.bc.ca/commsvcs/planning/udp/Udp.html [accessed on March 21, 2011].

City of Winnipeg. 2005. Photo of Winnipeg, Wendy Stephenson, photographer. Winnipeg: Corporate Communications Division.

City of Yellowknife. 2005. Photo of Yellowknife, Sherman Hines, photographer. Yellowknife: Economic Development.

Clatworthy, Leskiw and Associates. 1990. *An Evaluation of the Winnipeg Core Area Agreement Tripartite Model.* Winnipeg: Clatworthy, Leskiw and Associates.

Cleveland, Harland. 1989. "Control: The Twilight of Hierarchy, New Management." In *Creative Organization Theory*, Gareth Morgan. Newbury Park: Sage, pp. 121-123.

Cliff, Amanda. 2007. "Planning a New Prescription for Health," *Ontario Planning Journal*, January-February, pp. 11-12.

Clutterbuck, Peter and Marvyn Novick. 2003. *Building Inclusive Communities: Cross-Canada Perspectives and Strategies.* Ottawa: Federation of Canadian Municipalities and Laidlaw Foundation, p. 5.

Clutterbuck, Peter, Christa Freiles and Marvyn Novick. 2005. "Meeting the Civic Challenges of Social Inclusion: Cross-Canada Findings and Priorities for Action," *Inclusive Cities*, pp. 26, 39, 40.

Cohen, Andrew. 2007. *The Unfinished Canadian: The People We Are.* Toronto: McClelland & Stewart.

Commission on Global Governance. 1995. *Our Global Neighborhood.* New York: Oxford University Press, pp. 2, 93.

Congress for New Urbanism. 2007. *School Choice: A Remedy for Sprawl*, Chicago: Congress for New Urbanism.

Conseil du paysage québécois, www.paysage.qc.ca/cpq.htm [accessed on March 21, 2011].

Cook, Jeffrey. 2008. "Building on Traditions of the Past: The Rise and Resurgence of First Nations Comprehensive Community Planning," *Plan Canada*, summer, pp. 13-17.

Courchene, Thomas J. and Donald Savoie, eds. 2003. *The Art of the State: Governance in a World Without Frontiers.* Montreal: Institute for Research on Public Policy, p. 415.

Crookal, Paul. 2004. "From Government On-Line to Service Transformation, Interview with Helen McDonald, Federal Government's Acting Chief Information Officer," *Canadian Government Executive*, October-November, pp. 5-6.

Crowhurst, Suzanne H. 2006. "What Constitutes True Urbanism," *Urban Land*, March, p. 110.

Cullingworth, J.B. 1972. *Communication and Understanding in Planning Research: The Case of the Scottish Planning Exchange.* Toronto: University of Toronto, Department of Urban and Regional Planning, Papers on Planning and Design, No. 18, p. 4.

D'Auray, Michelle, Maryantonnett Flumian and Tony Valeri. 2003. "From Ideas to Action: Toward Seamless Government," Toronto: KTA Centre for Collaborative Government, Policy, Politics and Governance, October.

Davies, Libby. 2003. "Planning Vancouver: A Political Perspective," *Plan Canada*, autumn, pp. 34-36.

Deacon, James. 2004. "A Trillion-Dollar Pipe Dream," *Maclean's*, November 8, p. 40.

Denhez, Mark. 2003. "Why Bother with Heritage Anyway?" *Plan Canada*, summer, pp. 14-15.

De Souza, Mike. 2006. "Service Canada Could Spin Off into Separate Department," *The Hill Times*, January 16, p. 18.

Dingwall, John. 2004. "Leadership in Municipal Planning — The Healthy Choice," interview with Gerry Thompson (former CEO, Waterloo Region), *Canadian Government Executive*, August-September, pp. 7-8.

Donnelly, Jim. 2006. "Commercial Builders Slow to Go Green," *Ottawa Business Journal*, February 20, p. 10.

Downs, Anthony. 1994. *New Visions for Metropolitan America.* Washington/Cambridge: The Brookings Institution/Lincoln Institute of Land Policy, pp. 15, 202, 367.

Drucker, Peter F. 1993. *Post-Capitalist Society.* New York: Harper Business, pp. 159, 212.

Duany, Andres and Elizabeth Plater Zyberk. 1991. *Towns and Town-Making Principles.* New York: Rizzoli.

Dubé, Pierre and François Lapointe. 1999. "L'urbanisme au Canada : Regard sur les années 1990," *Urbanité*, printemps, pp. 12-14.

Dubuc, Alain. 2005. "Santé: Une recette magique," *Le Droit*, October 16, p. 29.

Dyer, Gwynne. 2006. "Croissance non durable," *Le Droit*, February 25-26, p. 27.

Ebersohn, Dick *et al.* 2005. "Imagine CALGARY: A 100-Year Vision for Sustainability," *Plan Canada*, winter, p. 40.

Economist, The. 1988. "A Survey of Canada — Bleeding-Heart Conservatives," October 8.

Economist, The. 2003. "Survey of the Internet Society — Digital Dilemmas," January 25, pp. 41-42.

Economist, The. 2004a. "Philanthropy — Doing Well and Doing Good," July 31, p. 59.

Economist, The. 2004b. "Technology Quarterly, The Rise of Green Building," December 4, p. 17.

Economist, The. 2005a. "A Survey of Nanotechnology — Small Wonders," January 1.

Economist, The. 2005b. "A Survey of Consumer Power — Crowned at Last," April 2.

Economist, The. 2005c. "Environmental Economics: Are You Being Served?" April 23, pp. 76-78.

Economist, The. 2005d. "Peace, Order and Rocky Government — A Survey of Canada," December 3.

Economist, The. 2006a. "A Survey of the World Economy — The New Titans," September 16.

Economist, The. 2006b. "A Survey of Talent — The Battle for Brainpower," October 7.

Economist, The. 2007a. "A Special Report on Technology and Government: The Electronic Bureaucrat," February 16, p. 4.

Economist, The. 2007b. "A Survey of Cities — The World Goes to Town," May 5.

Economist Intelligence Unit. 2010. *Liveable Cities: Challenges and Opportunities for Policymakers*, commissioned by Philips, p. 21.

Eisenstadt, S.N. and A. Shachar. 1987. *Society, Culture, and Urbanization*. Newbury Park: Sage.

Ekos Research Associates. 2006. *Building Effective Relationships Between Canadians and their Governments*. Ottawa: Ekos Research Associates.

Elliot, Deni, ed. 1986. *Responsible Journalism*. Beverly Hills: Sage.

Environmental Design Research Association. 2003. *EDRA/Places Planning Award for Places*, First Nations Community Planning Project. http://www.edra.org/index.php?option=com_content&task=view&id=321&Itemid=187 [accessed on March 22, 2011].

European Sustainable Cities & Towns Campaign. 1994. *The Charter of European Cities and Towns Towards Sustainability — Aalborg Charter*. Brussels: European Sustainable Cities & Towns Campaign.

External Advisory Committee on Cities and Communities. 2006. "From Restless Communities to Resilient Places: Building a Stronger Future for All Canadians," final report. Ottawa: Infrastructure Canada, June, pp. 17, 29, 35-42, 46.

Faga, Barbara. 2006. *Designing Public Consensus: The Civic Theater of Community Participation for Architects, Landscape Architects, Planners, and Urban Designers*. Hoboken: John Wiley & Sons.

Fagan, Brian. 2004. *The Long Summer: How Climate Changed Civilization*. New York, Basic Books, pp. xiv-xvi.

Falardeau, Jean-Charles. 2004. "Roots and Values in Canadian Lives." In *Visions of Canada: The Alan B. Plaunt Memorial Lectures 1958-1982*, eds. Bernard Ostry and Janice Yalden. Montréal: McGill-Queen's University Press, pp. 75-98.

Filipi, Diane and Jim Chappell. 2008. "New Places for an Informed Public," *Urban Land*, March, pp. 83, 85-86.

Flannery, Tim. 2005. *The Weather Makers: How We Are Changing the Climate and What It Means for Life on Earth*. Toronto: Harper-Collins.

Florida, Richard. 2002. *The Rise of the Creative Class*. New York: Basic Books.

Florida, Richard. 2008. *Who's Your City? How the Creative Economy is Making Where to Live the Most Important Decision of Your Life*. Toronto: Vintage Canada, p. xviii.

Foot, David and Daniel Stoffman. 1996. *Boom, Bust and Echo*. Toronto: MacFarlane, Walter, Ross, pp. 130-131, 157-158, 198.

Forester, John. 2006. "Making Participation Work when Interests Conflict," *Journal of the American Planning Association*, autumn, pp. 447-456.

Forsey, Eugene. 1980. *How Canadians Govern Themselves*. Ottawa: Government of Canada, pp. 20-37.

Freedman, Arthur M. 1997. "The Undiscussable Sides of Implementing Transformational Change," *Consulting Psychology Journal: Practice and Research*, pp. 51-76.

Friedman, Avi. 1996. "Flexible Planning Strategies: The La Prairie Experiment," *Plan Canada*, March, pp. 33-42.

Friedman, Avi. 2002. *Planning the New Suburbia: Flexibility by Design*. Vancouver: UBC Press.

Friedman, Avi. 2003. "Ideas for the Homefront." In *Fueling the Future: How the Battle over Energy is Changing Everything*, eds. Andrew Heintzman and Evan Solomon. Toronto: Anansi, pp. 310-321.

Friedman, Avi. 2005. *Homes Within Reach: A Guide to the Planning, Design, and Construction of Affordable Homes and Communities*. Hoboken: John Wiley & Sons.

Friedman, Avi. 2007. *Sustainable Residential Development: Planning and Design for Green Neighborhoods*. New York: McGraw Hill.

Friedman, Avi, Jennifer E. Steffel and Jasmin S. Frechette. 1998. "Planning for Suburban Evolution," *Plan Canada*, July, pp. 35-44.

Friedman, Thomas L. 1999. *The Lexus and the Olive Tree: Understanding Globalization*. New York: Farrar, Straus, Giroux.

Frisken, Frances, ed. 1994. *The Changing Canadian Metropolis: A Public Policy Perspective,* volume 2. Berkeley/Toronto: Institute of Governmental Studies, University of California/Canadian Urban Institute.

Frolick, Larry. 2005. "Suburbia's Last Stand," *The Walrus*, November, pp 44-45.

Frood, Peter. 2003. "The Historic Places Initiative: A National Framework to Conserve Canada's Built Heritage," *Plan Canada*, summer, pp. 29-32.

Gaboury, Paul. 2005. "Service Canada," *Le Droit*, September 3, p. 6.

Galbraith, Jay. 1989. "The Innovating Organization, Organizational Dynamics." In *Creative Organization Theory: A Book*, Gareth Morgan. Newbury Park: Sage, pp. 143-149.

Gariépy, Michel and Michel Marié, eds. 1997. *Ces réseaux qui nous gouvernent?* Montreal: L'Harmattan.

Garnaud, Emmanuelle. 2004. "La dette — Un fardeau pour nos enfants?" *L'Actualité*, October 1, p. 25.

Geddes, John. 2004. "How to Make Our Cities Work," *Maclean's*, January 19, pp. 20-22.

Gehl, Jan. 2010. *Cities for People*. Washington, D.C.: Island Press.

Gendron, Louise. 2007. "Attention, les vieux arrivent!" Entrevue avec Réjean Hébert, gériatre, *L'Actualité*, December 1, p. 23.

Gertler, Len. 2005. "Regional Planning in Canada," *Plan Canada*, autumn, p. 24.

Gillis, Charlie. 2004. "The War Between Town and Country," *Maclean's*, November 29, pp. 52-54.

Gillis, Charlie. 2005. "Kyoto Shell Game," *Maclean's*, February 28, pp. 18-21.

Gladwell, Malcom. 2002. *The Tipping Point — How Little Things Can Make A Big Difference*. Boston: Little, Brown and Company.

Goldberg, Michael A. and John Mercer. 1986. *The Myth of the North American City: Continentalism Challenged*. Vancouver: UBC Press, pp. 123, 144, 251, 252, 257.

Goldsmith, Stephen and William D. Eggers. 2004. *Governing by Network: The New Shape of the Public Sector*. Washington, D.C.: Brookings Institutions Press, pp. 98, 111.

Gordon, David L.A. 2001. "Weaving a Modern Plan for Canada's Capital: Jacques Gréber and the 1950 Plan for the National Capital Region," *Urban History Review*, March, pp. 41-63.

Gordon, David L.A. 2005. "The 1950 Plan for the National Capital: An Example of Vision in Planning," *Plan Canada*, autumn, pp. 18-21.

Gordon, David L.A., ed. 2006. *Planning Twentieth-Century Capital Cities*. London: Routledge.

Gore, Al. 2006. *An Inconvenient Truth — The Planetary Emergency of Global Warming and What We Can Do About It*. New York: Rodale.

Government of Canada. 1993. *Rôles et compétences de base des spécialistes de l'apprentissage dans un contexte d'apprentissage continu*. Ottawa: Government of Canada, p. 2.

Government of Ontario. 2004. *A Growth Plan for the Greater Golden Horseshoe*. Toronto: Government of Ontario, pp. 1-2.

Grant, Jill. 1999. "Can Planning Save the Suburbs," *Plan Canada*, September-October, p. 17.

Grant, Jill. 2002. "Mixed Use in Theory and Practice — Canadian Experience with Implementing a Planning Principle," *Journal of the American Planning Association*, winter, pp. 71-84.

Grant, Jill and Jaime Orser Smith. 2006. "Visions for a Common Future," *Plan Canada*, spring, pp. 16-19.

Greenberg, Ken and Frank Lewinberg. 1996. "Reinventing Planning in Toronto," *Plan Canada*, May, pp. 26-27.

Gregg, Allan R. 2004a. "Aging Is As Aging Does," *Maclean's*, January 19, p. 44-45.

Gregg, Allan R. 2004b. "Why Don't People Vote?" *Maclean's*, April 5, p. 42-43.

Gwyn, Richard. 2005. "Canadians Want to Know How Newcomers Will Be Turned into Canadians," *The Hill Times*, October 19, p. 9.

Gwyn, Richard. 2007. "Slum Cities in Developing World Are Growing at an Alarming Rate," *Embassy*, March 21, p. 7.

Halifax Regional Municipality. 2005. Photo of Halifax, Corinne Hartley-Robinson, photographer. Halifax: Corporate Communications Office.

Hall, Edward. 1969. *The Hidden Dimension*. New York: Anchor Book.

Hall, Peter. 1998. *Cities in Civilization*. London: Weidenfell and Nicolson, pp. 987-988.

Harivel, Colin and Colette Anderson. 2008. "First Nations Comprehensive Community Planning — A Good Investment for Canada," *Plan Canada*, summer, pp. 29-31.

Harvey, David. 1990. *Condition of Post-Modernity*. Oxford: Blackwell, p. 202.

Hausen, Michael von, Larry Pollock and Thomas Mahler. 2005. "Calgary's Midtown: Actively Shaping a 100-Year Vision," *Plan Canada*, spring, pp. 46-49.

Heilbroner, Robert and Lester Thurow. 1994. *Economics Explained*. New York: Touchstone.

Heilbroner, Robert. 1995. *Visions of the Future*. New York: Oxford University Press.

Heintzman, Andrew and Evan Solomon, eds. 2003. *Fueling the Future: How the Battle over Energy is Changing Everything*. Toronto: Anansi, p. 369.

Held, David and Christopher Politt. 1986. *New Forms of Democracy*. London: Sage, p. 12.

Heller, Peter. 2003. *Who Will Pay? Coping with Aging Societies, Climate Change, and Other Long Term Fiscal Challenges*. Washington, D.C.: International Monetary Fund, pp. 3-4.

Hesselbein, Frances, Marshall Goldsmith and Richard Beckhard, eds. 1997. *The Organization of the Future*. The Drucker Foundation. San Francisco: Jossey-Bass Publishers.

Hitchcock, John and Anne McMaster, eds. 1983. *The Metropolis: Proceedings of a Conference in Honour of Hans Blumenfeld*. Toronto: Centre for Urban and Community Studies, University of Toronto.

Hodge, Gerald and David L.A. Gordon. 2008. *Planning Canadian Communities*. Toronto: Thomson Nelson, pp. 65, 113-114, 123.

Hodges, Louis W. 1986. "Press Responsibility: A Functional Perspective." In *Responsible Journalism,* Deni Elliott, ed. Beverly Hills: Sage, pp. 20-21.

Hodgson, Corinne. 2005. "New Research Puts Spotlight on Link Between Transportation and Health," *Ontario Planning Journal*, March-April, p. 25.

Hoenigman, Vince. 2003. "Homelessness in a Progressive City," *Urban Land*, January, p. 51.

Homer-Dixon, Thomas. 2000. *The Ingenuity Gap*. Toronto: Knopf, p. 396.

Homer-Dixon, Thomas. 2003. "Bringing Ingenuity to Energy." In *Fueling the Future: How the Battle over Energy is Changing Everything,* Andrew Heintzman and Evan Solomon, eds. Toronto: Anansi, pp. 16-25.

Homer-Dixon, Thomas. 2006. *The Upside of Down: Catastrophe, Creativity, and the Renewal of Civilization*. Toronto: Knopf.

ICLEI — Local Governments for Sustainability, http://www.iclei.org [accessed on March 22, 2011].

Ignatieff, Michael. 2004. *The Lesser Evil: Political Ethics in an Age of Terror*. Toronto: Penguin, pp. 2-3, 5.

Indian and Northern Affairs Canada. 2006. *CCP Handbook: Comprehensive Community Planning for First Nations in British Columbia*. BC Region: Indian and Northern Affairs Canada.

Institute of Public Administration of Canada. 2004. Innovative Management Award — Vancouver Agreement. http://www.ipac.ca/InnovationAwards [accessed on March 22, 2011].

Iyer, Pico. 2004. "Canada: Global Citizen," *Canadian Geographic*, November-December, pp. 64, 66.

Jacobs, Jane. 1961. *The Death and Life of Great American Cities*. New York: Vintage Books, pp. 150-151.

Jacobs, Jane. 1984. *Cities and the Wealth of Nations: Principles of Economic Life*. New York: Vintage Books, pp. 39, 232.

Jacobs, Jane. 2000. *The Nature of Economies*. Toronto: Random House.

Jacobs, Jane. 2004. "The Changing Economy of Canada." In *Visions of Canada: The Alan B. Plaunt Memorial Lectures 1958-1982*, eds. Bernard Ostry and Janice Yalden. Montreal: McGill-Queen's University Press, pp. 249-272.

Janigan, Mary. 2003. "A Scandalous Waste," *Maclean's*, July 21, p. 41.

Jock, Richard, Mary Simon, Graham Fox and Marcia Nickerson. 2004. *Finding an Aboriginal Digital Voice*. Toronto: KTA Centre for Collaborative Government, Policy, Politics & Governance, July, pp. 1-2.

Katz, Peter. 1994. *The New Urbanism: Toward an Architecture of Community*. New York: McGraw-Hill.

Keating, Michael. 2003. "The Territorial State: Functional Restructuring and Political Change." In *The Art of the State: Governance in a World Without Frontiers,* eds. Thomas J. Courchene and Donald J. Savoie. Montreal: Institute for Research on Public Policy, p. 340.

Keeble, Ronald M. 2006. "Barriers to Employment: The Experience of Internationally Trained Planning Professionals Immigrating to Ontario," *Ontario Planning Journal*, April-May, pp. 26-28.

Keohane, Robert O. and Elinor Ostrom. 1995. *Local Commons and Global Interdependence*. London: Sage, p. 21.

Kerwin, Larkin. 2004. "The More Thou Searchest, the More Thou Marvel: The Role of Canadian Science." In *Visions of Canada: The Alan B. Plaunt Memorial Lectures 1958-1982*, eds. Bernard Ostry and Janice Yalden. Montreal: McGill-Queen's University Press, pp. 487-497.

Kingwell, Mark. 2008. *Concrete Reveries — Consciousness and the City*. Toronto: Penguin Canada, p. 11.

Kitchen, Harry M. 2002. *Municipal Revenue and Expenditure Issues in Canada*. Toronto: Canadian Tax Foundation, p. 331.

Kouchner, Martin. 2004. "Les Entretiens Jacques Cartier," *Le Devoir — Recherche*, September 18, p. 1.

Laborit, Henri. 1971. *L'Homme et la Ville*. Paris: Flammarion.

Lacombe, Réal, Julie Levesque and Louis Poirier. 2002. "Villes et villages en santé au Québec — Une idée qui a porté fruit," *Plan Canada*, October-November-December, pp. 15-17.

L'Actualité. 2005. "Choc 2013 — Le grand défi démographique," série de reportages sur le déclin démographique au Québec.

Landry, Charles. 2002. *The Creative City: Toolkit for Urban Innovation*. London: Earthscan, pp. 17, 205-207, 253, 269.

Landry, Charles. 2006. *The Art of City Making*. London: Earthscan, pp. 5, 14, 19, 215, 238, 247, 257, 262, 291, 292, 300, 311, 313, 315, 325, 329-330, 330, 410-411, 413, 424.

Lang, Reg. 2003. "Expect the Unexpected," *Ontario Planning Journal*, September-October, pp. 5-7.

Langdon, Philip. 2006. "Developers Form Institutes to Keep New Urban Ideals Alive," *New Urban News*, September, p. 1.

Lapointe, François. 1999. "Vers des collectivités viables: Colloque international sur les enjeux du 21ième siècle pour un développement durable des agglomérations — Sommaire des échanges et délibérations," *Urbanité*, automne, pp. 25-26.

Lapointe, François and Pierre Dubé. 2000. "A Century of Urban Planning and Building in Canada's Capital Region," *Plan Canada*, April-May-June, pp. 18-19.

Larousse. 2000. *Le Petit Larousse Illustré*, Paris, p. 551.

Larsh, Susan, Frances Shamley and Lorna Heidenheim. 2002. "Working Together for Healthy Communities," *Plan Canada*, October-November-December, pp. 13-14.

Lash, Harry. 1976. *Pour une planification humaine*. Ottawa: Ministère d'État — Affaires urbaines Canada, pp. 10-13.

Leadlay, Christina. 2005. "Cities Expect to Have a Say on Foreign Policy," *Embassy*, October 19, pp. 1, 7.

Lebreux, Marlene. 2004. "Un bon coach dans le sport comme dans la vie," *Le Droit*, October 2, A46.

Leeming Dan, Diane Riley and Dena Warmar. 2006. "Public Health and Welfare: An Urban Planning Perspective," *Ontario Planning Journal*, January-February, p. 8.

Lefebvre, Christine and Ève Wertheimer. 2006. "An Indispensable Reference for Heritage Conservation: The Standards and Guidelines for the Conservation of Historic Places in Canada," *Plan Canada*, spring, pp. 41-43.

Lefebvre, Mario and Natalie Brender. 2006. *Canadian Hub Cities: A Driving Force of the National Economy*. Ottawa: The Conference Board of Canada.

Lenihan, Donald G. 2006a. "Technology in Federal Government: Measuring Progress and Impact of New Technology on Government," *The Hill Times*, January 16, p. 22.

Lenihan, Donald G. 2006b. "Challenge Now Is to Show Canada 2020 Really Has Something New to Say About Being Progressive," *The Hill Times*, June 26, p. 11.

Lenihan, Donald G. and Graham Fox. 2004. "Democratic Renewal: Solutions in Search of a Problem," *The Hill Times*, November 7.

Lenihan, Donald G. and Graham Fox. 2005a. "What We Need to Know to Renew Our Democracy," *The Hill Times*, September 21, p. 41.

Lenihan, Donald G. and Graham Fox. 2005b. "Framing Canada," *The Hill Times*, October 31, p. 10.

Lenihan, Donald G. and Graham Fox. 2006. "Open Federalism and the National Conversation," *The Hill Times*, February 6, p. 8.

Levitt, Rachelle L. 2009. "What Makes a City a City?" *Urban Land*, July, p. 16.

Lewis, Paul. 1997. "La planification des transports dans la région de Montréal: La recherche de la cohérence." In *Ces réseaux qui nous gouvernent?* eds. Gariépy, Michel and Michel Marié. Montreal: L'Harmattan, pp. 291, 292, 298.

Lightbody, James, ed. 1995. *Canadian Metropolitics — Governing our Cities.* Toronto: Copp Clark Ltd.

Lithwick, N.H and Gilles Paquet, eds. 1968. *Urban Studies: A Canadian Perspective.* Toronto: Methuen Publications, p. 274.

Local Governments for Sustainability. 2000. "Local Initiatives Award for Governance in Sustainable Development, Hamilton-Wentworth's Vision 2020" http://www.iclei.org/index.php?id=1875 [accessed on March 22, 2011].

Lockwood, Charles. 2007. "The Green Quotient: Q & A with William A. McDonough," *Urban Land*, January, p. 118.

Loheed, Philip N. and Brandy H.M. Brooks. 2006. "New Places for a New Age," *Urban Land*, March, p. 94.

Lopes, Sandra and Yves Poisson. 2005. "Building our Cities — The Importance of Immigration," *Public Policy Forum*.

London, Mark. 1998. "Tourism and the Lachine Canal," *Plan Canada*, January, pp. 14-18.

London, Mark. 2003. "Heritage Preservation and the Lachine Canal Revitalization Project," *Plan Canada*, summer, pp. 33-35.

Lord, Marie-Linda. 2004. "Bilingualism and Diversity in Postmodern Moncton." In *Our Diverse Cities,* ed. Caroline Andrew. Ottawa: Metropolis Project, Number 1, spring, p. 93.

Lorinc, John. 2006. *The New City: How The Crisis in Canada's Urban Centres Is Reshaping the Nation.* Toronto: Penguin, pp. 6, 11, 14, 19, 58, 112, 182, 190, 213, 228, 252, 267.

Lorius, Antony. 2004. "How to Meet the Challenge of Planning for Employment Land," *Ontario Planning Journal*, November-December, p. 3.

Lynch, Kevin. 1969. *L'image de la cite.* Paris: Dunod, pp. 2-5, 6.

MacQueen, Ken. 2005. "Victory with a Spanking," *Maclean's*, May 30, p. 38.

Makula, Peter. 2004. "The Engineering Development Program — Developing Successful Successors," *Road Talk*. Toronto: Ministry of Transportation, p. 6.

Mannell, Laura and Heather Ternoway. 2008. "The Need to Do More: Advancing Planning with First Nation Communities," *Plan Canada*, summer, pp. 21-23.

Marion, Russ. 1999. *The Edge of Organization: Chaos and Complexity Theories of Formal Social Systems.* Thousand Oaks, CA: Sage.

Marshall, Robert. 2005. "The Innovative Urge — Creative Juices," *Maclean's 100 Special Commemorative Issue, Leadership and Dreamer — Canada's Greatest Innovators and How They Changed The World.*

Mau, Bruce and Institute without Boundaries. 2004. *Massive Change.* New York: Phaidon Press Inc.

McAffee, Ann *et al*. 1995. "Vancouver's City Plan — People Participation in Planning," *Plan Canada*, May, pp. 15-16.

McArthur, John W. 2009. "The Great Generalists," *Global Brief*, fall, p. 49.

McClean, Don and Bob Korol. 2004. "Some Measures of Sustainability of Urban Neighbourhoods: A Case Study in Hamilton, Ontario," *Plan Canada*, spring, pp. 19-21.

McGregor, Sarah. 2005. "Granatstein's Immigration Views Cause Some Unease," *Embassy*, November 11, p. 3.

McLennan, Jason F. 2004. *The Philosophy of Sustainable Design.* Kansas City: Ecotone.

McLuhan, Marshall. 1962. *The Gutenberg Galaxy.* New York: Mentor.

McLuhan, Marshall *et al*. 1977. *The City as Classroom: Understanding Language and Media.* Agincourt: Book Society of Canada.

McWhinney, Will. 1992. *Paths of Change: Strategic Choices for Organizations and Society.* Newbury Park: Sage.

Melamed, Sara. 2003. "A National Brownfield Redevelopment Strategy: Reflections on an Opportunity for Canada," *Ontario Planning Journal*, March-April, pp. 5-6.

Metro Vancouver. 1996. *The Liveable Region Strategic Plan.* Vancouver: Greater Vancouver Regional District.

Metro Vancouver. 2005. *The Liveable Region Strategic Plan Annual Report.* Vancouver: Greater Vancouver Regional District.

Michailidis, John. 2004. "The Creation of a GTA Agricultural Action Plan," *Ontario Planning Journal*, January-February, p. 5.

Micklethwait, John. 2010. "Tremble Leviathan," *The Economist: The World in 2011*, p. 17.

Milloy, John and Maryantonnett Flumian. 2006. "Redoing Federalism Via Service Delivery," *CIO Government Review*, March, p. 4.

Mills, Lara. 2004. "Music Bridge — Leaving a Footprint in British Columbia, Presto!" *The National Arts Centre Orchestra Newsletter*, pp. 2-3.

Miller, David. 2004. "Canada's Cities: A Time of Opportunity," The 2004 Donald Gow Lecture. Kingston: School of Policy Studies, Queen's University, April 30, p. 6.

Miller, Glenn. 1996. "RexRedux: Deregulation Aims to Give New Lease on Life to 'Kings Areas' of Downtown Toronto," *Plan Canada*, July, p. 38.

Miller, Glenn and John Farrow. 2008. "Economic Development Strategies in the Face of Climate Change." Presentation to the Canadian Institute of Planners Conference on Climate Change, Iqaluit, July.

Miller, John. 2008. "Energy Bill Shines Light on Things to Come," *Urban Land Green*, spring, pp. 62-63.

Mintzberg, Henry. 2004. *Managers, Not MBA — A Hard Look at the Soft Practice of Managing and Management Development.* San Francisco: Berrett-Koehler Publishers Inc., pp. 142, 254.

Mintzberg, Henry. 2009. *Managing.* San Francisco: Berrett-Kochler.

Morgan, Gareth. 1988. *Riding the Waves of Change: Developing Managerial Competencies for a Turbulent World.* San Francisco: Jossey-Bass Publishers, pp. 15, 89-90, 101, 130.

Morgan, Gareth. 1989. *Creative Organization Theory: A Book.* Newbury Park: Sage, pp. 122-123.

Morgan, Gareth. 1993. *Imaginization: The Art of Creative Management.* Newbury Park: Sage.

Morgan, Gareth. 1998. *Images of Organization.* Thousand Oaks, CA: Sage, pp. 4, 92, 101.

Moule, Lawrence. 2007. "The Importance of Being Partners — How Shared Governance Can Eschew Old Norms," *CIO Government Review*, March, p. 12.

Nasmith, Karen, Ann Joyner and Mary Neuman. 2005. "Sustainability from the Ground Up: Affordable Design at Regent Park to Leave Smaller Ecological Footprint," *Ontario Planning Journal*, March-April, pp. 28-30.

National Capital Commission. 1996. *A Plan for the National Capital Greenbelt*. Ottawa: National Capital Commission.

National Capital Commission. 1999a. *Plan for Canada's Capital*. Ottawa: National Capital Commission.

National Capital Commission. 1999b. *A Capital in the Making*. Ottawa: National Capital Commission.

National Capital Commission. 2004. "Life-Cycle Management Module," *Integrated Asset Management Information System Manual*. Ottawa: National Capital Commission.

National Capital Commission. 2005a. *Capital Core Area Sector Plan*. Ottawa: National Capital Commission, pp. 171-173.

National Capital Commission. 2005b. *Gatineau Park Master Plan*. Ottawa: National Capital Commission.

National Capital Commission. 2005c. *Strategic Transportation Initiative*. Ottawa: National Capital Commission.

National Capital Commission. 2007. Photo of Ottawa-Gatineau.

National Capital Planning Commission. 2003. *The National Capital Urban Design and Security Plan*. Washington, D.C.: National Capital Planning Commission.

Natural Resources Canada. 2005. "Population Density-2001," *The Atlas of Canada*. Ottawa: Natural Resources Canada.

Natural Resources Canada. 2008. Satellite Image of Canada. *The Atlas of Canada*. Ottawa: Natural Resources Canada.

National Round Table on the Environment and the Economy (NRTEE). 1996. *Forger un consensus pour un avenir viable: Des principes à la pratique*. Ottawa: NRTEE.

National Round Table on the Environment and the Economy (NRTEE). 2003. *Environmental Quality in Canadian Cities — The Federal Role*. Ottawa: NRTEE, p. 59.

New Urban News. 2006. "Biking to Work: Lessons from Canada," July-August, p. 7.

New York Center for Architecture, http://cfa.aiany.org/index.php?section=center-for-architecture [accessed on March 23, 2011].

Nyberg, Eugene. 2004. "Innovation and Energy — Putting Fiscal Policy to Work: Economic Prosperity Can No Longer Be Divorced From Environmental Stewardship," *The Hill Times*, October 4, p. 20.

Ostry, Bernard and Janice Yalden, eds. 2004. *Visions of Canada: The Alan B. Plaunt Memorial Lectures 1958-1982*. Montreal: McGill-Queen's University Press.

Palermo, Frank, ed. 2003. *First Nations Community Planning Model*, 2nd ed. Halifax: Cities and Environment Unit, Faculty of Architecture and Planning, Dalhousie University.

Palermo, Frank, ed. 2003. *First Nations Community Planning Workbook*. Halifax: Cities and Environment Unit, Faculty of Architecture and Planning, Dalhousie University.

Panel on the NCC Mandate Review. 2006. *The National Capital Commission: Charting a New Course*. Ottawa: National Capital Commission.

Paquet, Gilles. 2004. *Pathologies de gouvernance : Essais de technologie sociale*. Montreal: Liber, p. 108.

Parks Canada. 2008. *Lachine Canal National Historic Site of Canada*. Ottawa: Parks Canada. http://www.pc.gc.ca/lhn-nhs/qc/canallachine/index_E.asp [accessed on March 23, 2011].

Parks Canada. 2008. "Lachine Canal," *Directory of Designations of National Historic Significance of Canada*. Ottawa: Parks Canada. http://www.pc.gc.ca/apps/lhn-nhs/det_E.asp?oqSID=0636&oqeName=Lachine+Canal&oqfName=Canal+de+Lachine [accessed on March 23, 2011].

Parolek, Daniel G., Karen Parolek and Paul Crawford. 2008. *Form-Based Codes — A Guide for Planners, Urban Designers, Municipalities, and Developers*. Hoboken, N.J.: John Wiley and Sons.

Pavillon de l'Arsenal, http://www.pavillon-arsenal.com [accessed on March 23, 2011].

Pearce, Bill. 1995. "Hamilton-Wentworth Region's Sustainable Community Initiative," *Plan Canada*, September, pp. 26-27.

Peters, John. 2003. "Aboriginal Perspective on Planning in Canada — Decolonizing the Process: A Discussion with Four Aboriginal Practitioners," *Plan Canada*, summer, pp. 39-41.

Planetizen. 2007. *Contemporary Debates in Urban Planning*. Washington, D.C.: Island Press, www.planetizen.org [accessed on March 26, 2011].

Pollitt, Christopher. 2003. "New Forms of Public Service: Issues in Contemporary Organizational Design." In *The Art of the State: Governance in a World Without Frontiers*, eds. Thomas J. Courchene and Donald J. Savoie. Montreal: Institute for Research on Public Policy.

Postman, Neil. 1999. *Building a Bridge to the 18th Century: How the Past Can Improve Our Future*. New York: Vintage Books.

Pressman, Norman. 1995. *Northern Cityscape: Linking Design to Climate*. Yellowknife: Liveable Winter Cities Association.

Pressman, Norman. 1996. "Urban Form for Stressful Climates," *Plan Canada*, March, pp. 30-32.

Pressman, Norman. 2004. *Shaping Cities for Winter: Climatic Comfort and Sustainable Design*. Prince George: Liveable Winter Cities Association.

Pressman, Norman. 2005. "La notion d'hivernité : Apprivoiser la glace et la neige " In *Sensations urbaines : Une approche différente à l'urbanisme,* ed. Mirko Zardini. Montreal: Centre Canadien d'Architecture et Lars Mueller Publisher, pp. 128-141.

Prigogine, Ilya and Isabelle Stengers. 1979. *La nouvelle alliance : Métamorphose de la science*. Paris: Gallimard.

Prime Minister's Caucus Task Force on Urban Issues. 2002. *Canada's Urban Strategy: A Blueprint for Action*, Final Report. Ottawa: Prime Minister's Caucus Task Force on Urban Issues, November, pp. 6, 21.

Proactive Information Services Inc. 2000. *Winnipeg Development Agreement: Evaluation of the Organizational Model — Final Report*. Winnipeg: Proactive Information Services Inc.

Procos, Dimitri. 1976. *Mixed Land Use: From Revival to Innovation*. Stroudsburg: Dowden, Hutchinson & Ross, p. viii.

Punter, John. 2003. *The Vancouver Achievement*. Vancouver: UBC Press, p. 182.

Quindlen, Anna. 2004. "Put 'Em in a Tree Museum," *Newsweek*, August 23, p. 74.

Ralston Saul, John. 1994. *The Unconscious Civilization*. Toronto: Anansi, p. 116.

Ralston Saul, John. 1997. *Reflections of a Siamese Twin: Canada at the End of the Twentieth Century*. Toronto: Viking, p. 69.

Ralston Saul, John. 2001. *On Equilibrium*. Toronto: Penguin-Viking, p. 14, 178.

Ravetz, Joe. 2000. *City Region 2020: Integrated Planning for a Sustainable Environment*. London: Earthscan.

Richardson, John. 2004. "Between Obligation and Refusal: Some Thoughts on a Process of Inclusion and the Role of Municipalities." In *Our Diverse Cities,* ed. Caroline Andrew. Ottawa: Metropolis Project, Number 1, spring, pp. 172-173.

Roberts, David G. and Michael Sobel. 2004. "Redevelop with Schools in Mind," *Urban Land*, October, p. 18.

Roberts, Wayne. 2006. "Taxshift — Beginning of a Movement," *Ontario Planning Journal*, January-February, pp. 32-33.

Robinson, Ira and Gerald Hodge. 1998. "Canadian Regional Planning at 50: Growing Pains," *Plan Canada*, May, p. 13.

Romanow, Roy J. 2006. "A House Half-Built," *The Walrus*, June, pp. 48-54.

Rosan, Richard M. 2004. "Urban Design Is About Creating Great Places," *Urban Land*, August, p. 133.

Rosan, Richard M. 2007. "The Traffic/Housing Equation," *Urban Land*, April, p. 46.

Roy, Jeffrey and John Langford. 2008. "Creating a Collaborative Ethos Across Jurisdictions," *Canadian Government Executive*, January, p. 10.

Russell, Peter H. 2004. *Constitutional Odyssey — Can Canadians Become a Sovereign People?* Third Edition. Toronto: University of Toronto Press.

San Francisco Urban Center, http://www.spur.org [accessed on March 24, 2011].

Saunders, Doug. 2010. *Arrival City: The Final Migration and Our Next World*. Toronto: Alfred A. Knopf Canada.

Science Council of Canada. 1971. *Cities for Tomorrow: Some Application of Science and Technology to Urban Development*. Ottawa: Science Council of Canada, pp. 33, 40.

Senge, Peter *et al.* 2008. *The Necessary Revolution — How Individuals and Organizations Are Working Together to Create a Sustainable World*: New York: Doubleday.

Sheridan, Mike. 2004. "Rethinking Building Security," *Urban Land*, September, p. 136.

Sherwood, David. 2002. "The State of the Healthy Communities Movement in Canada," *Plan Canada*, October-November-December, pp. 11-12.

Simpson, Jeffrey, Mark Jaccard and Nic Rivers. 2007. *Hot Air: Meeting Canada's Climate Change Challenge*. Toronto: McClelland & Stewart.

Skelton, Ian, ed. 2003. "Perspectives on a Canadian Urban Strategy," *Canadian Journal of Urban Research/Canadian Institute of Planners*.

Sloane, David Charles. 2006. "From Congestion to Sprawl: Planning and Health in Historical Context," *Journal of the American Planning Association*, winter, pp. 10-15.

Smith, Barry E. and Susan Haid. 2004. "The Rural-Urban Connection: Growing Together in Greater Vancouver," *Plan Canada*, spring, pp. 36-39.

Smith, P.J. 1995. "Governing Metropolitan Change." In *Canadian Metropolitics — Governing our Cities, ed.* James Lightbody. Toronto: Copp Clark Ltd, p. 169.

Société du Havre de Montréal. 2004. "Le Havre de Montréal — Vision 2025." Montreal: Société du Havre de Montréal, p. 3.

Solomon, Daniel. 2003. *Global City Blues*. Washington, D.C.: Island Press.

Spaxman, Ray. 1994. "The Planning of South False Creek," *Plan Canada*, July, pp. 76-79.

Spielman, Seth *et al.* 2006. "Interdisciplinary Planning for Healthier Communities: Findings from the Harlem Children's Zone Asthma Initiative," *Journal of American Planning Association*, winter, pp. 100-108.

Statistics Canada. 2001. "Portrait ethnoculturel du Canada : Une mosaique en évolution," *Recensement 2001- série "analyses."* Ottawa: Statistics Canada.

Statistics Canada. 2002. "Le Canada en statistiques : Population urbaine et rurale, par province et territoire," *Recensements du Canada 1851-2001*. Ottawa: Statistics Canada.

Stead, W. Edward and Jean Garner Stead. 1992. *Management for a Small Planet*. Newbury Park: Sage, p. 6, 16.

Sully, Lorne, Livia Kellett, Joseph Garcea and Ryan Walker. 2008. "First Nations Urban Reserves in Saskatoon: Partnerships for Positive Development," *Plan Canada*, summer, pp. 39-42.

Sykes, J.B., ed. 1980. *The Concise Oxford Dictionary of Current English*. Oxford: Clarendon Press, pp. 162, 245, 560, 1280.

Talbot, Michael. 1991. *The Holographic Universe*. New York: Harper Collins, p. 49.

Tapscott, Don and Anthony D. Williams. 2006. *Wikinomics: How Mass Collaboration Changes Everything*. Toronto: Penguin/Portfolio.

Tarnay, Stella and Ed McMahon. 2005. "Toward Green Urbanism," *Urban Land*, June, p. 54-59.

Task Force on Housing and Urban Development. 1969. *Report*. Ottawa: Task Force on Housing and Urban Development.

Taylor, Charles. 1991. *The Malaise of Modernity*. Toronto: Anansi.

Thompson, Susan. 2002. "Meaning of Home: Developing a Responsive and Humane Planning Practice," *Plan Canada*, January-February-March, p. 13.

Toffler, Alvin. 1970. *Future Shock*. New York: Bantam Books.

Tomic, Sinisa. 2003. "Hamilton Urban Braille System: Urban Design for an Aging Society," *Plan Canada*, spring, pp. 41-43.

Tota, Kasio. 2003. "The Old/New Neighbours — Breaking Ground in Collaborative Land Use Planning Between First Nations and Local Governments," *Plan Canada*, winter, pp. 31-33.

TRANS — Joint Transportation Committee Serving the National Capital Region, http://ncr-trans-rcn.ca [accessed on March 24, 2011].

Treasury Board of Canada. 2003. *Canada's Performance: Annual Report to Parliament.* Ottawa: Treasury Board of Canada, p. 24, 25, 50.

Treasury Board of Canada. 2004. *Canada's Performance: Annual Report to Parliament.* Ottawa: pp. 5-2 of 15, 8-1 of 16, 4-2 of 19, 5-13 of 15.

TRIEC — Toronto Region Immigrant Employment Council, http://www.triec.ca [accessed on March 24, 2011].

Trist, Eric. 1983. "Referent Organization and the Development of Inter-Organizational Domains", *Human Relations*, pp. 269-284.

Trudel, Jonathan. 2004. "Les vieux, ça rapporte!, entrevue avec Richard Lefrançois, auteur de *Les nouvelles frontières de l'âge*, Les Presses de l'Université de Montréal," *L'Actualité*, May 15, pp. 22-24.

Trudel, Jonathan. 2005a. "Le progrès recule-t-il?, entrevue avec Philip Longman, New American Foundation," *L'Actualité*, March 15, p. 22.

Trudel, Jonathan. 2005b. "Les années zéro," *L'Actualité*, March 15, p. 26.

Underwood, Anne. 2005. "Leadership & Innovation — Designing the Future: Interview with William McDonough, author of *Cradle to Cradle with Michael Braungart*," *Newsweek*, May 16, pp. 40-45.

United Nations. 1999. *World Habitat Awards, 1999 — The Grow Home, Montreal, Avi Friedman.* New York: United Nations. http://www.worldhabitatawards.org/winners-and-finalists/project-archive.cfm?offset=97&lang=00 [accessed on March 24, 2011].

United Nations. 2000. *UN — Habitat, 2000 Dubai International Best Practices Award to Improve the Living Environment, Creating a Sustainable Community: Hamilton-Wentworth's Vision 2020.* New York: United Nations. http://www.bestpractices.org/ [accessed on March 24, 2011].

United Nations. 2004. *UN — Habitat, 2004 Dubai International Best Practices Award to Improve the Living Environment, First Nations Community Planning Project.* New York: United Nations. http://www.bestpractices.org/ [accessed on March 24, 2011].

United Nations. 2007. *World Population Prospects: The 2006 Revision Population Database.* New York: United Nations, Department of Economic and Social Affairs, Population Division.

United Nations. 2008. *Public Service Awards, 2005 — Europe and North America-Canada-Vancouver Agreement.* New York: United Nations. http://www.unpan.org/dpepa_psaward.asp [accessed on March 24, 2011].

Urban Land Institute. 2005. "High Performance Building," *Urban Land — Green Technology*, October.

Vastel, Michel. 2005. "On peut tirer du bon des Américains, " *Le Droit*, January 22, p. 23.

Vickers, Geoffrey. 1995. *The Art of Judgement: A Study of Policy Making.* Thousand Oaks, CA: Sage, pp. 16, 35.

Ville de Montréal. 2005. Photo of Montreal, Annie Bissonnette, photographer. Montreal: Direction des communications et relations avec les citoyens.

Wade, Tracey L. 2008. "Comprehensive Community Planning in the Atlantic Region: Where Do We Go From Here," *Plan Canada*, summer, pp. 18-20.

Walker, Ryan. 2005. "Reflections on Planning with the Urban Aboriginal Community," *Plan Canada*, winter, pp. 38-41.

Ward, Stephen V. 2002. *Planning the Twentieth-Century City — The Advanced Capitalist World.* Chechester: John Wiley & Sons.

Watts, Ronald L. 2003. "Managing Interdependence in a Federal Political System." In *The Art of the State: Governance in a World Without Frontiers*, eds. Thomas J. Courchene and Donald J. Savoie. Montreal: Institute for Research on Public Policy, pp. 123, 128, 135-136.

Warman, Dena, Dan Leeming and Diane Riley. 2006. "The Changing Demography of Canadian Communities: New Answers Needed," *Ontario Planning Journal*, July-August, pp. 8-11.

Wells, Paul. 2004. "Power to the People," *Maclean's*, January 26, pp. 18-21.

Wenger, Etienne. 1998. *Communities of Practice: Learning, Meaning, and Identity.* Cambridge, MA: Cambridge University Press, p. 119.

Wenger, Etienne, Richard McDermott and William M. Snyder. 2002. *Cultivating Communities of Practice.* Boston: Harvard Business School Press, pp. 6, 229-230.

Western Economic Diversification Canada. 2004. *Canada-Manitoba-Winnipeg Agreement for Community and Economic Development* Winnipeg: Western Economic Diversification Canada.

Western Economic Diversification Canada. 2005. *The Vancouver Agreement 2005 — An Urban Development Agreement Among Canada-British Columbia-Vancouver Regarding Economic, Social, Health and Community Development in the City of Vancouver.* Vancouver: Western Economic Diversification Canada. http://www.vancouveragreement.ca/TheAgreement.htm [accessed on March 24, 2011].

Western Economic Diversification Canada. 2008. *Urban Development Agreements.* Ottawa: Western Economic Diversification Canada.

Wheatley, Margaret and Myron Kellner-Rogers. 1998. "Bringing Life to Organizational Change," *Journal of Strategic Performance Measurement*, April-May, quoted in F. Capra, 2002, p. 113.

Wilson, Jeffrey and Mark Anielski. 2004. *Ecological Footprints of Canadian Municipalities and Regions.* Ottawa: Federation of Canadian Municipalities, p. 5-7.

Witty, David R. 1994. "Healthy Communities: A CIP Initiative," *Plan Canada*, July, pp. 116-117.

Witty, David R. 2002. "Healthy Communities: What Have We Learned?" *Plan Canada*, October-November-December, pp. 9-10.

Wyman, Max. 2004. *Culture Matters.* Ottawa: University of Ottawa, pp. 5-6.

Young, Kathryn. 2006. "Density Is Key, but a Tough Sell," *The Ottawa Citizen*, March 4, p. 12.

Zakaria, Fareed. 2004. "No Security, No Democracy," *Newsweek*, May 24, p. 37.

Zardini, Mirko, ed. 2005. *Sensations urbaines : Une approche différente à l'urbanisme.* Montreal: Centre Canadien d'Architecture et Lars Mueller Publisher.

Zussman, David. 2008. "Networked Public Service," *Canadian Government Executive*, May, p. 34.

ACKNOWLEDGEMENTS

Although written between 2004 and 2010, the manuscript has been in the making for more than a decade, at least. It has benefited from many readings but also many conversations and collaborations with professional colleagues, professors, friends and relatives. Below, I initially identify a number of people to whom I owe an intellectual debt in the course of my professional development and career. They are: Pierre Blanchard, Pierre De Blois, Serge Filion, André Guibord, Richard Lalande, Jean Paré, Léon Ploegaerts, Georges Potvin, Larry Spencer, Denis St-Onge, and Nick Tunnacliffe.

I would like to acknowledge also the following individuals whose friendship and individual achievements over the years have inspired me and have contributed in important ways to the writing of this manuscript: Bill Boss, Gisèle and Jean-Pierre Rousselle, André and Francine Lessard, Philippe and Ginette Paquin, and Michael P.J. and Marjorie Kennedy.

I wish to express my gratitude to several individuals from whom I have received precious support, comments and/or suggestions on earlier versions of this book: Denise Amyot, Caroline Andrew, Larry Beasley, Marni Cappe, David Gordon, Ruth Hubbard, Murio Lapointe, Glenn Miller, Eric Nelson, Michael O'Hearn, Gilles Paquet, Eugene Parent, Richard Scott, Lori Thornton and David Witty. A very special thank you must go to Richard Scott, who not only reviewed the manuscript but also provided very valuable initial editing support.

Many thanks are due to the marvellous people at the National Capital Commission who, in several ways, have influenced directly or indirectly the project, including existing and former staff of the Capital Planning Branch, existing or former members of the Executive Management Committee, and existing and former members of the Advisory Committee on Planning, Design and Realty. Thank you must go as well to Michel Céré, David Malkin and Hélène Pageot for their help in the early research and production of the document. Michel Céré made a significant contribution to the creation of the graphic "look and feel" of the book, which inspired and energized me to move forward.

Finally, I must thank my wife Marie for her unwavering support and help in making this book a reality.

ABOUT THE AUTHOR

I am an urbanist. I live close to downtown Ottawa, on a former brownfield site, in a mixed land use and high density area, and enjoy my walk to work!

With almost twenty years at the National Capital Commission (NCC), I have led the preparation of several long range strategic plans, some in collaboration with municipal, provincial and federal partners. The plans include the Plan for Canada's Capital (1999), the Greenbelt Master Plan (1996), the Gatineau Park Master Plan Review (2005), the Capital Core Area Sector Plan (2005) and the Strategic Transportation Initiative (2005). The Greenbelt Master Plan and the Capital Core Area Sector Plan have been recognized by awards for Planning Excellence given by the Canadian Institute of Planners. In addition, I was assigned to Transport, Infrastructure and Communities Canada to support the work of the panel on the mandate review of the National Capital Commission (2006), which allowed me to explore a "grand vision". In the Capital Planning and Real Asset Management Branch (CPRAM), I have contributed to the establishment of the strategic orientations of the branch and provided leadership and direction in a broad range of sectors of activity, including transportation and the implementation of the approval authorities of the NCC.

As Vice President, Capital Planning, my responsibilities include the realization of the NCC Planning Framework through the preparation of long range strategic capital plans, the application of the land use, design and realty transaction approval authorities as conferred to the NCC by the National Capital Act, and the coordination of the collaboration with the provinces and the municipalities in the National Capital Region for all current and long-term planning matters.

Before joining the NCC, I was principal project planner at the City of Ottawa for two years. In the 1980s, with a new Masters in Planning from the University of Ottawa under my arm, I worked in Saint-Jérôme, Québec, where I was director of planning for the city, involved as coordinator of Neighborhood Improvement programs and responsible for the preparation of the first regional plan for the new regional municipality.

I began my professional career with Campeau Corporation as a real estate analyst right out of university.

My passion for healthy, resilient and sustainable cities has led me to be a member of several management boards, including more recently the Association of Professional Executives of the Public Service of Canada (APEX) (2000-2006), where I led the "Healthy Leaders en Santé" initiative. With l'Ordre des urbanistes du Québec (OUQ), I launched a professional liaison program with university students and graduates in urbanism, and led the preparation of the first strategic and communications plans for the OUQ. More recently, I chaired the 2001 Conference of the OUQ in Gatineau, the theme of which was "Youths and urbanism". The OUQ recognized my contribution to urbanism in Québec with the Hans Blumenfeld Award in November 2003. I maintain my accreditations with the Canadian Institute of Planners, Ordre des urbanistes du Québec, and the Ontario Professional Planners Institute.

When I am not working, I enjoy the many benefits of living in a multicultural city, richly endowed with natural beauty.

Other titles by
INVENIRE BOOKS

4. James Bowen (ed.)   2009
   The Entrepreneurial Effect: Practical Ideas
   from Your Own Virtual Board of Advisors

3. Gilles Paquet   2009
   Scheming Virtuously: The Road to
   Collaborative Governance

2. Ruth Hubbard   2009
   Profession: Public Servant

1. Robin Higham   2009
   Who de we think we are? Canada's reasonable
   (and less reasonable) accommodation debates

To order copies, please contact Commoners' Publishing
at sales@commonerspublishing.com

www.ingramcontent.com/pod-product-compliance
Lightning Source LLC
Chambersburg PA
CBHW041549030426

42334CB00006B/103